Animals, Food, and Tourism

Food is routinely given attention in tourism research as a motivator of travel. Regardless of whether tourists travel with a primary motivation for experiencing local food, eating is required during their trip.

This book provides an interdisciplinary discussion of animals as a source of food within the context of tourism. Themes include the raising, harvesting, and processing of farm animals for food; considerations in marketing animals as food; and the link between consuming animals and current environmental concerns. Ethical issues are addressed in social, economic, environmental, and political terms. Chapters are theoretically grounded in frameworks of ethical theory, critical theory, ecofeminism, environmental theory, political economy, cultural theory, and the Global Sustainable Tourism Criteria. Several chapters explore contradicting and paradoxical ethical perspectives, whether those contradictions exist between government and private sector, between tourism and other industries, or whether they lie within ourselves.

This book wrestles with a range of issues such as animal sentience, the environmental consequences of animals as food, viewing animals solely as an extractive resource for human will, as well as the artificial cultural distortion of *animals as food* for tourism marketing purposes. It will appeal to tourism academics and graduate students as a reference for their own research or as supplementary material for courses focused on ethics within tourism.

Carol Kline is Associate Professor of Hospitality and Tourism Management at Appalachian State University, USA, in the Department of Management. Her research interests focus broadly on tourism planning and development and tourism sustainability, but cover a range of topics such as foodie segmentation, craft beverages, agritourism, wildlife-based tourism, animal ethics in tourism, tourism entrepreneurship, niche tourism markets, and tourism impacts to communities.

Routledge Ethics of Tourism

Series edited by Professor David Fennell

This series seeks to engage with key debates surrounding ethical issues in tourism from a range of interdisciplinary perspectives across the social sciences and humanities. Contributions explore ethical debates across socio-cultural, ecological, and economic lines on topics such as: climate, resource consumption, ecotourism and nature-based tourism, sustainability, responsible tourism, the use of animals, politics, international relations, violence, tourism labor, sex tourism, exploitation, displacement, marginalization, authenticity, slum tourism, indigenous people, communities, rights, justice, and equity. This series has a global geographic coverage and offers new theoretical insights in the form of authored and edited collections to reflect the wealth of rcsearch being undertaken in this sub-field.

For a full list of titles in this series, please visit www.routledge.com/Routledge-Ethics-of-Tourism-Series/book-series/RET

1 **Animals, Food, and Tourism**
Edited by Carol Kline

2 **Tourism Experiences and Animal Consumption: Contested Values, Morality, and Ethics**
Edited by Carol Kline

3 **Wild Animals and Leisure: Rights and Wellbeing**
Edited by Neil Carr and Janette Young

4 **Domestic Animals, Humans, and Leisure: Rights, Welfare, and Wellbeing**
Edited by Janette Young and Neil Carr

5 **New Moral Natures in Tourism**
Edited by Kellee Caton, Lisa Cooke and Bryan Grimwood

Animals, Food, and Tourism

Edited by Carol Kline

Routledge
Taylor & Francis Group
LONDON AND NEW YORK

First published 2018
by Routledge
2 Park Square, Milton Park, Abingdon, Oxon OX14 4RN

and by Routledge
711 Third Avenue, New York, NY 10017

Routledge is an imprint of the Taylor & Francis Group, an informa business

British Library Cataloguing-in-Publication Data
A catalogue record for this book is available from the British Library

Library of Congress Cataloging-in-Publication Data
A catalog record for this book has been requested

ISBN: 978-1-138-29160-7 (hbk)
ISBN: 978-1-315-26520-9 (ebk)

Typeset in Times New Roman
by Apex CoVantage, LLC

Contents

Figures

Tables

Contributors

Anders Angerbjörn is a Professor and Chair in Ecology in the Zoological Department at Stockholm University in Sweden. Angerbjörn has a focus on arctic and subarctic ecology, often with a conservation biology perspective. He has been studying arctic foxes for many years. He studies predator and prey populations, focusing on other carnivores in the mountain region such as gyrfalcon, golden eagle, rough-legged buzzard, and wolverine, and he also studies dolphins, porpoises, and seals.

Giovanna Bertella is Associate Professor at UiT The Arctic University of Norway in the School of Business and Economics in Tromsø (Norway). Her research interests focus on tourism. Topics covered in her research include: rural tourism, tourism networking and innovation, tourism entrepreneurship, nature-based tourism, animals in tourism, and sustainability. The geographical settings investigated in her research include northern Norway and Italy.

Bryan Blankfield is Assistant Professor-in-Residence in the Honors College at the University of Nevada, Las Vegas, USA. His research and published work focuses on presidential rhetoric, civic engagement, and animal studies. He is completing a book project on how President Franklin Delano Roosevelt's dog, Fala, became a useful centerpiece in the communicative practices between FDR and citizens. His essays on Fala have appeared in *Rhetoric & Public Affairs* (Summer 2016) and *Rhetoric Society Quarterly* (Winter 2017).

Jane Bone, Ph.D., is Senior Lecturer at Monash University, Australia. She is interested in innovative theories and methodologies relating to ethics, education, tourism, and animal studies. Her work in tourism focuses on critical issues in human and more-than-human animal rights. Her recent publications have featured posthuman theory, new materialist theories, and ideas from Deleuze and Guattari, and these approaches continue to contribute to the fields she is involved in through her research.

Kate Bone, Ph.D., is an interdisciplinary research scholar and Lecturer at Monash University in Australia. Her research interests include the sociology of tourism, sociology of wellbeing, sociology of work, and organizations. Kate's publications within the tourism field have examined spiritual retreat tourism, citizenship and education, voluntourism, animal and women's' rights, and ethical travel.

Kelly Bricker is Professor and Director of Parks, Recreation, and Tourism at the University of Utah, USA. She has research and teaching interests in ecotourism, sense of place, community development, natural resource management, value of nature-based experiences, and the impacts of tourism. She has authored and edited *Sustainable Tourism & the Millennium Development Goals: Effecting Positive Change*. Dr. Bricker serves the boards of the Global Sustainable Tourism Council, The International Ecotourism Society, The Multi-Stakeholder Advisory Committee of the United Nations World Tourism Organization 10YFP for sustainable development, and the Tourism and Protected Area Specialist Group of the IUCN. With partners in OARS and her husband, she developed an ecotourism operation called Rivers Fiji.

Georgette Leah Burns (B.Sc. (hons), M.Sc., Ph.D.) is Head of the Discipline of Society and Environment in the Griffith School of Environment, and a foundation member of the Environmental Futures Research Institute at Griffith University, Australia. Her work as an environmental anthropologist involves exploring the ethics and management of human–wildlife interactions in nature-based tourism settings, with fieldwork spanning countries as diverse as Iceland and Australia. She is the author of numerous books and journal articles on this topic.

Max Elder is an Associate Fellow at the Oxford Centre for Animal Ethics, an international think-tank that pioneers ethical perspectives on animals. He is also a researcher in the Food Futures Lab at the Institute for the Future, a 50-year-old think-tank that specializes in long-term forecasting. Max has published numerous articles and book chapters on topics ranging from fish ethics and dietary trends to the nature of evil and the philosophy of Louis CK.

Cadi Y. Fung is a doctoral candidate in the Department of Geography, Environment, and Spatial Sciences at Michigan State University, USA. As an animal geographer, she is especially interested in the relationships between humans and threatened/endangered animals, animals in captivity, and animals exploited by humans (for tourism, entertainment, lab research, and other means). Her previous work in the animal entertainment and tourism industry drives her desire to learn about the influence of perceptions, culture, economics, and political landscapes on these relationships. Her dissertation research focuses on human–wildlife conflict in the Brazilian Amazon as it pertains to subsistence fishers, local tourism operators, and the Amazon river dolphin.

Sandra Granquist is Head of Seal Research at the Icelandic Seal Center in Hvammstangi and a seal specialist at the Marine and Freshwater Research Institute in Iceland. Granquist holds a Ph.D. in behavioral ecology from the Zoological Department at Stockholm University and her main research interests are animal population dynamics, interdisciplinary management of wildlife, and anthropogenic interactions with wildlife, such as how tourism affects animal behavior and ecology.

Kent Henderson is a Ph.D. candidate in the Department of Sociology at Stony Brook University, USA. His interests are environmentalism and political economy with a broader agenda of examining how the global economy shapes or limits environmental policies and outcomes. His current research is on international development finance and global environmental norms.

Hin Hoarau-Heemstra is an Associate Professor at Nord University Business School in Bodø, Norway. Her Ph.D. dissertation (2015) is about knowledge, reflexivity, and innovation in nature-based tourism. Most of her teaching focuses on tourism management, innovation, and business ethics. Her current research interests include innovation, knowledge management, and sustainability in the tourism experience and public sector. She contributed to the edited books *Open Tourism – Open Innovation, Crowdsourcing and Co-Creation Challenging the Tourism Industry* (2016), *Handbook of Research on Innovation in Tourism Industries* (2014), and *Culture, Development and Petroleum – An Ethnography of the High North* (2014). She has recent journal publications in: *Tourism and Hospitality Research, Annals of Tourism Research* and *Scandinavian Journal of Hospitality and Tourism.*

Chantelle Jobberns is a Ph.D. candidate at the University of Technology Sydney (UTS), Australia, in the UTS Business School. She works in the area of ethics in sustainable tourism. She received her honors degree at UTS for a thesis titled "Animal Rights in Ecotourism: A Case Study of Whale Watching" and has published a number of papers in this field of research. Her work engages with the rights of animals and ecotourism, focused on the rights of whales in contemporary society.

Leah Joyner is a graduate student in the Parks, Recreation, and Tourism Ph.D. program at the University of Utah, USA. Her academic research interests include sustainable tourism, agritourism, voluntourism, visitor impact management, agriculture and protected landscapes, consumer purchasing decisions, and culinary tourism. Leah has previously served as the Education Coordinator for The Carolina Farm Stewardship Association, the oldest and largest sustainable agriculture organization in the Southeast USA. For several years, she coordinated CFSA's annual farm tours, which connect thousands of consumers with local, sustainable farmers in their communities. Leah holds an M.S. in Sustainable Tourism from East Carolina University, a B.A. in Sustainable Development, and a B.S. in Technical Photography from Appalachian State University. She has worked with farmers and tourism industry partners on agritourism development projects both in the USA and internationally.

Carol Kline is Associate Professor of Hospitality and Tourism Management at Appalachian State University, USA, in the Department of Management. Her research interests focus broadly on tourism planning and development and tourism sustainability, but cover a range of topics such as foodie segmentation, craft beverages, agritourism, wildlife-based tourism, animal ethics in tourism, tourism entrepreneurship, niche tourism markets, and tourism impacts to communities.

Kristin M. Lamoureux is an accomplished professional with twenty years of experience as an educator, researcher, and practitioner in tourism and hospitality. She is also a passionate animal rights advocate. In addition to being a professor of tourism, she has also been involved in projects focusing on sustainability around the world. She has served as a consultant for the U.S. government, World Bank, the UN World Tourism Organization, the Ecotourism Society, and Conservation International, among others. She holds a Ph.D. in Strategic Planning and Public Policy, a Master of Tourism, and a Graduate Certificate in Animal Studies.

Álvaro López López is Professor and Researcher of Geography of Tourism at the National Autonomous University of Mexico (UNAM). He received his doctorate in geography at the same institution and completed a postdoctoral fellowship at the University of Waterloo in Canada. His recent publications focus on animal ethics and food consumption as part of the tourist experiences, the perception of tourists in dark tourism sites and the role of local populations in tourist development. His research interests include geography of tourism, animal ethics and geography, local development and tourism, and sex tourism. He is currently coordinating a research project about dark tourism spaces in Mexico and has just completed a course on animal ethics.

Elin Lilja Öqvist has a master's degree in marine biology from Stockholm University, Sweden. Her master's thesis was an interdisciplinary study focused on the knowledge and opinions of tourists about hunting and tourism focused on marine mammals in Iceland. Elin has worked as a whale watching guide in Iceland and is currently working with nature-based activity development in Norway. Her research interests are on the interactions between tourism and marine mammals.

Gino Jafet Quintero Venegas is a Ph.D. candidate in geography at the National Autonomous University of Mexico (UNAM). His research interests include geography of tourism, regional integration, and anthrozoogeography: links between tourism and animal welfare. His recent publications center on animal ethics and food consumption as part of the tourist experiences, bullfighting as a cultural element of dark tourism, and transport and tourist integration in Central America. He is currently at the final phase of his Ph.D. and works as a high school teacher of human geography and economic geography at the Modern American School in Mexico City.

Rose Sayre is a Ph.D. candidate in the Department of Sociology at Stony Brook University, USA. Her research interests include environmental sociology, sociology of disaster, and sustainable development. Her current work focuses on the effect of political and economic policies on disaster vulnerability, including vulnerability to the predicted negative impacts of global warming cross-nationally.

Michael Wearing is Senior Lecturer in the Social Work Program at the School of Social Sciences, Faculty of Arts and Social Sciences, University of New South Wales, Australia. Michael is both a social worker and interdisciplinary sociologist who has had 30 years of involvement in social research and social policy in Australia. His teaching and research reflect his interests in interdisciplinary theory and policy ideas, and in social work practice. Michael has researched in the areas of social inequality, comparative social policy, youth studies and youth services, mental health and professional practice, ecotourism and globalization, public opinion, and the welfare state.

Stephen Wearing is Conjoint Professor at the University of Newcastle (UoN), Australia. His research and projects are in the area of Leisure and Tourism Studies, with a Ph.D. focused on sustainable forms of tourism. Stephen has made seminal contributions in many areas including ecotourism, volunteer tourism and community development; the importance of community-based approaches in the leisure, recreation, and tourism sector has formed the focus of his research. He is a prolific scholar and his work ranks among the top professors in the world for publications in sustainable tourism and leading research journals in that field. He has been recognized by the American Psychological Association (APA) with a "highly commended" for one of his papers. The World Leisure Organisation awarded him the George Torkildsen Literary Award International Innovation Prize in research and scholarly endeavors in 2016 and he was the recipient of the 2016 Emerald Citations of Excellence Award for "Volunteer Tourism: A Review" (*Tourism Management*).

Acknowledgments

I first wish to acknowledge David Fennell's support with the two books, *Animals, Food, and Tourism* and *Tourism Experiences and Animal Consumption: Contested Values, Morality, and Ethics*. Without his endorsement of the concept and assistance with the early framing, I would have never known the joy of working with such an outstanding cadre of authors nor bringing to bear a project of this magnitude. Between these two volumes and twenty-six chapters, I have gotten to work with authors supremely skilled in critical scholarship. I am grateful to them for entrusting their work to me as well as their patience as the project moved through its various stages. Thank you to Faye Leerink at Routledge for her keen guidance at the outset of the project.

My colleagues at Appalachian State University have been nothing but supportive of my research stream on animals and tourism, and in particular I must name Dr. Jacqui Bergman and Dr. Dana Clark. I am also fortunate to have lifelong friend-mentors, both retired and from other institutions, who continue to generously provide professional guidance and inspiration, as well as new friend-colleagues I met through attending the Oxford Centre for Animal Ethics' 2016 summer school on the topic of Eating Animals.

My mom instilled an ethic of care in our family regarding animals and my dad demonstrated how much fun a creative and intellectual project can be. My husband Brian shares my interest in animals and is tremendously encouraging of my work. Most importantly, however, I thank Hamilton, Ursa, Private, and Makana for all their love.

Reviewer acknowledgments

Animals, Food, and Tourism and *Tourism Experiences and Animal Consumption: Contested Values, Morality, and Ethics* could not have been completed without the expertise of our reviewers. Thank you to the following individuals for offering their time, guidance, and careful eyes to the project.

Suzanne Ainley, Senior Consultant Rural Research, The Ainley Group

Adam PH Amir, Earth, Ocean & Atmospheric Science Department, Florida State University

Sean Beer, Department of Tourism and Hospitality, Bournemouth University

Tracy Berno, Department of Culinary Arts, Auckland University of Technology

Azade Ozlem Calik, Tourism and Travel Services, Ankara University

Neil Carr, Department of Tourism, University of Otago

Kellee Caton, Department of Tourism Management, Thompson Rivers University

Christina T. Cavaliere, School of Business, Stockton University

Gülsel Çiftc, Tourism and Hospitality Management, Namık Kemal University

Lauren N. Duffy, Department of Parks, Recreation, and Tourism Management, Clemson University

Tricia Dutcher, Conservation Education Division, Nevada Department of Wildlife

José-Carlos García-Rosell, Multidimensional Tourism Institute (MTI) and Faculty of Social Sciences, University of Lapland

Brian Garrod, Aberystwyth Business School, Aberystwyth University

Bryan S. R. Grimwood, Department of Recreation and Leisure Studies, University of Waterloo

Hannah C. Gunderman, Department of Geography, University of Tennessee, Knoxville

Guðrún Helgadóttir, School of Business, University College of Southeast Norway and Department of Rural Tourism, Hólar University College

Patrick J. Holladay, School of Hospitality, Sport and Tourism Management, Troy University

Lee Jolliffe, Faculty of Business, University of New Brunswick

Leah Joyner, Department of Health, Kinesiology, and Recreation, University of Utah

Tori A. Kleinbort, Department of Parks, Recreation and Tourism Management, Clemson University

Tamara K. Kowalczyk, Department of Accounting, Appalachian State University

Matthew Liesch, Department of Geography and Environmental Studies, Central Michigan University

Ziene Mottiar, School of Hospitality Management and Tourism, Dublin Institute of Technology

Todd C. Patterson, History and Geography Department, East Stroudsburg University and Humanities & Social Sciences, Northampton Community College

Lisa J. Powell, Institute for Resources, Environment, & Sustainability, University of British Columbia and Department of Geography, University of the Fraser Valle

Andrea Presotto, Department of Geography and Geosciences, Salisbury University

Paul C. Quigley, Environmental GIS and Agricultural Sustainability, Independent Scholar

Dirk Reiser, Faculty of Society and Economics and Sustainable Tourism Management, Rhine-Waal University of Applied Sciences

Jillian M. Rickly, Nottingham University Business School, University of Nottingham

R. Cody Rusher, Industrial-Organizational Psychology and Human Resource Management, Appalachian State University

Tarja Salmela, Multidimensional Tourism Institute (MTI) and Faculty of Social Sciences, University of Lapland

Christopher Serenari, Wildlife Management Division, North Carolina Wildlife Resources Commission

Susan L. Slocum, Tourism and Events Management, George Mason University

Kristin L. Stewart, Independent Scholar

Caroline Winter, Faculty of Higher Education, William Angliss Institute

1 Introduction to *Animals, Food, and Tourism*

Kristin M. Lamoureux

Since the beginning of humankind, across all societies and cultures, humans have maintained deep and dependent relationships with non-human animals. The relationship between non-human animals, be they wild or domestic, companion or service, and their human counterparts is extensive, touching nearly every facet of the human experience. Indeed, the role animals have had in the human story is so ubiquitous that it is often taken for granted. Regardless of the whether non-human animals have served as companions, shelter, tools, transportation, entertainment, and most importantly, as food, the story of human existence is also one of human–animal relationships.

Given the profound dependence humans have had and continue to have on animals, it is not surprising that an area as diverse as tourism would also engage animals in an equally profound and widespread manner (Markwell, 2015). Animals – alive, dead or as symbols – are arguably the single largest contributor to the tourism experience. What would a trip to Disney feel like if all animal representations were removed? If a visit to Disney were devoid of Mickey, Minnie, and Pluto, would Disney's hold of child's fascination remain intact? Or would trips to safari destinations like South Africa, Kenya, or Tanzania continue to exist as iconic 'bucket list' destinations without wildlife viewing opportunities? Whale-watching, birdwatching, horseback riding, camel races, zoo and aquarium visits, and the like – all tourism major tourism activities dependent on a human–animal interaction.

Further, what would the impact be on the tourism experience if, for example, a visit to Cuzco no longer entailed savoring a freshly made fish ceviche before braving the hike to Machu Picchu; or a trip to a rodeo in the United States without sampling the local barbeque; or sampling fish balls in Hong Kong; or sipping yak's milk on the high plains of the Tibetan Plateau? All of these experiences and many more are so deeply entrenched in the tourism experience that it would be almost impossible for some to contemplate a visit to these destinations without tasting their iconic dishes or, more bluntly, the animal, or parts thereof, from which these flavors are derived.

To this end, while the body of literature documenting human–animal interactions has grown, this book seeks to make a meaningful, theoretically grounded contribution to this growing body of knowledge by specifically focusing on the little studied, but significant aspect of animals as food as part of the tourism experience. Animals as food or as food for animal attractions is one of the most, if not the most, significant and pervasive use of animals in tourism. The research that each of these authors presents, provides insight into various aspects of this topic, raises awareness, and asks the reader to think critically about them. Future researchers, students, and the public are invited to question the ethical implications of the use of animals as food as well as the potential opportunities to educate, adapt behavior, and consider the sustainability of these activities.

As humans, we live with, love, and respect animals. At the same time, we target, entrap, maim, and slaughter animals. The paradox of these human–animal relationships, which allows us to feed our children chicken strips while entertaining them with an endearing *Sesame Street* Big Bird episode, is complex. These relationships grow even more complex when individuals are removed from their day-to-day activities to partake in a tourism experience. The suspension of traditional ethical norms, the desire to explore the exotic, or to partake in the authentic experience, all serve as incentives to experience the destination with little concern for the consequences of these actions. If, as an industry, tourism seeks to exploit these actions by failing to protect the animals that are so integral to the experience, the tourism sector will once again continue to metaphorically and quite literally kill the goose that laid the golden egg.

Human–animal relationships and the tourism experience

Anthrozoology or the study of human–animal relationships has grown rich with insight on a broad range of topics. The study of the broad array of human–animal interrelationships and their constant evolution is well documented. As DeMello (2010) outlined in his seminal work on this topic, the study of human–animal relationships and the implications of these relationships has an important role across disciplines. The deep social and cultural implications of these diverse relationships provide a fascinating platform from which to delve into their ever-changing nature. These complex relationships, full of inconsistencies and ambiguities, have been considered through the lens of many distinct disciplines, including animal welfare, food security, human health, and biodiversity conservation, among others (e.g. Cohen & Avieli, 2004; DeMello, 2010; Franklin, 1999; Herzog, 2010; Serpell, 1996).

Over the last several decades, the study of human–animal relationships within the tourism context has also emerged. Contributing to the depth and breadth of the emerging body of knowledge of anthrozoology, research on this topic, albeit nascent compared to the study of human–animal relationships in other disciplines, has begun to develop, and much like tourism itself, is diverse and complex in nature (e.g. Carr, 2009; Fennell, 2012; Markwell, 2015). Carr (2009) argues that the relevance of animals as part of the tourism experience will become increasingly more important as trends in tourism and leisure activities change, as well as human relationships with animals evolve. Thus, it is imperative that animal welfare also be factored prominently in this discussion.

From a theoretical perspective, the study of animals in tourism has emerged and evolved during the past thirty years. Human–animal relationships in the tourism space first emerged out of the conservation, wildlife-viewing, and ecotourism literature. Academics and conservationists sought to make the argument that wildlife had an inherent value, not as sentient beings, but rather as attractions upon or within which the tourism industry could develop. For example, the researchers argued that a live shark or lion had a greater economic value as a tourism attraction or hunting subject over one that had been killed for food (Davis & Tisdell, 1999; Shackley, 1996). This was followed by the emergence of wildlife tourism (e.g. Boo, 1990; Lovelock, 2008; Topelko & Dearden, 2005); hunting and game tourism (e.g. Baker, 1997; Barnes, Burgess, & Pearce, 1992);and niche topics like birdwatching, safari photography tourism, and gorilla watching (e.g. Blom, 2000; Moscardo, 2000), just to name a few. In the last decade, the literature has taken a decided turn toward the issue of animals in tourism and the ethical implications (e.g. Burns, 2015; Fennell, 2012; World Society for the Protection of Animals, 2012).

Today, research around human–animal interactions in tourism has moved beyond the conservation literature to a much wider breath of topics. From a destination management perspective, researchers have explored the relevance and ethics of animals as icons or symbols for tourism marketing (Bertella, 2013; Tremblay, 2002). Others have explored issues of policies and governance of animals exploited or engaged in tourism (Duffy & Moore, 2010; Lovelock, 2015). Of course, research around the use of animals in captivity has garnered significant interest, possibly contributing to changes in what are deemed acceptable practices in this space (e.g. Ventre & Jett, 2015; Wearing & Jobberns, 2015).

Entire tomes have been published on the topics of animal welfare and tourism (e.g. Markwell, 2015) and animal ethics in the tourism space (e.g. Fennell, 2012). At the same time, popular opinion is also shifting. Large companies such as Expedia/Travelocity have enacted policies to monitor animal attractions sold on their site. SeaWorld has announced that it will phase out its captive orca breeding programs and Barnum & Bailey Circus will cease operations after several years of poor ticket sales and pressure to disband their large animal programs.

There is no question that the study of human–animal interactions in the tourism space has progressed. Major industry shifts have been seen, such as those discussed below. Significant contributions have been made in theoretical research. However, the issue of animal consumption, animal food chain exploitation, and the general welfare of animals used as food remains largely unexplored.

Animals as food in the tourism experience

As the body of knowledge around human–animal relationship in the leisure and tourism space has grown, little attention has been paid to the role of animals as food in the tourism experience. Even the United Nations World Tourism Association (UNWTO) Global Code of Ethics makes no mention of the ethical implications of animal consumption either as food or as food for attractions (Fennell, 2014).

A cursory review of the study of animals as food within the tourism experience yields, with a few notable exceptions (e.g. Fennell 2012, 2014; Mkono, 2015), very little results. In his review of human–animal relationships, Markwell (2015) found that within the tourism experience, animals as food are typically considered commodities, along with animals as apparel, traditional medicine, and souvenirs. In this model, animals as food are not included in either the pre-travel or post-travel experience. Carr (2009) argues that there is a distinct need to integrate emerging theories around animal rights into the unique reality of the tourism experience that has traditionally been tailored to focus on the desires of the human population above all else.

Traditionally, animals as part of the tourism experience are largely found within culinary tourism. There is no shortage of research around the value of food as part of a tourism experience, whether this be as a means to promote culinary tourism or to attract the "foodie" market, or simply as a commodity used to enhance the overall tourism experience (e.g. Ab Karim & Chi, 2010; Boniface, 2003; Horng &Tsai, 2010; Long, 2004). However, there is little to no mention of the animal as a sentient being, rather than simply the dish resulting from its death. The consumption of animals, either whole or in part, is systematically sterilized. To question where our food comes from would raise unsettling issues surrounding the morality of such consumption (Fennell, 2012).

From the popular press, for years, travel magazines such as *Conde Nast* and culinary magazines such as *Gourmet*, have positioned the notion of experiencing local delicacies as almost a "rite of passage" or an elite activity, something beyond the "touristy" experience. Tourism marketers contribute to the idea of typical foods, either created or traditional, as an experience that allows travelers a unique opportunity to immerse themselves in the location through a culinary experience.

Alternative tourism and its implications on animals as food

In addition to the unsettling lack of attention to the animal as more than a commodity within the tourism experience, it is also important to consider the dichotomy that now exists between this push for an alternative, authentic, or transformational tourism, and the implications that these growing trends have on animals used as food and the animal food chain.

As conservation and sustainability started percolating in tourism research, so did the slow but rising concern for an alternative to the growth in "mass tourism." As tourism tastes evolve, so does the movement away from the large-scale generic tourism experience, to what is often called a more authentic experience. Academics, practitioners, and the tourists themselves were looking for something "greener." Thus, several decades of research and consumer demand led to an increased awareness of the environmental impact of tourism, as well as greater concern regarding the social ills bred through poorly planned tourism, and an overall push to a tourism experience that is less "touristy" and more "authentic" (e.g. Wood, 2002).

Tourists are encouraged to partake in what is commonly known as typical foods, native foods, local foods, or *comida tipica*, all terms which invoke a sense of place (Hashimoto & Telfer, 2006; Sidali, Kastenholz, & Bianchi, 2015; Torres, 2002). Gastronomy is often used to foster a sense of place or belonging within the destination. Visitors are afforded the opportunity for an authentic experience by stepping out from the "tourist" label and experience the destination like a local. To many, breaking bread with the locals or eating traditional foods affords them the much more valued opportunity to feel like a pseudo-local or worldly "traveler." As Fennel and Maxwell (2015) noted, even those organizations offering ecotourism experiences, who score well on sustainable practices, often do no better than others when considering the ethical implications of their animal food sourcing. In some ways, this type of tourism may be preferred to larger-scale tourism development; it does not, however, release the visitor or the host from an ethical responsibility toward the animal on the plate.

While the topics covered in this tome vary across the issue of tourism and food, several of the authors of the chapters speak to the concept of "typical foods" as part of the tourism experience. In each case, the animal presented is a food authentic to that area, either because of tradition or through intense marketing. In some cases, these dishes have existed as a staple of local diets for decades. However, with the influx of tourism seeking the "authentic" or the special, the animals that are sacrificed for these dishes are now being pushed beyond local consumption, and often well out of the context of the traditional aspects of its origin. The authors make the argument that these cuisines are, in fact, sentient beings, first and foremost, rather than simply commodities within the typical tourism experience.

One interesting trend within sustainable tourism that may offer promise in the area of animals as food is that of transformational tourism. Advocates argue that transformational tourism has the power to change human behavior and make a positive impact on the world (Reisinger, 2015). It is assumed that this positive impact goes beyond benefits to humans. For tourism to truly be transformational, and thus have a positive impact on the world, it is imperative that it not cause suffering to any of the sentient beings, non-human animals included, that are involved. Although this is a fairly new tourism trend, it is an opportunity for the tourist and the provider to think more deeply about all of the impacts of tourism. At some point, it is inevitable that humans, with their desire to create a positive impact on the world, will have to take a look inward at the suffering their own existence is creating through consumption.

As Fennell (2012) argues, humans often prefer to turn a blind eye to the origins of their food, as to do otherwise would force us to consider the morality of such consumption. It is difficult to probe too deeply because to acknowledge animal suffering, we would also have to implicate ourselves as consumers. However, if a larger portion of the traveling population were to actually consider the impacts of animals as food offered as part of the tourism experience, then an outcome would be greater awareness, and hopefully, consumer rejection of these commodities, either in their pre-trip decision making or post-trip reflection.

While the trends mentioned above, paired with the growing body of knowledge of animal welfare in the tourism experience, does provide some hope, a significant shift is necessary. Not only is there a need to rethink the need for animal consumption, but also, specific to tourism, there is a need to shift away from the traditional hedonistic model of tourism consumption where the entire experience is designed to provide pleasure to the consumer (Carr, 2009), to one that encompasses a wider, more holistic appreciation for the other sentient beings impacted by the tourist experience.

Animals, Food, and Tourism book structure

The book is made up of eleven cases exploring animals and their role as food within the tourism experience. Several of the authors focus on a specific example of an iconic dish, often so ingrained in the tourism experience that to not partake might be considered unthinkable by those familiar with the destination. Imagine a trip to Maine that does not involve a bright red lobster dipped in melted butter or a trip into the Nordic region without a bit of roasted reindeer? The examples of such dishes are prevalent in tourism marketing and messaging, while rarely, if ever, actually referring to the animal, or animal part, that was sacrificed for the sake of the dish.

Several authors go beyond a specific example to explore the ethics of animals as food within the tourism experience, seeking to not only understand the history of this evolution but also how the tourism industry might better align the goals of sustainable tourism with the need to feed the tourist. If as a society, humans on both the supply and demand side of tourism are asking the sector to be more "responsible," "authentic," "sustainable," or the like, then do we not have a moral and global responsibility to align these emerging intentions with the animal welfare reality of the foods consumed by the tourist, which some might argue is one of the most important aspects of the travel experience?

The volume begins in Chapter 2 with Blankfield presenting an in-depth analysis of a pivotal essay by David Foster Wallace titled "Consider the Lobster" featured in *Gourmet* magazine in 2004. This pivotal piece, which was intended to be simply a review of the popular Maine Lobster Fest, instead took *Gourmet* readers, for the first time in its history, on an ethical exploration of the consumption of lobster as part of the festival. Through a textual analysis of the Wallace article, Blankfield demonstrates how the author provided a model for the application of gustatory ethics for the magazine's readers, as well as an opportunity to look with a critical eye upon their own tourism experiences. Breaking from the typical *modus operandi* of *Gourmet*, as well as many other culinary and tourism popular press pieces, the Wallace article forces the reader to consider the animal, its pain, its means of death, and the resulting ethical complications, rather than simply consider the taste of the dish.

There are animals that humans eat and others that humans play with, and sometimes they are the same. In Chapter 3, Burns, Öqvist, Angerbjörn, and Granquist explore the curious division of consumptive versus non-consumptive human–animal interactions. Drawing from two case studies of tourist interactions with marine mammals in Iceland, where the animals fall into both categories for the tourist, the researchers attempt to understand why some tourists may object to whale or seal hunting and may enjoy watching them in the wild, yet express an interest in eating these same beings as part of their tourist experience. They further explore the implications for the future of whaling, whale and seal watching, and hunting in Iceland and at a global level.

In Chapter 4, Quintero and López introduce the reader to the Mexican custom of *cabrito* or baby goat consumption. The manner in which the *cabrito* is raised and ultimately slaughtered is quite cruel, yet tourists are eager to partake in the dish. The authors argue that this is an example of culinary tourism where the tourist may not be fully aware of the cruelty involved, or may choose to ignore it for the sake of trying the dish, thus suspending an ethical standard that they may hold themselves to in a non-tourist situation. Tourists "behaving badly" is not a new concept. The idea that vacation affords the tourist the opportunity to do things they might not otherwise do is well documented. Therefore, it is of no surprise that this behavior would extend into culinary practices. Partaking in local traditional dishes often fosters the sense of place that is valued by the tourist. Through the lens of the *cabrito* example, the authors explore the issue of animal food production for widespread tourism consumption and the shared responsibility in this unethical practice.

In Chapter 5, Fung introduces a slightly different aspect of animals as food in the tourism sector. The author presents the case of the Amazon River dolphin. While this animal may be consumed by locals and tourists, it also has evolved into a tourist attraction. Visitors to the Brazilian Amazon are afforded the opportunity to feed the wild dolphins. This activity has become a popular tourist attraction, however because the dolphins are wild, attracting them requires a large number of fish. These fish are caught in tremendous numbers with little regard to their wellbeing. Not only is this practice ill-fated for the fish, it is also unsustainable and can exacerbate conflict between subsistence farmers who already view the dolphin as competition. Stepping back, the author discusses the ethics of utilizing one animal as food to attract other animals offered as part of the tourist experience.

In Chapter 6, Bertella focuses on the absence of animal-derived food from tourists' plates and how such an absence can be understood from an ecofeminist perspective. The author provides an in-depth analysis of veganism and the vegan food experience, introducing the concept of the "foodscape," which highlights the relationship between food, the spatial context of its supply chain, and the subjects who engage in food-related activities. The questions raised through the introduction of these theories are then addressed by the development of a case study of two vegan holiday country houses in Italy and the role animals play in that experience. The author concludes that tourism experiences that embrace the vegan lifestyle promote and reinforce values such as care and respect, and in doing so, raises the enormously import question of what values are reinforced with tourism food experiences that reject or ignore veganism.

In Chapter 7, Sayre and Henderson examine the impact that agritourism, specifically farm visits, has in fostering human–animal connections through interaction. They explore the notion that interacting with farm animals affords the visitor a greater awareness of the animal itself and features prominently in how the experience is appreciated by the tourist. Utilizing social media, specifically Yelp reviews, the authors argue that exposure to animals through farm visits features prominently in positive reviews, as does ethical production techniques. This research furthers the discussion on the importance of direct education regarding farmed animals as food so that humans can better understand the origins of their food, and thus, hopefully make better decisions.

In Chapter 8, Bricker and Joyner focus on linking sustainable food production with the principles of sustainable tourism. Their chapter frames this issue by contrasting the current state of the meat industry in the U.S., and in particular confined animal feeding lots, with the principles of sustainable tourism, through the lens of the Global Sustainable Tourism Criteria. In their review, they present the potential ramifications of factory farming on tourism, as well as a case study for sustainable management practices on pasture-raised pork in North Carolina, USA. They argue that for sustainable tourism development to be truly sustainable, a significant element of the tourism product – food production – must be considered.

In Chapter 9, Hoarau-Heemstra introduces the topic of reindeer tourism among the indigenous Sami people of the Nordic region. Responding to the growing interest in indigenous tourism in general, and specifically to the rise in tourist demand in that region, paired with the challenges of climate change, some of the Sami people elected to engage in tourism as an economic opportunity and cultural exchange. Hoarau-Heemstra presents the case of the Inga family reluctantly becoming engaged in tourism by allowing visitors to their reindeer farm. As opposed to some of the other cases presented previously, this chapter begins from the assumption that the Sami culture carries a moral responsibility toward the care of its animals. Thus, the case explores the realities for this one Sami family as they struggle with the challenges and impacts of introducing tourism to their farm while still protecting the wellbeing of their reindeer. Of course, this issue of a native population and their relationship to their animals is not unique to the Sami culture and is one that should be considered as researchers explore these topics further.

Coastal tourism is a popular tourism experience, and seafood often features prominently in that experience. In Chapter 10, Elder and Kline discuss the tremendous implications related to seafood tourism. The oceans are facing unprecedented pressure. Overfishing, pollution, and overpopulation are causing tremendous strain. The increasing popularity of coastal culinary tourism poses a particular threat. The authors argue that in addition to the matter of sentience as it relates to aquatic animal consumption, seafood tourism – and seafood consumption in general – has far-reaching implications for public health, conservation, and economic viability. They conclude with some innovative potential solutions to this problem.

In Chapter 11, Bone and Bone juxtapose the issue of animals as marketing icons and animals as food in Australia. Through a content analysis of tourism marketing materials for the city of Melbourne, the authors demonstrate the concerning practice of showcasing animals to then present them as food for the tourist. The region is experiencing a growth in agritourism, supported by the local government seeking to diversify its tourism offerings. At the same time, the authors also discuss "live export trade," or the disturbing practice in Australia whereby millions of farm animals are sent to countries for agricultural purposes, with little regulation protecting their wellbeing. The authors, taking a posthuman perspective, argue that tourism, as a potential contact zone where human and non-human animals meet, presents an opportunity for interspecies awareness and understanding.

In Chapter 12, Wearing, Wearing and Jobberns explore the complex relationship between Japanese whaling practices and the practice of whale meat consumption by tourists. At a time when Japan is under increasing global pressure over their whaling programs, and the Japanese population has significantly turned away from the consumption of whale products, there is still a prevalence of whale meat on the menu in traditional tourism restaurants. Through the lens of ecotourism, the authors explore how whale watching as a tourism experience has impacted the global and local conservation of whales and other marine species. They then turn their research back to the Japanese situation, which in spite of consistent criticism, continues to engage in whale capture and consumption, often under the guise of tourism. They pose the important question of whether, in this situation, as well as in others, there is the possibility of introducing an alternate ethical valuing system to contrast the dominant force of the economic value of the utilitarian view. The question of whether ethics in animal consumption will ever outweigh or even factor into the overall use of animals as a tourism "product" is of primary importance in this evolution of animal welfare related to consumption.

Finally, in Chapter 13, Kline completes the analysis by outlining the major themes drawn from each of the chapters, as well as identifying potential implications for tourism. Through this, and the careful considerations of the contributions by the book's authors, she identifies further areas of research.

References

Ab Karim, S., & Chi, C. G. Q. (2010). Culinary tourism as a destination attraction: An empirical examination of destinations' food image. *Journal of Hospitality Marketing & Management*, *19*(6), 531–555.

Baker, J. E. (1997). Trophy hunting as a sustainable use of wildlife resources in southern and eastern Africa. *Journal of Sustainable Tourism*, *5*(4), 306–321.

Barnes, J., Burgess, J., & Pearce, D. (1992). Wildlife tourism. In *Economics for the wilds: Wildlife, wildlands, diversity and development* (pp. 136–151). London: Earthscan Publications Limited.

Bertella, G. (2013). Ethical content of pictures of animals in tourism promotion. *Tourism Recreation Research*, *38*(3), 281–294.

Blom, A. (2000). The monetary impact of tourism on protected area management and the local economy in Dzanga-Sangha (Central African Republic). *Journal of Sustainable Tourism*, *8*(3), 175–189.

Boniface, P. (2003). *Tasting tourism: Travelling for food and drink.* Farnham: Ashgate Publishing Ltd.

Boo, E. (1990). Ecotourism: The potentials and pitfalls. In *Ecotourism: The potentials and pitfalls* (Vol. 1). Washington, DC: World Wildlife Fund.

Burns, G. L. (2015). Animals as tourism objects: Ethically refocusing relationships between tourists and wildlife. In K. Markwell (Ed.), *Animals and Tourism: Understanding Diverse Relationships* (pp. 44–59). Bristol: Channel View Publications.

Carr, N. (2009). Animals in the tourism and leisure experience. *Current Issues in Tourism, 12*(5–6), 409–411.

Cohen, E., & Avieli, N. (2004). Food in tourism: Attraction and impediment. *Annals of Tourism Research, 31*(4), 755–778.

Davis, D., & Tisdell, C. A. (1999). Tourist levies and willingness to pay for a whale shark experience. *Tourism Economics, 5*(2), 161–174.

DeMello, M. (2010). *Teaching the animal*. New York: Lantern Books.

Duffy, R., & Moore, L. (2010). Neoliberalising nature? Elephant-back tourism in Thailand and Botswana. *Antipode, 42*(3), 742–766.

Fennell, D. A. (2012). *Tourism and animal ethics*. London: Routledge.

Fennell, D. A. (2014). Exploring the boundaries of a new moral order for tourism's global code of ethics: An opinion piece on the position of animals in the tourism industry. *Journal of Sustainable Tourism, 22*(7), 983–996.

Fennell, D. A., & Markwell, K. (2015). Ethical and sustainability dimensions of foodservice in Australian ecotourism businesses. *Journal of Ecotourism, 14*(1), 48–63.

Franklin, A. (1999). *Animals and modern cultures: A sociology of human-animal relations in modernity*. London: SAGE.

Hashimoto, A., & Telfer, D. J. (2006). Selling Canadian culinary tourism: Branding the global and the regional product. *Tourism Geographies, 8*(1), 31–55.

Herzog, H. (2010). *Some we love, some we hate, some we eat*. New York: HarperCollins Publishers.

Honey, M. (1999). Who owns paradise? In *Ecotourism and sustainable development*. Washington, DC: Island Press.

Horng, J. S., & Tsai, C. T. S. (2010). Government websites for promoting East Asian culinary tourism: A cross-national analysis. *Tourism Management, 31*(1), 74–85.

Long, L. M. (Ed.). (2004). *Culinary tourism*. Lexington: University Press of Kentucky.

Lovelock, B. (2008). Ethical travel decisions travel agents and human rights. *Annals of Tourism Research, 35*(2), 338–358.

Lovelock, B. (2015). Troubled-shooting: The ethics of helicopter-assisted guided trophy hunting by tourists for Tahr. *Animals and Tourism: Understanding Diverse Relationships, 67*, 91. Bristol: Channel View Publications.

Markwell, K. (Ed.). (2015). Birds, beasts and tourism: Human – animal relationships in tourism. *Animals and Tourism: Understanding Diverse Relationships, 67*, 1–26. Bristol: Channel View Publications.

Mkono, M. (2015). 'Eating the animals you come to see': Tourists' meat-eating discourses in online communicative texts. *Animals and Tourism: Understanding Diverse Relationships, 67*, 211–226. Bristol: Channel View Publications.

Moscardo, G. (2000). Understanding wildlife tourism market segments: An Australian marine study. *Human Dimensions of Wildlife, 5*(2), 36–53.

Reisinger, Y. (2015). *Transformational tourism: Tourist perspectives*. Oxfordshire: CABI.

Serpell, J. (1996). *In the company of animals: A study of human-animal relationships*. New York: Cambridge University Press.

Shackley, M. L. (1996). *Wildlife tourism*. Andover: Cengage Learning EMEA.

Sidali, K. L., Kastenholz, E., & Bianchi, R. (2015). Food tourism, niche markets and products in rural tourism: Combining the intimacy model and the experience economy as a rural development strategy. *Journal of Sustainable Tourism*, *23*(8–9), 1179–1197.

Topelko, K. N., & Dearden, P. (2005). The shark watching industry and its potential contribution to shark conservation. *Journal of Ecotourism*, *4*(2), 108–128.

Torres, R. (2002). Toward a better understanding of tourism and agriculture linkages in the Yucatan: Tourist food consumption and preferences. *Tourism Geographies*, *4*(3), 282–306.

Tremblay, P. (2002). Tourism wildlife icons: Attractions or marketing symbols? In *CAUTHE 2002: Tourism and hospitality on the edge; Proceedings of the 2002 CAUTHE conference* (p. 624). Lismore: Edith Cowan University Press.

Ventre, J., & Jett, J. (2015). *Killer whales, theme parks and controversy: An exploration of the evidence* (Vol. 67, pp. 128–145). Bristol: Channel View Publications.

Wearing, S., & Jobberns, C. (2015). From free Willy to Seaworld: Has ecotourism improved the rights of whales? *Animals and Tourism: Understanding Diverse Relationships*, *67*, 75–98. Bristol: Channel View Publications.

Wood, M. E. (2002). *Ecotourism: Principles, practices and policies for sustainability*. Paris Cedex: United Nations Environmental Program.

World Society for the Protection of Animals. (2012). *The contribution of animal welfare and tourism for sustainable development*. Heredia: WSPA.

2 The gustatory ethics of "Consider the Lobster"

Bryan Blankfield

In 2003, the editors of *Gourmet*, an upscale culinary magazine dedicated to "fine living," invited David Foster Wallace, an American novelist, to go on assignment at the annual Maine Lobster Festival (MLF) and report about the event. His essay, "Consider the Lobster," was nothing they expected. Although Wallace begins rather benignly with a description of the festival's reputation as "one of the best food-themed festivals in the world" (2004, p. 50) and all the different types of lobster one might eat there, he quickly leaves these matters and launches into an ethical discussion of lobster neurology – whether or not they can feel pain – and ends by challenging readers of *Gourmet* to think deeply about lobster consumption.

Wallace's article was a steep departure from *Gourmet*'s standard fare. Since its founding in 1940, *Gourmet* had grown a reputation for high end culinary escapism. Readers expected to be whisked around the globe to the finest Parisian bistros, Italian vistas, and New York City restaurants. Randal Oulton writes, "[*Gourmet*] sold a fantasy; they sold you what you might create in your life, if only for one brief moment in early summer's dappled sunlight or mid-autumn's moonbeams on the bay" (2010, para. 2). *Gourmet* gradually expanded its focus in the 1980s to include American regional dishes, but the glossy-paged magazine remained devoted to its "romantic treatment of food" (Oulton, 2010, para. 13). It was against this literary and cultural milieu that Wallace contemplated the ethics of lobster consumption.

"Consider the Lobster" was published during a moment of redefinition for *Gourmet*. In 1999, Ruth Reichl, a former restaurant critic for *The New York Times*, was hired as *Gourmet*'s chief editor. According to fellow restaurant critic Jay Rayner, Reichl wanted to transform *Gourmet* into "the New Yorker of food, which many of us took to mean that she was going to stuff it full of staggeringly long, wonderfully in-depth, capricious, whimsical pieces" (2009, para. 6). In this respect, Wallace was an ideal contributor to Reichl's vision of the magazine. During the 1990s, Wallace had gained national prominence after *Infinite Jest*, a thousand-page piece of fiction riddled with over 300 footnotes, became a bestseller. Wallace also generated a cult following for his unique style of literary journalism, which Christoph Ribbat characterizes as "more baffled than excited, a persona more interested in the moral issues raised by . . . the event" (2010, p. 192). In a 1998 interview, Wallace described his method as "notic[ing] stuff that everybody else notices but they don't really notice that they notice" (Socca, 2012, p. 86).

Over the past two decades, many disciplines have been stimulated by the "animal turn," namely an increased attention to the study of animals and our relationships with them. David Fennell (2011), however, notes the paucity of scholarship bridging tourism and animal studies, especially those with an ethical perspective. Even within my own discipline of Communication Studies, scholars are only recently beginning to address the animal turn (Atkins-Sayre, 2010; Blankfield, 2016; Davis, 2011; Goodale & Black, 2010; Hawhee, 2011; Muckelbauer, 2011) and the rhetorical dimensions of food (Conley, 2015; Cramer, Greene, & Walters, 2011; Eckstein & Young, 2015; Rice, 2015; Stokes & Atkins-Sayre, 2016). In this chapter, I advance scholarly conversations on tourism, animal ethics, and rhetoric through a close-textual analysis of Wallace's lobster article. I argue that "Consider the Lobster" functions simultaneously as a treatise on tourism, a theorization of gustatory ethics, and a rhetorical performance that provides readers with a model for enacting gustatory ethics and critical tourism in their own lives.

In light of the diverse scholarly approaches in this edited volume, I would like to briefly expand upon my methodology. By rhetoric I refer to the creative use of symbolic language to influence thought and action. In the two millennia since rhetoric was theorized in Ancient Greece, many different definitions have proliferated. Wallace's essay illustrates Donald C. Bryant's belief that rhetoric operates by "*adjusting ideas to people and of people to ideas*" (1953, p. 413, emphasis original). According to Bryant, "difficult and strange ideas have to be modified without being distorted or invalidated; and audiences have to be prepared through the mitigation of their prejudices, ignorance, and irrelevant sets of mind without being disposed of their judgments" (1953, p. 413). In my analysis, I pay special attention to the ways in which Wallace adapts his observations to readers of *Gourmet*.

Tourism

In 1961, Daniel Boorstin bemoaned a historic shift in American travel experiences. No longer did most people experience the world as travelers. Instead, they had become tourists, pursuing artificial "pseudo-events." Although analyses of tourism have become more sophisticated in recent decades (Holden, 2000; MacCannell, 1999; Pezzullo, 2007; Urry, 2002), there still remains a disdain of tourists held by scholars of tourism, locals of tourist hotspots, and even tourists themselves, the latter of whom are prone to griping about *other* tourists (Bowman, 1998; MacCannell, 1999). One common complaint is that the presence of tourists undermines the authenticity of a locale. Throughout its publication history, *Gourmet* contributed to this form of excursionist snobbism in its valorization of high-end cultural settings, as opposed to kitschy tourist locales. Above all else, readers of *Gourmet* were invited to envision themselves as travelers in the know.

Wallace echoes Boorstin's critique of artificial pseudo-events and disdain for tourists. In his exposition of the MLF, he notes, "Tourism and lobster are the midcoast region's two main industries . . . and the Maine Lobster Festival represents less an intersection of the industries than a deliberate collision, joyful and lucrative and loud" (2004, p. 50). Whereas an editor of a rival epicurean magazine eagerly promoted the Festival, Wallace calls it a "commercial demotic event" (2004, p. 56) – hardly high praise for readers of *Gourmet*. Yet Wallace suggests that tourism may nonetheless be a personally rewarding enterprise.

Tourism is popularly imagined as a pleasurable, leisurely activity, but Wallace counters this assumption. In his view, tourism involves a more active and somewhat critical view of one's new environment. Wallace ventures that it "probably really is good for the soul to be a tourist, even if it's only once in a while. Not good for the soul in a refreshing or enlivening way, though, but rather in a grim, steely-eyed, let's-look-honestly-at-the-facts-and-find-some-way-to-deal-with-them way" (2004, p. 56 n6). Rather than relaxing one's senses to his or her surroundings, Wallace suggests that tourism amplifies them. This amplification comes at a price, however. The more one observes, the more she is confronted by her own insignificance. Wallace writes,

> My personal experience has not been that traveling around the country is broadening or relaxing, or that radical changes in place and context have a salutary effect, but rather that intranational tourism is radically constricting, and humbling in the hardest way – hostile to my fantasy of being a real individual, of living somehow outside and above it all.
>
> (2004, p. 56 n6)

Part of the problem is that one recognizes him or herself as merely one cog in the greater economic system that is tourism. Put more simply, "As a tourist, you become economically significant but existentially loathsome, an insect on a dead thing" (2004, p. 56 n6).

This critical view of tourism is found in his appraisal of the Festival itself. Wallace employs painfully long sentences, which imitate his description of the Festival as "full of irksome little downers" (2004, p. 55). He complains that the MLF does not

> give you near enough napkins, considering how messy lobster is to eat, especially when you're squeezed onto benches alongside children of various ages and vastly different levels of fine-motor-development – not to mention the people who've somehow smuggled in their own beer in enormous aisle-blocking coolers, or who all of a sudden produce their own plastic tablecloths and try to spread them over large portions of tables to try to reserve them (the tables) for their little groups.
>
> (2004, p. 55)

His belabored style encourages readers to dwell on the many ways the MLF falls short of expectations. In so doing, he challenges the idyllic fantasies often promoted by *Gourmet*. This section on the Festival is fairly short, however. To employ a food metaphor, it serves as an appetizer, providing an audience with a taste of what is yet to come. Wallace turns next to the actual consumption of lobster.

Gustatory ethics

Implicit throughout "Consider the Lobster" is Wallace's theorization of a gustatory ethics. By gustatory ethics, I refer to a thoughtful concern about one's predilections for particular foods. It is an ethics grounded in both senses of the word "taste" – consumption and a refined enjoyment grounded in judgment. As such, gustatory ethics falls within the domain of the gourmet. As Wallace illustrates, this refined judgment examines many aspects of the food in question. The gourmet should understand where their food has come from, its former livelihood, how it was butchered or killed, and ultimately prepared. Even cultural attitudes toward the food and its long-term sustainability may be relevant. Much like a connoisseur of fine wine, a gourmet abiding by Wallace's gustatory ethics revels in slowing down, embracing complexity, and savoring all the details. The flipside, of course, is whether one can fully savor their meal upon having researched it thoroughly. This is the pleasure and peril of being a gourmet. It goes beyond pleasing one's taste buds by enlisting one's mind.

Wallace begins his article by describing the locale, the Festival's glowing reputation, and lists the nine lobster dishes one might eat there. Instead of tantalizing his audience with provocative descriptions of these different dishes, or even how to cook them, Wallace educates his readers about the etymology of the word lobster, the class and phylum it belongs to, and provides a short history lesson of American attitudes toward these crustaceans. When he finishes, readers learn that "lobsters are basically giant sea-insects," "garbagemen of the sea," "chewable fuel," and only recently considered fine dining (2004, p. 55). Wallace notes how "some colonies had laws against feeding lobsters to inmates because it was thought to be cruel and unusual, like making people eat rats" (2004, p. 55). Only after listing these encyclopedic details does Wallace comment on how lobster tastes. This appraisal, however, is limited to the following solitary sentence: "[lobster] meat is richer and more substantial than most fish, its taste subtle compared to the marine-gaminess of mussels and clams" (2004, p. 55). Despite the Festival's promotion of lobsters as a healthier option than chicken, Wallace points out that "the common practice of dipping the lobster meat in melted butter torpedoes all these happy fat-specs, which none of the Council's promotional stuff ever mentions, any more than potato-industry PR talks about sour cream and bacon bits" (2004, p. 55 n5). Thus, even before Wallace poses any ethical dilemmas about lobster consumption, he invites readers to reconsider their previous views of lobsters.

To get a better sense of Wallace's rhetoric, we may compare it with an earlier account of a lobster entrée in *Gourmet* magazine. During her 1965 visit to Prunier, a restaurant in Paris, food critic Naomi Barry writes, "*Homard au Champagne* is lobster at its most luxurious. A live lobster weighing a scant pound and a half is cut into slices an inch thick" (2004, p. 157). Significantly, Barry quickly glosses over the lobster's death. Within one sentence, the live lobster simply transforms into inch thick slices. No mention of killing the lobster is made. She continues,

> After the slices have been browned in butter and seasoned with salt and pepper, half a bottle of very dry Champagne and a little fish stock are poured in, and a whole truffle is added. The pan is covered and the lobster cooked gently for twenty minutes. Then it is removed and shelled, and the meat and truffle are sliced thin and placed in a warmed, covered dish.
>
> (2004, p. 157)

Wallace has none of this. Indeed, his entire article challenges repeatedly the idea that there is anything gentle or casual about cooking lobsters.

Wallace explores the ethical dimensions of lobster consumption midway through his essay by considering the views of People for the Ethical Treatment of Animals (PETA), local residents, and the Maine Lobster Promotion Council. None of their stances are wholly satisfactory to Wallace, however. PETA is dismissed for its "simplistic and self-righteous" rhetoric (2004, p. 62 n13), such as "Lobsters are extraordinarily sensitive," "To me, eating a lobster is out of the question" (2004, p. 60), and "Being Boiled Hurts" (2004, p. 60 n10); as well as reliance on celebrities such as Mary Tyler Moore. Although these simplistic statements and celebrity endorsements have contributed greatly to PETA's popularity (Simonson, 2001), they do not wrestle with complexity. They are non-reflexive declarations. Wallace does not find the opposing views of the Maine Lobster Promotion Council or the locals, who largely echo the Festival's arguments, much better. He discredits them for advancing "false or fuzzy," albeit "more sophisticated" sounding claims (2004, p. 62).

Wallace adopts a scientific and philosophical approach while parsing the ethical conundrum of lobster consumption. In so doing, he avoids accusations of undue sentimentality. For instance, in response to Festival tracts, which assure tourists that "There's a part of the brain in people and animals that lets us feel pain, and lobsters' brains don't have this part," Wallace points out that this belief is "incorrect in about 11 different ways" (2004, p. 60) and gives a cogent discussion of the cerebral cortex, brain stem, and nociceptors. He then explains why nearly every way of preparing lobster, whether putting it in boiling water, incrementally increasing the temperature as one might cook a frog, microwaving, tearing the lobster apart with one's bare hands, or mercy-killing by stabbing the lobster's head, do not work and/or are potentially painful for the lobster. Although he concedes that lobsters' nervous systems are less advanced, since they cannot make or absorb "natural opioids like endorphins and enkephalins," he counters that this may make pain even more intolerable for them. "It could be," Wallace writes, "that their lack of endorphin/enkephalin hardware means that lobsters' raw subjective experience of pain is so radically different from mammals' that it may not even deserve the term *pain*" (2004, p. 63). It is doubtful whether readers of *Gourmet* had ever encountered discussions of neurological components such as cerebral cortexes, ganglia, or endorphins in the magazine before.

A thorough gustatory ethics may advance one's understanding of the world. While noting how lobsters' claws are "banded to keep them from tearing one another up under the stresses of captivity" (2004, p. 60), Wallace highlights similar practices in other food industries. "It's not clear to me," he writes, "whether most *Gourmet* readers know about debeaking, or about related practices like dehorning cattle in commercial feedlots, cropping swine's tails in factory hog farms to keep psychotically bored neighbors from chewing them off, and so forth" (2004, p. 60 n8). Significantly, Wallace adds, "It so happens that your assigned correspondent knew almost nothing about standard meat-industry operations before starting work on this article" (2004, p. 60 n8). His comment reveals how applying a gustatory ethic to one dish may inform the rest of one's diet.

Wallace repeatedly makes recourse to science and philosophy in his consideration of lobsters, but "Consider the Lobster" is not completely innocent of attitudinal leanings. He frequently incorporates language intended to enlist his readers' sympathy for lobsters. Similar to the tactics Wendy Atkins-Sayre observed in PETA's rhetoric, Wallace invites his audience to identify with these crustaceans. He compares a lobster with its claw on a "kettle's rim" to "a person trying to keep from going over the edge of a roof" (2004, p. 62). He doubles down on this personification several sentences later, noting, "The lobster . . . behaves very much as you or I would behave if we were plunged into boiling water (with the obvious exception of screaming)" (2004, p. 62). Even more dramatically, Wallace notes near the end of his essay that "if you, the Festival attendee, permit yourself to think that lobsters can suffer and would rather not, the MLF can begin to take on aspects of something like a Roman circus or medieval torture-fest" (2004, p. 64).

A rhetorical performance

In the conclusion to *Tourism and Animal Ethics*, David Fennell poignantly summarizes the chief dilemma facing each person who thinks deeply about his or her food. He writes,

> We do not want to ask questions about where our food comes from in an effort to avoid the personal anxiety this creates in deciding whether or not it is morally justifiable to comsume [sic] it. We do not want to probe deeper into questions about animal captivity because this unlocks a whole series of emotions that might not correspond with our pursuit of enjoyment. These questions are suppressed so we are able to enjoy what we might otherwise classify as wrong. We choose not to vilify these institutions . . . because in doing so we must certainly vilify ourselves.
>
> (2011, p. 248)

Part of what makes "Consider the Lobster" so striking is that Wallace wrestles candidly with these concerns. After likening the Festival to a "Roman circus or medieval torture-fest," he writes,

> Does that comparison seem a bit much? If so, exactly why? . . . My own immediate reaction is that such a comparison is hysterical, extreme – and yet the reason it seems extreme to me appears to be that I believe animals are less

> morally important than human beings; and when it comes to defending such a belief, even to myself, I have to acknowledge that (a) I have an obvious selfish interest in this belief, since I like to eat certain kinds of animals and want to be able to keep doing it, and (b) I have not succeeded in working out any sort of personal ethical system in which the belief is truly defensible instead of just selfishly convenient.
>
> (2004, p. 64)

Significantly, despite his lengthy probing into the ethical dimensions of lobster consumption, Wallace does not provide readers with any definite answers. He neither condones nor admonishes completely the killing of these crustaceans. Instead, he admits that "what I really am is confused" (2004, p. 64).

In light of this edited collection's aim, which is to better encourage ethical reflections on animals as food and tourism, Wallace's inability to offer any definite answers presents an unavoidable question: What value, if any, can scholars and readers derive from Wallace's essay? Does his gustatory ethics ultimately reveal itself as an aesthetic exercise? Is his essay all fun and no function? By refusing to provide any definite answers, Wallace models a mode of inquiry that readers can pursue further. His essay is thus a rhetorical performance that invites readers to consider the lobster and teaches them how to question the ethical choices implicit in their eating habits. Moreover, Wallace does so without devolving into "a PETA-like screed" (2004, p. 64). This detail is especially noteworthy insofar as PETA often serves as the animal rights movement's de facto representative; such popularity creates a limited view of what an ethical relationship with animals and food should be. Despite PETA's reasonable concern for the humane treatment of animals, its message is often easily dismissed by critics because of its frequent reliance on over-the-top rhetoric.

The success of Wallace's rhetorical performance hinges on his meandering style, which allows him to question assumptions that readers hold about lobsters. Wallace admits early on, "everyone knows what a lobster is. As usual, though, there's much more to know than most of us care about" (2004, p. 55). He derives his knowledge of lobsters and the MLF from a wide host of sources, ranging from encyclopedias, interviews with locals, books, newspapers, scientists, philosophers, and personal observation. With each piece of knowledge, Wallace links together a series of complex and uncomfortable observations. This approach encourages a nuanced ethical stance and self-reflection in readers because their stances become seen as less tenable or even morally hospitable.

In a manner consistent with his general writing style, but unusual for *Gourmet*, Wallace's essay is full of footnotes, which often comprise over one fourth of the page. These footnotes force readers to slow down, engage multiple facets, and think more deeply about the subject material. When questioned about his reliance on footnotes during a 1998 interview, Wallace explained,

> Look, I'm not a great journalist, and I can't interview anybody. But what I can do is slice open my head for you, and let you see a cross-section of an

> averagely bright person's head. And in a way, the footnotes I think are better representations of thought patterns and fact patterns.
>
> (Socca, 2012, p. 86)

Footnotes highlight potential avenues of thought, which may run counter, adjacent, and perpendicular to Wallace's main focus. At times, he even places footnotes within footnotes. For instance, Wallace subdivides footnote 13 with two parenthetical N.B. while navigating his own complicated views of PETA.

Of course, whether these footnotes slow the reader down depends on how the essay is read. If one merely reads the essay without pausing at each footnote, and instead reads each footnote afterward, the effect is diminished. Nonetheless, Wallace's heavy reliance on antithesis throughout his essay insures a similar effect for those who either ignored the footnotes or skimmed them after. Wallace routinely presents and then challenges common beliefs about lobsters. For instance, he states, "[lobsters are] good eating. Or so we think now" (2004, p. 55). His negative description of the MLF counters the high appraisal made by a rival magazine's senior editor. He offers a contrast between the Festival's fuzzy propaganda and scientific research. Similarly, while describing the pain that lobsters feel, he fluctuates from the possibility that they may not feel pain at all to suggesting that they do. Each attempt to posit a more ethical method of lobster preparation is confronted with scientific data that suggests the lobster still suffers.

Although Wallace's language leans heavily in support of not eating lobsters, he refrains from prohibiting the consumption of lobster. Instead of giving any definite answers to the ethical dilemmas posed by the Festival, he simply confronts the reader with more questions. (Of the nineteen sentences in his final section, over half – eleven – are questions.) The essay itself ends in abeyance. In his final two sentences, he writes,

> These last couple queries, though, while sincere, obviously involve much larger and more abstract questions about the connections (if any) between aesthetics and morality, and these questions lead straightaway into such deep and treacherous waters that it's probably best to stop the public discussion right here. There are limits to what even interested persons can ask of each other.
>
> (2004, p. 64)

This may seem like a cop-out, but this unresolved conclusion illustrates the tourist component of a gustatory ethics. Tourism, for Wallace, is not an easy enterprise. It is not intended to make you feel good about yourself, like a simple resolution would. Tourism invites you into uncharted territory and forces you to recognize how quickly your expertise ends and goes no further.

Conclusion

Unlike most *Gourmet* articles, Wallace does not present readers with an idyllic view of his travel experience or food. He performs a mode of rhetorical inquiry.

Instead of encouraging escapism, he reframes tourism as an arduous opportunity for moral introspection. Instead of describing a succulent entrée, he focuses on the creature and what it might experience when becoming such a dish. Indeed, if Wallace ate lobster while at assignment at the Maine Lobster Festival, he never mentions it. In short, Wallace's article involves nothing less than a complete reversal in how we understand tourism, gourmets, and lobsters. From a rhetorical perspective, Wallace invites us to read lobsters as subjects and not simply objects – or in the more common parlance of rhetorical critics, as texts instead of the context. "Consider the Lobster" illustrates Nathan Stormer's observation that, "Texts are recognized within networks that privilege them as such. . . . They are linguistic to those few who read them and not to them who ignore them" (2004, p. 276). How we treat animals or, in this case, lobsters, is often a matter of how we read them.

This lesson in gustatory ethics may be applied profitably in future tourism studies that center on animals as food. What cultural knowledge, for instance, shapes and promotes a tourist's experience of a particular regional dish? How does the romantic portrayal of food by epicurean magazines encourage certain forms of agritourism or restaurant practices? If Wallace can make a compelling case for considering the moral treatment of lobsters, how may a gourmet reconcile eating animals with more sophisticated pain mechanisms? By asking readers to consider the lobster, Wallace unleashes the possibility of a more expansive gustatory ethics.

References

Atkins-Sayre, W. (2010). Articulating identity: People for the ethical treatment of animals and the animal/human divide. *Western Journal of Communication*, *74*(3), 309–328.

Barry, N. (2004). Prunier. In R. Reichl (Ed.), *Remembrance of things Paris: Sixty years of writing from Gourmet* (pp. 154–158). New York: Modern Library.

Blankfield, B. (2016). 'A symbol of his warmth and humanity': Fala, Roosevelt, and the personable presidency. *Rhetoric & Public Affairs*, *19*(2), 209–244.

Boorstin, D. J. (1961). *The image: A guide to pseudo-events in America*. New York: Atheneum.

Bowman, M. S. (1998). Performing Southern history for the tourist gaze: Antebellum home tour guide performances. In D. Pollock (Ed.), *Exceptional spaces: Essays in performance and history* (pp. 142–158). Chapel Hill, NC: University of North Carolina Press.

Bryant, D. C. (1953). Rhetoric: Its functions and its scope. *Quarterly Journal of Speech*, *39*(4), 401–424.

Conley, D. (2015). M/Orality. *Communication and Critical/Cultural Studies*, *12*(2), 223–227.

Cramer, J. M., Greene, C. P., & Walters, L. (2011). *Food as communication: Communication as food*. New York: Peter Lang.

Davis, D. (2011). Creaturely rhetorics. *Philosophy & Rhetoric*, *44*(1), 88–94.

Eckstein, J., & Young, A. M. (2015). Cooking, celebrity chefs, and public chef intellectuals. *Communication and Critical/Cultural Studies*, *12*(2), 205–208.

Fennell, D. A. (2011). *Tourism and animal ethics*. London: Routledge.

Goodale, G., & Black, J. E. (2010). *Arguments about animal ethics*. Lanham, MD: Lexington Books.

Hawhee, D. (2011). Toward a bestial rhetoric. *Philosophy & Rhetoric*, *44*(1), 81–87.

Holden, A. (2000). *Environment and tourism*. London: Routledge.

MacCannell, D. (1999). *The tourist: A new theory of the leisure class*. Berkeley, CA: University of California Press.

Muckelbauer, J. (2011). Domesticating animal theory. *Philosophy & Rhetoric*, *44*(1), 95–100.

Oulton, R. (2010, December 8). Gourmet magazine. *Cook's Info*. Retrieved August 20, 2016, from www.cooksinfo.com/gourmet-magazine

Pezzullo, P. C. (2007). *Toxic tourism: Rhetorics of pollution, travel, and environmental justice*. Tuscaloosa, AL: University of Alabama Press.

Rayner, J. (2009, October 5). Gourmet magazine to close. *The Guardian*. Retrieved August 20, 2016, from www.theguardian.com/lifeandstyle/wordofmouth/2009/oct/05/food-and-drink-magazines

Ribbat, C. (2010). Seething static: Notes on Wallace and journalism. In D. Hering (Ed.), *Consider David Foster Wallace: Critical essays* (pp. 187–198). Los Angeles, CA: Sideshow Media Group Press.

Rice, J. (2015). Craft rhetoric. *Communication and Critical/Cultural Studies*, *12*(2), 218–222.

Simonson, P. (2001). Social noise and segmented rhythms: News, entertainment, and celebrity in the crusade for animal rights. *The Communication Review*, *4*(3), 399–420.

Socca, T. (2012). David Foster Wallace. In S. Burn (Ed.), *Conversations with David Foster Wallace* (pp. 82–88). Jackson, MI: University Press of Mississippi.

Stokes, A. Q., & Atkins-Sayre, W. (2016). *Consuming identity: The role of food in redefining the South*. Jackson, MS: University Press of Mississippi.

Stormer, N. (2004). Articulation: A working paper on rhetoric and taxis. *Quarterly Journal of Speech*, *90*(3), 257–284.

Urry, J. (2002). *The tourist gaze* (2nd ed.). London: SAGE Publications.

Wallace, D. F. (2004). Consider the lobster. *Gourmet*, *64*(8), 50–64.

3 When the wildlife you watch becomes the food you eat

Exploring moral and ethical dilemmas when consumptive and non-consumptive tourism merge

Georgette Leah Burns, Elin Lilja Öqvist, Anders Angerbjörn, and Sandra Granquist

Introduction

In the context of wildlife tourism, human experiences with other species are often divided into the binary categories of consumptive and non-consumptive interactions. What happens when the same person values a species, and interacts with it, in both categories? The aim of this chapter is to explore moral and ethical issues inherent in tourism experiences where tourists both watch and eat the same species. The work also seeks to contribute to filling an identified gap in the tourism literature concerning moral issues associated with the use of animals as food (Yudina & Fennell, 2013).

Although the chapter is primarily a theoretical piece, two case studies examining whale watching and whale eating, and seal watching and seal eating, in Iceland are included. These provide practical examples of the decision-making dilemmas when consumptive and non-consumptive forms of wildlife tourism merge. In discussing situations where the same species is both watched and eaten, we seek to explore the implications for tourism of this seemingly paradoxical human behavior. Understanding why tourists who state that the hunting of wildlife (in this case whales and seals) is unacceptable are willing to eat that same wildlife has implications for the future of the whale and seal industries in both their consumptive and non-consumptive forms in Iceland. More globally, understanding the underlying moral and ethical considerations that influence tourist behavior in this context has implications for the future of wildlife watching.

Humans, other animals, and tourism

Human and non-human animals have a long, complex, and essential history of interactions, in which the relationships formed vary temporally, spatially, and culturally. As Hal Herzog (2011) so simply, and eloquently, phrased it, there are “some we love, some we hate, and some we eat.” Inherent in these relationships are different ethical perspectives that provide the framework for individual, human consideration of what is right or wrong behavior.

Tourism is just one of the many ways humans engage with other animals, and in the context of tourism, human interactions with other animal species are no less broad and complex. We ride them, watch them, feed them, hunt them, photograph them, and eat them. These experiences are often divided into the binary categories of consumptive and non-consumptive activities (Bauer & Herr, 2004; Burns, 2015a; Higginbottom, 2004, Lovelock, 2015).

The division traditionally drawn between these two categories implies that consumptive activities, such as fishing and hunting, involve the deliberate killing of animals, while non-consumptive activities, such as wildlife watching, do not. Accordingly, wildlife watching is considered non-consumptive because the wildlife is not deliberately physically consumed, or killed, during the activity. When a species is eaten, however, it must first be killed: an activity that is consumptive. In some forms of consumptive wildlife tourism, the tourist is involved in the activity of killing the animal – such as in fishing or hunting experiences. When the wildlife is ordered on a plate at a restaurant, it is unlikely that the consumer was involved in the process of killing the animal. However, as Bratanova, Loughnan, and Bastian (2011, p. 195) claim, "Even when people do not actively contribute to the death of the animal, categorizing it as food leads to a reduction in capacity to suffer and subsequent moral standing."

A further distinction is that non-consumptive forms of wildlife tourism experiences are often considered more sustainable than consumptive forms (Mau, 2008; Walpole & Thouless, 2005; Wilson & Tisdell, 2001), although this is debated. Wildlife watching, for example, can lead to negative impacts on wild animals, affecting them both physiologically and behaviorally (Ellenberg, Setiawan, Cree, Houston, & Seddon, 2007; Granquist & Sigurjónsdóttir, 2014; Parsons, 2012). In contrast, consumptive tourism forms are sometimes discussed as sustainable in a wildlife management context – for example, when hunting is promoted as a "sustainable utilization of wildlife resources" (Akama, 2008, p. 85).

The simplistic dichotomy between consumptive and non-consumptive tourism activities is contentious, with some authors arguing that all forms of wildlife tourism are consumptive (Burns, 2015a; Mkono, 2015). One reason for this is because some interactions with wildlife can lead to unintended death for the animals. For example, on Australia's Fraser Island, interactions between tourists and dingoes have resulted in injury to humans and subsequent wildlife management decisions to kill dingoes (Burns, 2015a; Burns, Macbeth, & Moore, 2011). Interactions with non-lethal outcomes for the wildlife, however, have also been argued as a form of consumption (Higham & Hopkins, 2015; Higham, Bejder, Allen, Corkeron, & Lusseau, 2016). When wildlife is watched, it is framed as an object of the tourist's gaze, existing for the benefit of the tourist. In this commodification (Wearing & Jobberns, 2011), the wildlife is constructed as a product to be used, and thus consumed visually by the tourist (Burns, 2015a). Both in this context, and where the wildlife is considered a resource for human utilization and lethal consumption, an extrinsic value of the animal, stemming from a Judeo-Christian ethic that legitimizes our use of them, perpetuates. Thus, the concept of utility of the species may be most strongly connected with consumptive tourism practices (e.g., hunting and fishing) but can also be part of non-consumptive activities when animals are viewed as existing for the purpose of us watching them – as resources for our, human, pleasure.

What happens when the boundaries between consumptive and non-consumptive tourism are blurred, such as when the same species is valued for its use in both of these categories? Are Herzog's (2011) three types of human relationships with animals (love, hate, and eat) necessarily mutually exclusive? Certainly, individual difference exists between humans regarding how they classify their engagement with different species. For example, some people may hate dogs, others love them, and others choose to eat them. Similarly, rabbits are kept as pets by children, poisoned as pests by farmers, and eaten as a high protein food source by many people around the world (Szendrő, 2016; Dalle Zotte, 2014). These scenarios, where different people place the same animal in different categories (Bratanova et al., 2011, p. 196), are common across groups of people. Less common, however, particularly in the case of wildlife, is the same person valuing a species, and interacting with it, in more than one of these categories.

Some tourism involves experiences where tourists both watch and eat the same species. This occurs in Australia, for example, where visitors to the country are enticed by, and expect to see, the indigenous kangaroo (Higginbottom, Northrope, Croft, Hill, & Fredline, 2004) but can also select its flesh from some restaurant menus. Similar experiences occur in Iceland, where the popularity of whale watching is increasing while commercial whale hunting continues simultaneously, and whale meat is served in many restaurants. In the same country, riding the Icelandic horse is a popular tourism activity (Helgadóttir & Dashper, 2016; Sigurdardóttir & Helgadóttir, 2015), and its meat can be purchased for human consumption in grocery stores around the country. In discussing situations where the same species is both watched and eaten, our intention is not to determine what is right or what is wrong; rather we seek to explore the decision-making process for tourists and the implications for tourism of this behavior.

The dilemma of eating meat: cognitive dissonance and the meat-paradox

Literature from wildlife tourism, tourism ethics, and discourse surrounding the consumption of meat in contemporary society enables us to examine how attitudes toward animals are shaped and formed and the potential emotional and moral contradictions inherent in not wanting to harm species while simultaneously not wanting to give up use of animal products (Bulliet, 2005). This contradiction exists for many of us on a daily basis, though we do not often think about it consciously. For this reason, cognitive dissonance theory (Festinger, 1957) is a useful framework with which to disentangle this contradiction.

Cognitive dissonance theory tells us that individuals seek consistency among their beliefs and opinions. When there is inconsistency between attitudes or behaviors, something must change to eliminate any dissonance. Thus, cognitive dissonance often occurs when a person's behavior and beliefs are in conflict, and they disconnect mentally and/or emotionally from part of the experience. While the disconnect may be deliberate, it may not be conscious. It operates as a defense mechanism for practicing avoidance and denial (Joy, 2011) allowing, for example, those who oppose the harming of animals to consume their flesh. This accords with the work of Loughnan, Haslam, and Bastian (2010) and Loughnan, Bastian, and Haslam (2014) who describe a 'meat paradox' that highlights the moral dilemma involved in eating animals. "Eating animals is morally troublesome when animals are perceived as worthy of moral concern" (Loughnan et al., 2014, p. 105). Thus, to resolve this dilemma, Loughnan et al. (2010) assert that people withdraw moral concern for the species they are consuming.

A moral and ethical perspective

A discussion of morality is obviously, and necessarily, connected with ethics since ethics is concerned with moral values (Vaughn, 2008). Morals and ethics are essentially about determining the correct behavior in a given situation. In our interactions with non-human animals, the chosen right or wrong of an activity may be based on how we categorize the animal. We may categorize the same species for different purposes in different contexts, and each category we use "highlights certain attributes of the animal while deemphasizing those irrelevant to the category" (Bratanova et al., 2011, p. 196). Recent calls for greater attention to morals (Caton, 2012) and ethics in tourism generally (Burns, 2015b; Fennell, 2015; Lovelock & Lovelock, 2013), and wildlife tourism specifically (Burns, 2017; Burns, 2015a), is thus warranted as we strive to understand experiences where tourists both watch and eat the same species, as these activities entail different ethical and moral considerations.

Wildlife tourism activities, even non-lethal ones, are most frequently based on concern for maximizing pleasure for the tourist and profit for the operator, with industry concerns for wildlife often centered upon what is necessary to maintain their availability as a resource. That is, the philosophy underlining the tourism activity is anthropocentric and based on the utility of the wildlife, appreciating it for its extrinsic value (Burns et al., 2011). A more ecocentric philosophical approach, encompassing the wider ecosystem as a connected whole in which humans are less central, recognizes the potential of a more ethical and sustainable intrinsic value of wildlife (Burns, 2017; Burns et al., 2011). An argument is also made that recent societal changes, such as accepted labelling of the current geological era as the Anthropocene and the granting of intrinsic rights to the Whanganui River in New Zealand, pave the way for a shift to this type of approach in tourism (Burns, 2017).

The two case studies presented below provide examples that help us explore questions asked in this chapter that build on our ethical hypothesis about why, and how, tourists make decisions about engaging with wildlife through both consumptive and non-consumptive activities. The data draws on a larger study conducted by Öqvist (2016) on tourist experiences and perceptions of interacting with whales and seals in Iceland.

Case study one: whales and tourists in Iceland

Throughout the history of human interactions with whales, the overarching ethics in most interactions have been anthropocentric and based on extrinsic value. This legitimized the ideological construction of whales as a species for consumption, whether for use that resulted in the deliberate death of the whale, such as sustaining small scale indigenous populations and large scale commercial industry, or for non-lethal use as an object of tourism. Over the last few decades, systematic anthropomorphizing and personification of whales has increased the emotional response of humans to them (Einarsson, 2009), driven campaigns to cease lethal use, and promoted their non-lethal/non-consumptive use (Higham et al., 2016). In this "moral turn" (Caton, 2012), whales are increasingly afforded moral concern; however, even non-lethal use such as tourism is based on anthropocentrism and rarely acknowledges the potential intrinsic value of the species.

Recent authors examining whales and tourism focus on the shift from whale hunting to whale watching (e.g. Chen, 2011; Cunningham, Huijbens, & Wearing, 2012) and the potential of increasing watching as a tourist activity (e.g., Cisneros-Montemayor, Sumaila, Kaschner, & Pauly, 2010). Attention paid to destinations where hunting continues yet watching also thrives remains minimal and tends to debate whether these two activities can coexist (e.g., Higham & Lusseau, 2008). Examining the parallel occurrence of whale watching and whale eating in Iceland provides a practical example of the inherent dilemma in combining these forms of tourism, and assists to demonstrate the moral and ethical issues embedded within these different forms.

In Iceland, the popularity of whale watching is increasing annually while simultaneously commercial whale hunting continues. Whale watching formally commenced as a tourism activity in Iceland in 1999 and approximately 20% of all tourists who visit the country actively seek a whale watching experience (Icewhale, 2017). In 2014, almost 230,000 tourists engaged in whale watching and this number rose to around 270,000 in 2015 (Icewhale, 2017). The main species sighted are minke (*Balaenoptera acutorostrata*), followed by humpback (*Megaptera novaeangliae*) and the occasional blue whale (*Balaenoptera musculus*). Meanwhile, whale meat is served in Icelandic restaurants and can be purchased in stores around the country. Thus, Iceland is one of the few places in the world where both watching and eating whales is possible as part of the tourism experience.

In Öqvist's (2016) study, questionnaires were distributed to tourists on whale watching boats in Húsavík, northeast Iceland, between July and September 2015 (n=570). A similar questionnaire was distributed between September and October 2015 (n=153) in other parts of the country, targeting tourists who did not participate in whale watching activities and thus creating a control group against which results from whale watchers could be compared.

Only 5% of whale watchers and 4% of non-whale watchers thought commercial hunting of whales was an acceptable practice, while approximately half of the whale watchers thought whaling in any form was unacceptable. The main reasons cited for this negative response to killing whales was the perception that whale populations are threatened or endangered (26%) and the opinion that whaling is an unnecessary practice (24%) (Öqvist, 2016). These results match those found in studies of attitudes of whale watchers toward whaling both in Iceland and other parts of the world (e.g. Kuo, Chen, & McAleer, 2012; Parsons & Rawles, 2003; Wende & Gothall, 2008).

When asked if they would eat whale meat, 15% of whale watchers and a slightly higher proportion of non-whale watchers (20%) stated they were likely to eat whale meat if they had the opportunity. The main reason stated by whale watchers for wanting to eat whale meat was because it was considered exotic (74%) (Öqvist, 2016). In Iceland, whale meat is promoted to tourists as a novelty food and access to it through restaurants and stores has recently increased (Bertulli, Leeney, Barreau, & Matassa, 2014). Tourists are often motivated by a search for an experience different from their everyday life at home and this may explain why, for such a high percent of respondents, the perceived exoticness of whale meat was a contributing factor to their willingness to eat it.

The second highest reason given by whale watchers for wanting to eat whale meat was because they believed it to be an important Icelandic tradition (37%) (Öqvist, 2016). For many tourists, food is a critical part of their travel experience (Mkono, 2015), and they seek food that is considered unique or of special importance to their travel destination (Hall & Sharples, 2003). The notion of traditional consumption of whale meat in Iceland, however, has very little basis in fact. Basque hunters in the seventeenth century hunted whales near Iceland (Cunningham et al., 2012), but for most of settled Iceland's history since the ninth and tenth centuries, consumption of whale meat has been infrequent and based on opportunistic harvesting (Einarsson, 1987), as evidenced by the Icelandic term for a beached whale – *hvalreki*, akin to a windfall (Sigurjónsson, 1989). Traditional use of whales for food is mostly confined to blubber, treated to make it sour and served in mid-winter as a specialty dish (Altherr, 2003). Beyond this, Icelanders show little interest in eating whale meat (Einarsson, 2009).

Prior to the resumption of commercial whaling in Iceland, 91.4% of whale watchers surveyed by Parsons and Rawles (2003) said they would not take a whale watching trip in the country if Iceland resumed whaling. Since commercial whaling resumed in 2006, however, both the number of foreign visitors to Iceland and the number of those choosing to watch whales has increased. This suggests two things: (1) commercial whaling has not affected the popularity of whale watching in Iceland, and (2) tourist intention differs from actual behavior – unless tourists are unaware of the presence of commercial whaling in Iceland. To test awareness, Öqvist (2016) asked respondents if they knew whether whales were hunted in Iceland. The majority of whale watchers (63%) and non-whale watchers (62%) were aware that hunting occurs, while 18% of whale watchers and 4% of non-whale watchers were not. A considerable number (19% of whale watchers and 35% of non-whale watchers) were unsure.

Case study two: seals and tourists in Iceland

Similar to the situation with whales, anthropocentric ethics, based on extrinsic value, have dominated interactions between humans and seals throughout history across the world and informed longstanding, and widespread, perceptions of seals as a resource for human consumption. This is particularly true in Iceland. The first settlers arriving in Iceland from Norway and the British Isles during the "Age of Settlement" from 874 to 930AD (Kristjánsson, 1980, p. 441) encountered a harsh environment, dominated by volcanic eruptions and famine, joined later by dramatic climatic changes and plague (Burns, 2018). Against this backdrop, locally abundant colonies of harbor seals (*Phoca vitulina*) and grey seals (*Halichoerus grypus*) are likely to have been a critical resource for human survival (Hauksson & Einarsson, 2010). Seal flesh provided a source of food and bait. Blubber was used for oil, in cooking, as food for both humans and livestock, and in paint. Seal skins were used for clothing, shoes, bags, ropes, containers, decorations, and even for binding manuscripts (Kristjánsson, 1980).

The importance of seal products to assist human survival and subsistence in this northern periphery country is reflected in Icelandic culture. In addition to holding a prominent place in folklore (Puhvel, 1963), the role of seals is evident in the naming of places in Iceland, many of which date back to the earliest settlements (Kristjánsson, 1980). The city of Kópavogur, for instance, is derived from the old Norse word for seal pup, *kópar*, and the word for bay, *vogur*, to mean bay of seals.

As a consequence of consumptive use, many seal colonies were probably decimated in the first centuries of settlement (Valtýsson, n.d.). However, once seal hunting farms were registered and seal hunting rights became economically profitable due to increasing external demand for seal products, colonies were actively managed by landowners to ensure that hunting could continue (Kristjánsson, 1980; Valtýsson, n.d.). Approximately 6000 seals, mainly harbor seal pups, were killed annually in response to the fashion trend for seal furs (Valtýsson, n.d.) prior to the anti-sealing campaign in the 1970s. Although seals are still hunted in Iceland, the global shift in perception of appropriate seal consumption, combined with a reduction in the reliance on seal meat (Granquist & Hauksson, 2016) and a European Union ban on importing and commercializing seal products (Wegge, 2013), led to a significant reduction in hunting (Burns, 2018).

In recent years, attention has turned to seals as a source of tourism. The number of tourist arrivals to Iceland began steadily increasing in the mid-1960s (Jóhannesson & Huijbens, 2010), matching worldwide growth at that time. The greatest increases, however, have occurred since 2008 with foreign arrival numbers doubling between then and 2015, and an increase of 39% after 2015 leading to a 2016 total of 1,792,201 foreign arrivals (Icelandic Tourist Board, 2017). Mirroring this growth, seal watching has become a popular tourism activity. In 2005, the Vatnsnes peninsula in northwest Iceland, on which the town of Hvammstangi is located, began promoting itself as the "land of seals." "The deliberate, targeted, strategy to attract visitors yielded a ten-fold increase over ten years, with the recorded visitor numbers in Hvammstangi increasing from 2,200 in 2005 to 27,150 in 2015" (Burns, 2018, p. 59).

To determine the attitudes of seal watchers to eating seal meat as part of their tourist experience, Öqvist (2016) distributed an onsite questionnaire to 194 participants between July and October 2015 after they completed a seal watching boat trip from Hvammstangi. A further 153 participants who had not taken part in any seal watching while they were in Iceland completed a similar questionnaire between September and October 2015. The results revealed information about tourist awareness of seal hunting in Iceland, as well as their attitudes to hunting and willingness to eat seal meat, and allowed a comparison between seal watchers and non-seal watchers.

Fewer tourists in the seal-watching group (37%) than in the control group of non-seal watchers (55%) were aware that seal hunting occurred in Iceland. A similar, but slightly smaller, number of respondents in both groups (33% of seal watchers, 41% of the control group) said they did not know whether or not seal hunting occurred (Öqvist, 2016). This demonstrates a lower level of hunting awareness than for tourists who were asked a similar question about whale hunting. The contrasting higher awareness of whale hunting is likely due to the fact that whaling is undertaken commercially in Iceland while sealing is not, and the recent and extensive coverage of media attention afforded to whale hunting, both in Iceland and globally.

Respondents were also asked if they thought seals should be hunted. Approximately a third of both seal watchers (34%) and the control group (29%) were against seal hunting for any reason. For participants in the seal watching group who thought hunting should be permitted, scientific research was chosen as the most acceptable reason by (33%), followed by population control (19%) and maintaining cultural traditions (17%). This matched the control group, in which scientific research (33%) and population control (32%) were also the two most common responses for why hunting should be permitted. For participants who thought seal hunting should not be permitted, reasons included a prioritization of seal conservation (41% percent of seal watchers, 63% of the control group), and the opinion that seal hunting was simply an unnecessary practice (28% of seal watchers, 16% of control group). Other common reasons were that humans should not interfere with nature, and because respondents felt personal and emotional connections with seals.

Support for hunting of wildlife in general seems to be higher when people believe there are valid reasons to hunt the animals (Dandy et al., 2012). Commercial hunting of marine mammals for human consumption is most likely not considered a valid reason when there are other sources of food, and whales and seals are large, charismatic animals that people tend to care more about (Roberge, 2014). This is supported by Öqvist's (2016) study, where emotional and moral concerns about hunting both whales and seals were frequently mentioned by tourists in their responses for why marine mammals should not be hunted.

Whale meat is readily available to tourists in Iceland. Seal meat is not. Thus, it was not a surprise that only 1% of seal watchers and 2% of the control group in Öqvist's study (2016) had tasted seal meat whilst in Iceland. More revealing was the number of respondents who stated they were likely to try seal meat if the opportunity arose. 82% of the seal watchers and 69% of the control group stated they were unlikely to taste seal meat, while 11% of seal watchers and 18% of the control group were likely to try it. Thus, as may be expected, seal watchers were less likely to try seal meat than respondents in the control group. These figures are similar to, though slightly higher than, those for whale watchers and the non-whale watching control group (Öqvist, 2016).

The main motivation to taste seal meat was the same as for whale meat: that it was considered exotic. The option that "it's a tradition in Iceland and it's culturally important and interesting" was the second most common reason to taste both seal and whale (Öqvist, 2016). Hunting whales and seals are extremely important cultural and social events in many Arctic Inuit communities, but this is not the case for whales in Iceland (Cunningham et al., 2012; Tyrrell, 2007). Whales have been eaten in Iceland since the thirteenth century, but mainly as a source of protein when other options were scarce (Sigurjónsson, 1989), thus differing from the important early subsistence role of seals.

Results from the questions about willingness to taste whale and seal indicate that both seal and whale watchers were less likely to want to taste the meat of the animal they have watched. As discussed earlier, studies on meat eating and its relationship to animals show that people tend to withdraw moral concern by reducing mind attribution and the capacity to suffer of the animals they eat, and to cognitively separate the animals from the meat (Bastian, Loughnan, Haslam, & Radke, 2012; Hoogland, de Boer, & Boersema, 2005). Watching the animals in their natural habitat could make the separation between animal and meat more difficult and create a moral dilemma (Mkono, 2015). Participating in guided activities, as offered as part of the whale and seal watching boat experiences that tourists had undertaken prior to Öqvist's (2016) questionnaire, could also decrease incentives to eat these animals. During the boat trips, the animals are described as sentient beings and their life histories and individual features are described, and animals that are perceived to have minds and humanlike attributes are often considered more inappropriate for consumption (Ruby & Heine, 2012).

Discussion and conclusions

Tourism involving wildlife is traditionally divided into activities that are consumptive or non-consumptive, where the distinction between the two categories is based on whether or not the activity is intentionally lethal for the wildlife. In this division, wildlife watching is non-consumptive yet an activity in which the wildlife is eaten as part of the tourism experience is consumptive. Arguments against this simplistic divide into two categories highlight the ways tourism can be consumptive, in terms of using the wildlife as a resource and being the cause of impacts that are negative without being lethal. In this vein, Higham et al. (2016) convincingly argue that whale-watching is a consumptive form of non-lethal exploitation. Adopting this approach, watching whales and eating whales, and watching seals and eating seals, are all consumptive activities, so the ethical gap between watching and eating may not be as wide as originally conceived.

The two case studies, of whale and seal tourism in Iceland, explore situations in which tourists both watch and eat the same species as part of their tourism experience. Although most tourists are aware that commercial hunting of whales occurs in Iceland and think it is unacceptable, some are still willing to eat whale meat. To negotiate and overcome this contradiction, Iceland's tourists may be engaging in a form of disconnect or denial, as described in cognitive dissonance theory, that in turn allows them to suppress their moral concern for whales, as suggested in the meat paradox. Clearly the tourists have moral concern for both whales and seals, and deem them species worthy of emotional attachment, which in turn suggests they may afford them intrinsic value. The moral suppression then may be driven by the pursuit of personal satisfaction that accompanies the hedonism of tourism (Burns, 2015a), the desire to do something different and try something exotic that the traveler would not normally do or experience at home.

The dominance of this pursuit of hedonistic satisfaction within the tourism experience may be the psychological factor enabling individuals to at least temporarily modify their attitudes to fit their current behaviors. In this context, the state of cognitive dissonance may cause a change in, or at least a suspension of, attitudes toward eating whale or seal meat in an attempt to reduce the feelings of unease associated with inconsistences between compassionate attitudes toward whales and seals and the behavior of eating their flesh.

Most of the surveyed whale and seal watchers stated that whaling and sealing were unacceptable under any circumstances, suggesting an ethical stance that may stem from an appreciation of animals having intrinsic value. The willingness to eat whale and seal meat, however, contradicts this. As a food for consumption, the whales and seals are again, or still, appreciated dominantly for their extrinsic value and utility to humans.

Data presented here supports Loughnan et al.'s (2010) assertion that people suppress their moral concern for animals when they eat meat. Respondents stated that they have concern and are opposed to commercial whaling and seal hunting, yet, for some, this opposition is just that – stated and intentional, but does not translate into actual behavior. It has not led them to boycott a country in which they know whaling occurs, nor does it stop them from eating whale meat.

One critical difference between whales and seals can be found in the history of human–wildlife interactions in Iceland, namely the importance of seals for subsistence. This importance seems to correspond with an elevated state for seals in Icelandic culture that does not exist for whales. Icelanders know this history, but tourists do not. 17% of seal-watching tourists thought that seal hunting should continue for the reason of maintaining a cultural tradition, while 37% of the whale watchers thought that whale meat was an important cultural tradition (Öqvist, 2016).

Based on the notion of a strong dichotomy between consumptive and non-consumptive forms of wildlife tourism, a hypothesis that tourists who engage in non-consumptive (non-lethal) activities, such as wildlife watching, do not wish to also participate in consumptive activities might seem logical. The case studies presented here, of whale and seal watching in Iceland, show that such a hypothesis would be incorrect. At least for some tourists, watching and eating are not necessarily mutually exclusive activities. However, the reasons given for both supporting hunting and supporting eating are not necessarily based on fact. Tourists surveyed by Öqvist (2016) either lacked the knowledge to make informed decisions or were engaging in the practice of cognitive dissonance to enable them to both eat and watch the same species as part of their perceived exotic experience in an exotic location.

Our interactions with animals are complex and linked to attitudes that shape behaviors and perspectives. Those attitudes differ at individual and societal levels, and they are formed by a combination of many factors (Serpell, 2004). The chosen right or wrong of a wildlife tourism activity, be it consumptive or non-consumptive, is based on how we categorize the animal and, as these case studies demonstrate, we may categorize the same animal for different purposes in different contexts. The tourist who both watches whales and eats them, or watches seals and would like to taste them, is categorizing the same animal as two different things: entertainment and eating experience, while on the same holiday. Thus, for interactions with whales and seals, the paradox or contradiction is quite strong.

The overarching ethics in most interactions between humans and wildlife, whether consumptive or non-consumptive, remain anthropocentric and based on extrinsic value. Watching wildlife as a tourist activity may hold the potential to embody a more ecocentric and intrinsic philosophical stance, but framed as consumptive and subject to moral suppression in the face of contrasting categories of the wildlife (as food and as entertainment) suggests that this is not always realized.

References

Akama, J. S. (2008). Controversies surrounding the ban on wildlife hunting in Kenya: An historical perspective. In B. A. Lovelock (Ed.), *Tourism and the consumption of wildlife: Hunting, shooting and sport fishing* (pp. 73–86). London: Routledge.

Altherr, S. (2003). *Iceland's whaling comeback: Preparation for the resumption of whaling*. Report for Pro Wildlife, Whale and Dolphin Conservation Society, and the Humane Society of the United States.

Bastian, B., Loughnan, S., Haslam, N., & Radke, H. R. M. (2012). Don't mind meat? The denial of mind to animals used for human consumption. *Personal Social Psychology Bulletin, 38*, 247–256.

Bauer, J., & Herr, A. (2004). Hunting and fishing tourism. In K. Higginbottom (Ed.), *Wildlife tourism: Impacts, management and planning* (pp. 57–80). Gold Coast: Common Ground Publishing.

Bertulli, C. G., Leeney, R. H., Barreau, T., & Matassa, D. S. (2014). Can whale-watching and whaling co-exist? Tourist perceptions in Iceland. *Journal of the Marine Biological Association of the United Kingdom, 96*(4), 969–997.

Bratanova, B., Loughnan, S., & Bastian, B. (2011). The effect of categorisation as food on the perceived moral standing of animals. *Appetite, 57*, 193–196.

Bulliet, R. W. (2005). *Hunters, herders and hamburgers: The past and future of human-animal relationships*. New York: Columbia University Press.

Burns, G. L. (2015a). Animals as tourism objects: Ethically refocusing relationships between tourists and wildlife. In K. Markwell (Ed.), *Animals and tourism: Understanding diverse relationships* (pp. 44–59). Bristol: Channel View Publications.

Burns, G. L. (2015b). Ethics in tourism. In C. M. Hall, S. Gossling, & D. Scott (Eds.), *The Routledge handbook of tourism and sustainability* (pp. 117–126). London: Routledge.

Burns, G. L. (2017). Ethics and responsibility in wildlife tourism: Lessons from compassionate conservation in the Anthropocene. In R. Green & I. Borges de Lima (Eds.), *Wildlife tourism, environmental learning and ethical encounters: Ecological and conservation aspects* (pp. 213–220). Springer. doi: 10.1007/978-3-319-55574-4_13.

Burns, G. L. (2018). Searching for Resilience: Seal watching tourism as a resource for community development in Iceland. In A. A. Lew & J. Cheer (Eds.), *Tourism resilience and adaptation to environmental change* (pp. 69–85). Routledge Advances in Tourism Series. Oxon: Routledge.

Burns, G. L., Macbeth, J., & Moore, S. (2011). Should dingoes die? Principles for engaging ecocentric ethics in wildlife tourism management. *Journal of Ecotourism*, *10*(3), 179–196.

Caton, K. (2012). Taking the moral turn in tourism studies. *Annals of Tourism Research*, *39*(4), 1906–1928.

Chen, C. (2011). From catching to watching: Moving towards quality assurance of whale/dolphin watching tourism in Taiwan. *Marine Policy*, *35*, 10–17.

Cisneros-Montemayor, A. M., Sumaila, U. R., Kaschner, K., & Pauly, D. (2010). The global potential for whale watching. *Marine Policy*, *34*, 1273–1278.

Cunningham, P. A., Huijbens, E. H., & Wearing, S. (2012). From whaling to whale-watching: Examining sustainability and cultural rhetoric. *Journal of Sustainable Tourism*, *20*, 143–161.

Dalle Zotte, A. (2014). Rabbit farming for meat purposes. *Animal Frontiers*, *4*(4), 62–67.

Dandy, N., Ballantyne, S., Moseley, D., Gill, R., Quine, C., & Van Der Wal, R. (2012). Exploring beliefs behind support for and opposition to wildlife management methods: a qualitative study. *European Journal of Wildlife Research*, *58*(4), 695–706.

Einarsson, N. (1987). *Hvalvieðar við Ísland 1600–1939* (Whaling around Iceland 1600–1939). Reykjavik: Bókaútgáfá Menningarsjóðs.

Einarsson, N. (2009). From good to eat to good to watch: Whale watching, adaptation and change in Icelandic fishing communities. *Polar Research*, *28*, 129–138.

Ellenberg, U., Setiawan, A. N., Cree, A., Houston, D. M., & Seddon, P. J. (2007). Elevated hormonal stress response and reduced reproductive output in yellow-eyed penguins exposed to unregulated tourism. *General and Comparative Endocrinology*, *152*(1), 54–63.

Fennell, D. (2015). Ethics in tourism. In G. Moscardo & P. Benckendorff (Eds.), *Education for sustainability in tourism* (pp. 45–57). Berlin: Springer.

Festinger, L. (1957). *A theory of cognitive dissonance*. Stanford, CA: Stanford University Press.

Granquist, S. M., & Hauksson, E. (2016). *Management and status of harbour seal population in Iceland 2016: Catches, population assessments and current knowledge*. Reykjavik: Veiðimálastofnun [Institute for Freshwater Fisheries].

Granquist, S. M., & Sigurjónsdóttir, H. (2014). The effect of land based seal watching tourism on the haul-out behavior of harbour seals (*Phoca vitulina*) in Iceland. *Applied Animal Behaviour Science*, *156*, 85–93.

Hall, C. M., & Sharples, L. (2003). The consumption of experience or the experience of consumption? An introduction to the tourism of taste. In C. M. Hall, L. Sharples, R. Mitchell, N. Macionis, & B. Cambourne (Eds.), *Food tourism around the world: Development, management, markets* (pp. 1–24). New York: Butterworth-Heinemann.

Hauksson, E., & Einarsson, S. T. (2010). Review on utilization and research on harbor seal (*Phoca vitulina*) in Iceland. *NAMMCO Scientific Publications*, *8*, 314–353.

Helgadóttir, G., & Dashper, K. (2016). "Dear international guests and friends of the Icelandic horse": Experience, meaning and belonging at a niche sporting event. *Scandinavian Journal of Hospitality and Tourism*, *16*(4), 422–441.
Herzog, H. (2011). *Some we love, some we hate, some we eat: Why it's so hard to think straight about animals*. New York: Harper Perennial.
Higginbottom, K. (2004). Wildlife tourism: An introduction. In K. Higginbottom (Ed.), *Wildlife tourism: Impacts, management and planning* (pp. 1–14). Gold Coast: Common Ground Publishing.
Higginbottom, K., Northrope, C. L., Croft, D. B., Hill, B., & Fredline, E. (2004). The role of kangaroos in Australian tourism. *Australian Mammalogy*, *26*, 23–32.
Higham, J. E. S., Bejder, L., Allen, S. J., Corkeron, P. J., & Lusseau, D. (2016). Managing whale-watching as a non-lethal consumptive activity. *Journal of Sustainable Tourism*, *24*(1), 73–90.
Higham, J. E. S., & Hopkins, D. (2015). Wildlife tourism: "Call it consumption". In C. M. Hall, S. Gössling, & D. Scott (Eds.), *The Routledge handbook of tourism and sustainability* (pp. 280–293). London: Routledge.
Higham, J. E. S., & Lusseau, D. (2008). Slaughtering the goose that lays the golden egg: Are whaling and whale-watching mutually exclusive? *Current Issues in Tourism*, *11*, 63–74.
Hoogland, C. T., de Boer, J., & Boersema, J. J. (2005). Transparency of the meat chain in the light of food culture and history. *Appetite*, *45*, 15–23.
Icelandic Tourist Board (Ferðamálastofa). (2017). *Foreign visitor arrivals by air and sea to Iceland 1949–2016*. Retrieved from www.ferdamalastofa.is/en/recearch-and-statistics/numbers-of-foreign-visitors.
Icewhale. (2017). *Whale watching in Iceland: Number of passengers by year*. Retrieved from http://icewhale.is/whale-watching-in-iceland
Jóhannesson, G. T., & Huijbens, E. H. (2010). Tourism in times of crisis: Exploring the discourse of tourism development in Iceland. *Current Issues in Tourism*, *13*, 419–434.
Joy, M. (2011). *Why we love dogs, eat pigs, and wear cows: An introduction to carnism*. San Francisco, CA: Conari Press.
Kristjánsson, L. (1980). *Íslenzkir Sjávarhœttir* [Icelandic fisheries]. Reykjavik: Bókaútgáfa.
Kuo, H., Chen, C., & McAleer, M. (2012). Estimating the impact of whaling on global whale-watching. *Tourism Management*, *33*, 1321–1328.
Loughnan, S., Bastian, B., & Haslam, N. (2014). The psychology of eating animals. *Current Directions in Psychological Science*, *23*(2), 104–108.
Loughnan, S., Haslam, N., & Bastian, B. (2010). The role of meat consumption in the denial of moral status and mind to meat animals. *Appetite*, *55*, 156–150.
Lovelock, B. (2015). Consumptive and non-consumptive tourism practices: The case of wildlife tourism. In C. M. Hall, S. Gossling, & D. Scott (Eds.), *The Routledge handbook of tourism and sustainability* (pp. 165–174). London: Routledge.
Lovelock, B., & Lovelock, K. M. (2013). *The ethics of tourism: Critical and applied perspectives*. New York: Routledge.
Mau, R. (2008). Managing for conservation and recreation: The Ningaloo whale shark experience. *Journal of Ecotourism*, *7*(2–3), 208–220.
Mkono, M. (2015). 'Eating the animals you come to see': Tourists' meat-eating discourses in online communicative texts. In K. Markwell (Ed.), *Animals and tourism: Understanding diverse relationships* (pp. 211–226). Bristol: Channel View Publications.
Öqvist, E. (2016). *Whaling or watching, sealing or seeing? A study of interactions between marine mammal tourism and hunting in Iceland*. Master thesis, Stockholm University, Sweden.

Parsons, E. C. M. (2012). The negative impacts of whale-watching. *Journal of Marine Biology*, *2012*, 1–9.

Parsons, E. C. M., & Rawles, C. (2003). The resumption of whaling by Iceland and the potential negative impact in the Icelandic whale-watching market. *Current Issues in Tourism*, *6*(5), 444–448.

Puhvel, M. (1963). The seal in the Folklore of Northern Europe. *Folklore*, *74*, 326–333.

Roberge, J. (2014). Using data from online social networks in conservation science: Which species engage people the most on twitter? *Biodiversity Conservation*, *23*, 715–726.

Ruby, M. B., & Heine, S. J. (2012). Too close to home: Factors predicting meat avoidance. *Appetite*, *59*, 47–52.

Serpell, J. A. (2004). Factors influencing human attitudes to animals and their welfare. *Animal Welfare*, *13*, 145–152.

Sigurdardóttir, I., & Helgadóttir, G. (2015). Riding high: Quality and customer satisfaction in equestrian tourism in Iceland. *Scandinavian Journal of Hospitality and Tourism*, *15*(1–2), 105–121.

Sigurjónsson, J. (1989). To Icelanders, whales were a godsend. *Oceanus Magazine*, *32*, 29–36.

Szendrő, K. (2016). Consumer perceptions, concerns, and purchasing practices of rabbit meat in Hungary. *Journal of Food Products Marketing*, *22*(6), 683–693.

Tyrrell, M. (2007). Sentient beings and wildlife resources: Inuit, beluga whales and management regimes in the Canadian Arctic. *Human Ecology*, *35*, 575–586.

Valtýsson, H. Þ. (n.d.). Seals. *Icelandic Fisheries*. Retrieved from www.fisheries.is/main-species/marine-mammals/seals/

Vaughn, L. (2008). *Ethics: Moral reasoning and contemporary issues*. New York: W.W. Norton.

Walpole, M. J., & Thouless, C. R. (2005). Increasing the value of wildlife through non-consumptive use? Deconstructing the myths of ecotourism and community-based tourism in the tropics. In R. Woodroffe, S. Thirgood, & A. Rabinowitz (Eds.), *People and wildlife, conflict or co-existence?* (pp. 122–140). Cambridge: Cambridge University Press.

Wearing, S., & Jobberns, C. (2011). Ecotourism and the commodification of wildlife: Animal welfare and the ethics of zoos. In W. Frost (Ed.), *Zoos and tourism* (pp. 47–58). Great Britain: Short Run Press Ltd.

Wegge, N. (2013). Politics between science, law and sentiments: Explaining the European Union's ban on trade in seal products. *Environmental Politics*, *22*(2), 255–273.

Wende, B. D., & Gothall, S. E. (2008). *Match point: Watching versus catching. The influence of whaling for the whale watching tourism industry in Iceland*. MSc thesis, Goteburg University, Goteburg, Germany.

Wilson, C., & Tisdell, C. (2001). Sea turtles as a non-consumptive tourism resource especially in Australia. *Tourism Management*, *22*(3), 279–288.

Yudina, O., & Fennell, D. (2013). Eco-feminism in the tourism context: A discussion of the use of other-than-human animals as food in tourism. *Tourism Recreation Research*, *38*(1), 55–69.

4 The (unethical) consumption of a newborn animal

Cabrito as a tourist and recreational dish in Monterrey, Mexico

Gino Jafet Quintero Venegas and Álvaro López López

Introduction

Food as a cultural heritage consumption in Mexico is by no means an "innocent act" to which academic reflection should turn a blind eye, especially when it involves a breach of the ethical limits of animal welfare, as is the pain inflicted on sentient beings equipped with a central nervous system (Dawkins, 2006). The inflicting of pain on many species of animals, like the young goat, is part and parcel of the growth control necessary to maintain culinary standards. The human cruelty involved in this kind of suffering reaches a peak at the time of slaughter (Rinfret, 2009), a shared responsibility in which all players – including tourists – have their part.

Raising animals for consumption by tourists is becoming a widespread practice at many Mexican tourism destinations, as gastronomic specialties are one of the ways in which the notion of "place," in all its distinctive particularities, is constructed (Trauer & Ryan, 2005). Monterrey, one of the chief tourist destinations in northern Mexico, is associated with *cabrito* – or roasted kid – advertised as a delicacy of "*gran sabor*" (very tasty) no traveler to the city should miss (Expedia México, 2014). As an added-value opportunity to generate income, food production for tourists affects both local agricultural systems and food supply chains.

Consumption of roasted kid is an example of tourists' lack of ethical considerations when enjoyment of their holiday is their main concern. Although many tourists might not be fully aware of the animal suffering involved in the preparation of this expensive dish, their consumption of this exotic meat product reinforces their sense of power and social status. From an economic standpoint, humans exercise their "bio-power" over sentient non-humans, deliberately controlling the latter's physiological processes, as much in life as in death (Holloway & Morris, 2007; Rinfret, 2009). In the case of *cabrito*, in order to ensure its taste and tenderness, its diet must be strictly controlled, in utter disregard of the animal's welfare. By indulging in this culinary experience, even unknowingly, tourists assume their position of superiority over animals in general, exercising their "right" to self-gratification, regardless of any bioethical implications.

The analysis of culinary tourism in Mexico has been carried out mostly from an anthropocentric perspective, legitimizing – deliberately or not – various forms of animal abuse. As for research on the consumption of roasted kid, the dominant trend is to position animals as a resource at the mercy of human beings. Garza, Vera, and Kawas (1994), for example, make a cursory description of how the animal should be raised and slaughtered to obtain hefty profits, while Rodríguez and Cavazos (1990) analyze the possibilities for expansion of the roasted kid market in the metropolitan area of Monterrey, and Quiroz and Hernández (2014) investigate the mechanisms to increase the productivity of kid meat. Absent from the scene are works that tackle the issue from a post-humanist perspective, minimally acknowledging the fact that animals are sentient beings.

This chapter dwells on the consumption of kid meat for tourism and recreational purposes from a utilitarian standpoint, whose premise, according to Singer (1975), is that individual interests cannot supersede collective welfare. This means that no traveler ought to engage in any action that presupposes the suffering, mistreatment, and demise of animals for consumption, even if this means being deprived from tasting a "typical" product. This author rightly argues that the pleasures derived from tasting a dish cannot be above an animal's right to life and integrity. The mistreatment and suffering of animals are too high a price to pay for ephemeral pleasures that, far from adding up to world happiness, contribute to its decrease, thus lacking moral legitimacy (Singer, 1975).

This chapter explores the unethical situation in which the production and consumption of *cabrito*, a culinary product considered a "cultural expression" of Monterrey, is involved. To achieve this, a method that combined non-participant observation (Bryman, 2008) with the analysis of visual and written documents (especially those produced and reproduced in the so-called "social networks") was designed. Aware of the fact that discussing ethical issues directly with tourists would yield unreliable information, the authors of this article opted for the collection of opinions on the subject circulating in the web, from platforms such as Tripadvisor.com and Facebook. As Mkono (2011, p. 255) puts it, this environment "is more likely to generate honest, candid accounts as participants join the blogosphere of their own free will, and, because participants may assume pseudonymous or anonymous identities."

The following is organized into three sections. In the first section, a historical account on the cultural significance of the consumption of *cabrito* is presented, from its religious meaning, to its current secular recreational use. The second section analyzes how the consumption of this kind of meat is legitimized as a recreational practice related to tourism. Finally, the third section contains a discussion of the ethical implications of this, by no means exceptional, practice in the world of tourism today.

The consumption of kid meat in Monterrey: a gastronomic tradition

The extraordinary industrial, commercial, and financial momentum achieved by Monterrey (the third largest Mexican city) is partly explained by its proximity to the United States, and the strong global links it has developed (Figure 4.1). Monterrey enjoys international recognition as a business tourism destination (Sánchez, López, & Propín, 2005) with a cosmopolitan flavor and distinctive tourist attractions, including a gastronomy focused on meat products directly from neighboring farms, of which the famous *cabrito* is the most distinctive example (Expedia Mexico, 2014).

Wilkinson and Stara (1998) explain that *cabrito* is a 30- to 40-day-old kid that has been fed only with breast milk, at the exclusion of vegetable foods that could potentially harden its flesh or make it fibrous. The tenderness and flavor of this meat, similar to that of sheep and lamb yeanlings, has become a gourmet product in high demand for local as well as tourist consumption. Since meat quality is measured by the presence or absence of fat in the animal's kidneys (Hernández, 2000), a kid that has been fed with other foods will be subjected to a diet consisting of only oregano for two weeks before it is dispatched, so as to leach away kidney fat (Ansín et al., 2001). In observance to the method known as CAFO (Concentrated Animal Feeding Operations), the animal is confined throughout his short lifetime (Webb, Casey, & Simela, 2005).

Roasted kid, Monterrey's typical dish, has been consumed as a Judeo-Christian tradition for 450 years dating back to the arrival of the first Spanish settlers of Sephardic origin. They took to subsistence farming bringing along their own sheep and goats, and feeding them with Mesoamerican plant species, thereby starting a process of cultural miscegenation that would evolve into the cuisine of northern Mexico (Hernández, 2007; Garza, 1995). Nowadays, *Cabrito al Pastor* is a gourmet version of roasted kid closely linked to recreation and tourism.

Figure 4.1 Location of Monterrey City in Mexico
Source: Alejandrina De Sicilia, 2016.

Figure 4.2 *Cabrito* ready to be cut and served as a recreational meal in Monterrey
Source: Photo by Mariana Treviño Cantú.

Currently more than 300,000 kids a year are raised to meet the market demand of locals and visitors combined (Salinas et al., 2016). The animal is slaughtered within a few days after birth in a cruel and rudimentary way, by hanging it from its hind legs on a pole in a head-down position, then cutting his neck with a homemade knife to drain the blood on a tray (which will be used in the cooking process). There is always someone holding the animal to prevent it from moving out of suffering and pain, lest the adrenaline generated by its agitation affect the meat's taste. The animal's agony can be prolonged for several minutes of intense and constant bleating (Pawn, 2012; Lázaro, 2015).

Once the bleeding has stopped, the animal is cut and impaled upon a metal rod that runs longitudinally through its body from one of the legs (Figure 4.2). Then it is brought over the embers for slow roasting. Once done, it is cut and served at the table accompanied by guacamole and *frijoles charros* (freshly cooked beans) with onion, garlic, chili, bacon, sausage, and fried pork rinds, to be eaten along with wheat flour tortillas.

Legitimizing kid consumption in Mexico

Kid supply and demand as a tourist synecdoche

Cabrito is associated with Monterrey in a typical case of tourist synecdoche, which is a rhetorical figure used to express the notion that access to one of the meaningful parts of a whole (in this case a tourist space) is enough for a traveler to experience or get to know that whole (De Certeau, 2014). *Cabrito* and Monterrey are then tied in a metonymical type of relationship in which the whole is taken for its part and the part for the whole (Seto, 1999), so that eating the roasted kid amounts to "knowing" the city. Therefore the local dish is strongly promoted as a cultural and gastronomic element, and an essential part of the tourist experience (Gran Turismo, 2015).

Websites promoting the cuisine of northern Mexico position *cabrito* as the star: "when visiting Monterrey, don't miss the chance to experience this delicious specialty" (Murillo, 2016). *México Desconocido*, the well-established tourism magazine with national distribution, places *cabrito* at the top of the list of things to do in Monterrey:

> Surrender to the culinary delights that make Monterrey famous. There are several options in the city to savor cabrito, the maximum culinary expression of Nuevo León. El Rey del Cabrito is one of the best places to taste this delicious dish roasted in wood and seasoned with salt and other condiments.
> (México Desconocido, 2015)

Amid the plethora of restaurants specializing in kid dishes all over the city, the centrally located El Rey del Cabrito has the largest turnout, in view of its large number of gastronomic awards; it is popular among locals and tourists alike. Trip Advisor (2016) offers an array of comments on the iconic restaurant: "If you are visiting Monterrey, you can't miss *cabrito*," "coming to Monterrey and not eating *cabrito* is not recommended," and "Going to Monterrey and not getting to know this restaurant is not normal."

The dish as an element of identity

In November 2010, Mexican food was declared an intangible cultural heritage by UNESCO (2010), and thus roasted kid has made its way into the gastronomic offer of several central and southern locations in the country, since it is perceived as a traditional Mexican dish invested with "originality" (Cohen, 2005). It is not by accident that in July 2016 the prestigious Hacienda Los Morales restaurant in Mexico City celebrated its first "Festival del *Cabrito*," with an aim to promote this culinary tradition of northeastern Mexico, while diversifying Mexico City's gastronomy (Notimex, 2016).

As Monterrey strengthens its role as an economic and cultural center in northern Mexico, its tourist offer undergoes a notorious diversification, to the extent that the city is no longer dominated by business tourism, but features cultural tourism products, such as festivals and fairs, where consumption of *cabrito* is the norm. These activities have contributed to an increase in the number of visitors from regional, national, and international locations (Sánchez, López, & Propín, 2005).

On September 20, 2016, Monterrey celebrated its 420th anniversary as a city with activities meant to "attract the attention and gaze not only of *regiomontanos*, but also of those from the metropolitan area and neighboring states" (Gobiernos México, 2016, paragraph 6). At these festivities, the consumption of *cabrito* and other meat dishes is encouraged, for they are perceived as part of the local identity, an issue of the highest importance to local authorities, as evidenced in the rather chauvinistic speech of the city mayor at the time:

> We must invest in the city, show off our society's origins, our big city, a thriving city that can be visited for tourism, business or any other purpose; a safe city, a festive city where there is work, where there is prosperity; [we must] demonstrate all that at the national and international levels.
>
> (Tapia, 2016)

As part of the anniversary celebrations, the municipality organized a Gastronomy Fair, with the attendance of more than 6000 local residents. At the opening ceremony, 420 kilograms of meat were cut and the pieces distributed among the attendants, in direct allusion to the number of years the city has existed. Additionally, over two thousand meat dishes prepared with kid and pork were given away (Tapia, 2016). The mayor of Monterrey reportedly declared that the intention of the artistic, sporting, cultural, and civic activities was to encourage the sense of belonging and identity of *regiomontanos* (Tapia, 2016).

As the consumption of kid meat gets established as a distinctive feature of the local culture, and a "must-do" activity for tourists, the *cabrito* image undergoes a process of idealization and sublimation that extends to other aspects of the local culture. This can be seen, for example, in the "Silver Kid Award" at the Monterrey International Film Festival, where a figurine depicting a kid (alive and standing) is offered to the winners.

A pricy dish as a symbol of social prestige

Notwithstanding its important role in the local imagination, and its fame throughout the region and beyond, *cabrito* is by no means an everyday dish, and it remains mostly a special-occasion treat. It is a rather expensive dish reserved for celebrations such as christenings, weddings, birthdays, anniversaries, and graduation ceremonies, and it is usually linked to the intake of alcohol, mainly beer and tequila (a drink associated with the construction of masculinity in Mexico) (Lemle & Mishkind, 1989; Gaytán, 2010). A family of four at a restaurant can spend more than two thousand pesos (one hundred US dollars, approximately) on this dish, which in mid-2016 amounted to a little less than the minimum monthly wage in northern Mexico.

On account of its price – unaffordable to some and expensive to others, including tourists – this dish has been imbued with an aura of indulgence that reinforces the power and economic status of those who consume it – and, most notably, of those who offer it, typically a family patriarch at large gatherings (Gutmann, 2006). To offer *cabrito* at private parties or city restaurants is synonymous with economic power and social prestige, especially when the occasion involves many guests, as happens in ranches throughout the region, where binges of at least 150 people of local and foreign provenance are common during holidays (Napolitano, 2009; Lima, 2010).

Roasted kid-featuring feasts are usually held in large spaces (house patios, ranch yards) and they conform to a ritual where the male head of the host family plays the leading role (Berlanga, Lara, & Ramírez, 1999). On a huge circular broiler the bodies of ten to twenty previously slaughtered kids are placed (González, 2011) for all guests to see. The host then approaches the site to verify the quality of the meat and instruct the cooks as to the terms of the roast. In addition to the meat of this animal, other "cuts" may be offered, such as *arrachera* (hanger beefsteak). The roasting is carried out with mesquite wood, and the scent of meat is scattered with the smoke throughout the area, generating a festive atmosphere with a sense of abundance.

A *cabrito* feast usually begins with two entrances: the *principio de fritada* ("fry starter," a thick broth made of the kids' blood to which roasted offal is added), and a *taco* with pieces of the chopped kids' eyes and tongues (*Sin Embargo*, 2016). The term *cabrito* refers to the skewered and broiled body (Figure 4.2), pieces of which are served along with the bones, to be eaten with *guacamole* and *salsa*. Adults accompany the dish with tequila or beer. Depending on the type of celebration, other side dishes may be served along, such as *empalmes* (wheat flour tortillas stuffed with beans and the *asiento*, or fried pork lard and residues at the bottom of the cooking pot), or dried beef, previously roasted on a *comal*.

Cabrito has been spearheading gastronomic tourism in the city of Monterrey, a process that got momentum with the aforementioned UNESCO award to Mexican cooking. One of the goals of gastronomic tourism is to have visitors experience traditional dishes in special contexts and occasions, such as fairs and festivities (Hall & Sharples, 2003), and the consumption of *cabrito* conforms precisely to this approach, since the dish is hardly ever eaten separately in a restaurant or meeting; it is part of a festive environment filled with aromas, music, decorations, and the consumption of alcoholic drinks, all of which implies a high economic cost.

Notions such as "the discovery of the other" and "the pursuit of happiness," what Hiernaux (2002) interprets as the subjective desires of a society, are at the very center of the imaginary of tourism, and they are constantly used to motivate travelers. The social prestige derived from consuming the expensive *cabrito* goes precisely in this direction, and the old adage of "When in Rome" suffices to justify not only the act of conforming to the norm but also the search for "truly authentic" experiences, regardless of their ethical implications.

Restaurants that specialize in *cabrito*, and websites that promote the cuisine of Monterrey, resort to phrases like "the art of fine eating" and "food for kings, not to be missed in Monterrey" (Gran Turismo, 2015), dictums that appeal to those willing to experience a "new culinary adventure" (Quan & Wang, 2004), usually linked to the offer of a "special dish" (Nield, Kozak, & LeGrys, 2000). These phrases find an echo in the narcissism of sybaritic tourists, bent on an endless gratification of their own desires and interests, manifested in phrases like "I consume, therefore I am," or "I consume because I have everything at my fingertips and my unlimited desire to possess it" (Barcellona, 1992).

The unethical consumption of *cabrito* under scrutiny

The treatment afforded to the goat kid before it becomes an exotic dish for tourists

The authors of this article consider *cabrito* consumption to be a more-or-less unconscious act of complicity with unethical practices. As happens with the meat industry in general (be it large or small scale) animals are treated as "products," and subjected accordingly to continuous suffering from their birth to their death. In the case of *cabrito*, this cruelty is magnified by the various acts of torture afforded to the newly born kid during the first weeks of its life, in order to obtain from its meat the flavor and consistency characteristic of this dish. Culinary luxury is established as justification for these untenable acts, under any ethical standards.

In the Monterrey region, where goats have been providers of milk and meat for centuries, traditional keeping methods have been substituted by "scientific" ones in order to maximize both animal reproduction and size, something Galina, Pacheco, Silva, Palma, and Hummel (1995) consider a zootechnical achievement. However, with no regard whatsoever for the suffering inflicted on them, practices like artificial insemination are constantly being forced upon the animals throughout their lives (Salinas et al., 2016). Goats are raised and reproduced for various purposes: while females are destined to milking, males are earmarked for meat production (mainly barbecue meat) or as studs during their reproductive age. Finally, recently born kids (also known as "milk kids") are set apart for the obtention of tender meat for *cabrito*.

On the seventh day from their birth, kids are subjected to castration by "elastration," a rather cruel method, practiced throughout the American continent (Pollicino, Gandini, Perona, Mattoni, & Farca, 2007; Clark, Murrell, Fernyhough, O'Rourke, & Mendl, 2014), consisting of the placement of an elastic rubber band around the animal's testicles, so as to completely block blood circulation, as a consequence of which the scrotum and the testicles will fall off after ten to fourteen days (*Panorama Agropecuario*, 2015). Rollin (2003) refers to the growing concern about the use of this method in several countries, as the animals are exposed to over 24 hours of intense pain. In the UK, a law has been passed to prohibit this practice on goats, sheep, and calves over seven days of age, unless it is accompanied by anesthetics, something that is not observed in Mexico.

The treatment of animals as "resources" inevitably leads to unethical practices, since, as Terrazas, Serafin, Hernández, Nowak, and Poindron (2003) and Francione (2010) have pointed out, the secondary interests of consumers run counter to the primary interests of the affected beings. Within the ethical order of the humane treatment of animals, kids' primary interests are: to be free from pain and fear, to live in their community, and to behave according to their nature. Recently born kids need the presence of their mothers in order to discover the world they have arrived into and enjoy it (Terrazas et al., op. cit.). Furthermore, females should not be treated merely as biological machines destined to permanently give birth and breast-feed kids that will soon be taken away from them. *Cabrito* consumption in Monterrey is associated with the secondary interests of tourists who privilege the consumption of an exotic product in order to satisfy their expectations, without even thinking about the suffering experienced by the dead animal they have on their table.

Human–non-human power relations and the construction of masculinity

According to Sahlins (1997), the "totemic order" ranks animals depending on their value and their role in the sacred world. Although today the kid is not part of the sacred, its death functions as a sort of ritual sacrifice among those who eat it. Meat consumption has been associated with social privilege and the reinforcement of patriarchic values among humans (Sahlins, 1997; Kellman, 2000; Ruby & Heine, 2011). This is also true with power relations between humans and non-humans. By standing as arbiters of certain cultural practices, men seek to reinforce human dominance over other animals (Fessler & Navarrete, 2003).

Violence and patriarchal domination over non-human others, including the environment, plants, and animals, have been addressed by ecofeminism in an effort to release all sentient beings (human or not) from exploitation and abuse, asserting their fundamental right to life, their right to not be tortured, and their right to freedom (Adams & Gruen, 2015). The same domination mechanisms used to control women (including, though not limited to, violence, scorn, and submission) are used to dominate animals (Plumwood, 2000; Adams & Gruen, 2015), except that the relations of inequality between humans and non-humans are not exclusive to men: women are also dominant agents and exert their power (for example, economic power) over other humans and other animals.

According to Domínguez (2007) and Lewis (2009), among the several prototypes that have forged the imaginary of Mexican masculinity today are: the cowboy, the rancher, the horseman (*Charro*), the wrestler, and the football player. However, the ultimate masculine figure in the rural setting and many urban areas in the country is a hybrid cowboy-*Charro*-rancher, characterized, among other things, by the explicit use, consumption, and ruthless treatment of animals. The abundant and frequent consumption of meat – a diet often devoid of vegetables – is part and parcel of this prototype of masculinity predominant across Mexican society, whose imagination has assimilated to a certain extent the myth of the cowboy-*Charro*-rancher. This is especially true in the northern region of the country, where a variety of meats (including *cabrito*) is available throughout the year. The association of meat consumption to a special kind of virility (strength, sexual power) is evidenced in the opinions about *cabrito* on social networks. Examples of such associations are found in other parts of the world as well, including the archetypes of the "male hunter," the "ferocious Viking," and the "bloodthirsty warrior" (Heinz & Lee, 1998; Rothgerber, 2013).

There is some machismo implicit in the power to acquire luxury goods, as is the case of *cabrito*, and tourists who go for this culinary experience are not only exercising their power over the dead animal, but they are also contributing to the male supremacist discourse implicit in the handling of livestock in general. This is an activity that demands both physical force and the exercise of violence to corner and dominate the animals, especially under the extremely hot temperatures prevalent in the region, which can reach up to 45° C. The association of livestock rearing to male prowess is so strong that without the latter the food is regarded as being of inferior quality (Sobal, 2005).

At the Facebook site entitled (literally, "Prick Broilers") (2016), where the consumption of *cabrito* is encouraged, the delicacy is described in rhyme: "*cabrito lechal, mientras más inocente, más delicioso el animal!*" ("the more innocent the milk kid is, the more delicious its meat tastes"). The reference to the "innocence" of the recently born animal in this expression enhances the power relations involved in the practice of rearing and eating it. Meat eating is established here as the standard practice, and those who choose to refrain from eating *cabrito* for ethical reasons are treated with derision, and their masculinity is questioned, as illustrated by a "meme" on the same page. Superimposed over an image of a *cabrito* grill, a drawing of a man "retouching" his lips is accompanied by the legend "I don't eat *cabrito* because of the ugly way in which they are slaughtered" (Parrilleros Mamones (2016) (Figure 4.3). Clearly, concern over animal suffering is an attitude not befitting of a real man.

Among the comments elicited by this image, a woman invites to reconsider the concept of "macho:" "A macho is a man with feelings, capable of compassion for the suffering of other beings, rather than one who only thinks about his own pleasure," to which a man responded: "Here's the *Femi-Nazi*, so dull she can't understand black humor. A man saying 'oh . . . how ugly is their killing!', looks

Figure 4.3 Meme about *cabrito* consumption

Source: Parrilleros Mamones, 2016.

like the ultimate sissy. Tough luck, dude. . . . Does the lion kill his prey in a pretty way? This is the life cycle, humans provide food to the animals and there's nothing wrong in killing for eating, it's the most natural thing." Meat eating binges, including *cabrito* feasts, legitimize the power over animal otherness, reinforcing masculine values in men. Vegetarianism, by contrast, is perceived as unfit for men, reserved for the meek (Sobal, 2005; Rothgerber, op cit.).

Animals as property in the collective imagination

Zafrilla (2013) has argued that when it comes to our moral and legal obligations toward non-humans, we suffer from moral schizophrenia. Some people recognize that animals have significant moral interests, such as being free from fear and pain, and therefore it is morally wrong to inflict unnecessary suffering on them (Singer, 1975; Nussbaum & Sunstein, 2004). However, this ideology means little when, acting as a tourist, an individual feels entitled to everything money can buy. The ideology of "speciesism" conceives of unequal relations among species and assigns animals the status of human property, which in practical terms means that animal suffering is necessary to fulfill human interests, including economic benefit (Singer, 1975).

If animal rights (to life, to freedom from suffering, from fear) were taken seriously, and human–non-human relations were founded on their intrinsic rather than their extrinsic values, animals would not be treated as "resources" (Webster, 2001; Lynn, 1998). We must stop treating animals as objects and property, and subjecting them to a kind of treatment that would be inconceivable in the case of a human being, for they can feel fear and pain as much as humans can. For locals and tourists in Monterrey alike, the *cabrito* has more value as a dish than as a sentient being, something that is unlikely to change unless Mexican federal law is reformed to include the rights of livestock species and all other animals (Lira, 2016).

For as long as animals continue to be regarded as human property, the principle of equal treatment will never apply, as it didn't in the case of African slaves before the abolition of slavery (Hribal, 2003). Kids, for the time being, will continue to be seen as culinary objects that satisfy the palate of tourists, who seem to have little or no regard for their rights as sentient beings with cognitive properties.

Conclusions

The production of *cabrito* dishes in Monterrey raises two questions of moral order: (1) Is it right to raise and sacrifice animals, so locals and tourists can taste a dish considered part of a cultural heritage? (2) Would things be different if the killing process were carried out humanely? The recognition of animal rights dictates that the slaughter of animals is morally wrong in most cases (Singer, 1975; Regan, 1986).

Gastronomic tourism is linked to animal farming, which compromises the wellbeing of animals in various ways. Consisting basically of the rearing and slaughtering of animals, animal farming transgresses their most basic rights to life.

Moreover, as in capitalist economies the accumulation of capital leads to mass production, the conditions of confinement and crowdedness in which rearing is carried out deprives animals of the right to thrive in natural environments (or at least in decent conditions), the right to roam around freely, the right to be free from fear and pain, the right to live a healthy life without medical intervention, and the right to eat a natural diet and enjoy the social/family life typical of their species.

The consumption of *cabrito* responds to a trivial interest that has been blown out of proportion, misleading tourists into thinking of it as an act that leads to happiness – i.e., the pleasure of tasting and the satisfaction of the desire to experience something new. Few consumers, however, are aware of what this act means for the animals, and of the extraordinary abuse of power that is exercised on them, which causes them pain, agony, and stress, the exact reverse of happiness. One of the basic tenets of utilitarianism is that individual happiness (in this case the happiness of a tourist) cannot override collective welfare (in this case, the welfare of animals) (Bentham, 2009, Singer, 1975). An ethical consideration of gastronomic tourism would take into account the interests of other species and, in the case of *cabrito*, would prevent their suffering as newborn beings. Every visitor to Monterrey ought to be confronted with these decisions, and recognize the egotism, pride, and arrogance of the economic and power relations involved in the creation of "tourist experiences."

The production of *cabrito* for tourist consumption or as a traditional element on festive occasions has been legitimized by religious ideas and the personal right to "have some fun," in a society that affords masculinity the highest social rank, including the precedence over the rights of a newborn animal to life and to be free from suffering. However, attitudes on this issue do vary and can be classified into three different positions: while some people do not perceive the kid as a sentient being, but rather as a culinary product, others are aware of the implications of breeding and slaughtering a sentient being, but they will still consume *cabrito* because they are entitled to their tourist experience. Finally, there are those who, aware of the ethical implications of their actions, will refuse to eat *cabrito*, even if this means they will go back home with an "incomplete" tourist experience.

Lastly, as the "scientific" human being has been able to determine how to obtain the same nutrients (proteins) from plants, a truly ethical position about *cabrito* consumption would be not only to avoid eating this being but any kind of meat, especially when it involves the slaughtering of animals in the way kids are slaughtered. The claim that humans are omnivores, and at the top of the food chain, does not justify the slaughter of animals, nor does it justify their breeding in cruel environments, such as stables (Singer, 1975). The newborn kid is slaughtered with rudimentary methods and left to agonize in severe pain for several minutes, all in the name of obtaining an "exquisite" animal dish.

Note

1 From now on, and unless otherwise indicated, all direct translations from both text citations and reported speech from users of the internet sites consulted, have been done by the authors of this article.

Acknowledgment

This research was carried out under the project entitled "Dark Tourism in Mexico: An Interdisciplinary Social-Science Approach," financed by CONACYT, Mexico (CB-2014–01/Application No. 239653).

References

Adams, C., & Gruen, L. (2015). Introduction. In C. Adams & L. Gruen (Eds.), *Ecofeminism: Feminist intersections with other animals and the earth* (pp. 1–5). New York: Bloomsbury.

Ansín, O., Antonini, A., Castagnaso, H., Lacchini, R., Miceli, E., & Muro, M. (2001). Cabras criollas: producción de leche, ganancia de peso de los cabritos y efectos de la restricción nutricional en el tercio final de la gestación. *Producción Animal, 13*(1), 59–62.

Barcellona, P. (1992). *Postmodernidad y comunidad: El regreso de la vinculación social.* Madrid: Trota.

Bentham, J. (2009). *An Introduction to the Principles of Morals and Legislation.* 2nd edition. Mineola: Dover Philosophical Classics.

Berlanga, J., Lara, E., & Ramírez, C. (1999). *Las fiestas del dolor: un estudio sobre las celebraciones del Niño Fidencio.* Monterrey: Fondo Estatal Para La Cultura y Las Artes de Nuevo León.

Bryman, A. (2008). *Social research methods.* Oxford: Oxford University Press.

Clark, C., Murrell, J., Fernyhough, M., O'Rourke, T., & Mendl, M. (2014). Long-term and trans-generational effects of neonatal experience on sheep behaviour. *Biology Letters, 10*(7), 57–86.

Cohen, E. (2005). Principales tendencias en el turismo contemporáneo. *Política y sociedad, 42*(1), 11–24.

Dawkins, M. (2006). Through animal eyes: What behaviour tells us. *Applied Animal Behaviour Science, 100*(1), 4–10.

De Certeau, M. (2014). Spatial practices. In *The people, place, and space reader.* Osaka: Osaka People University.

Domínguez, H. (2007). *Modernity and the nation in Mexican representations of masculinity: From sensuality to bloodshed.* New York: Macmillan.

Expedia México. (2014). Itinerarios de Monterrey: rutas para todos los gustos [Blog]. *Expedia.mx.* Retrieved September 17, 2016, from https://blog.expedia.mx/itinerario-de-monterrey/

Fessler, D., & Navarrete, C. (2003). Meat is good to taboo: Dietary proscriptions as a product of the interaction of psychological mechanisms and social processes. *Journal of Cognition and Culture, 3*(1), 1–40.

Francione, G. (2010). Animal welfare and the moral value of nonhuman animals. *Law, Culture and the Humanities, 6*(1), 24–36.

Galina, M., Pacheco, D., Silva, E., Palma, J., & Hummel, J. (1995). Fattening goats with sugarcane sprouts, corn stubble, protein concentrate, molasses and urea. *Small Ruminant Research, 18*(3), 227–232.

Garza, C., Vera, G., & Kawas, G. (1994). Sacrificio y comercialización del cabrito en la ciudad de Monterrey. In *Memorias de la IX Reunión Nacional sobre Caprinocultura* (pp. 340–344). La Paz: Universidad Autónoma de Baja California Sur.

Garza, J. (1995). *Tierra de cabritos.* Mexico: Consejo Nacional para la Cultura y las Artes.

Gaytán, M. (2010). Drinking the nation and making masculinity: Tequila, Pancho Villa and the US media. In H. Gray & M. Gómez-Barris (Eds.), *Toward a sociology of the trace* (pp. 207–233). Minneapolis: University of Minnesota Press.

Gobiernos México. (2016). Anuncian festejos por el 420 aniversario de la fundación de Monterrey [online]. Retrieved May 1, 2017, from www.gobiernosmexico.com.mx/gobiernos-municipales/monterrey-nuevo-leon-anuncian-festejos-por-el-420-aniversario-de-la-fundacion-de-monterrey/

González, G. (2011). *El Rey del Cabrito: Bagaje gastronómico* [online]. Retrieved September 24, 2016, from http://bagajegastronomico.tumblr.com/post/7067930472/el-rey-del-cabrito

Gran Turismo. (2015). Cabrito: manjar de reyes, tienes que probarlo en Monterrey [online]. *Gran Turismo México*. La experiencia de tu vida. Retrieved September 16, 2016, from http://granturismomexico.com /tag/monterrey-tienes-que-visitarlo-y-comer-cabrito/

Gutmann, M. (2006). *The meanings of Macho: Being a man in Mexico City* (Vol. 3). Santa Barbara, CA: University of California Press.

Hall, C., & Sharples, L. (2003). The consumption of experiences or the experience of consumption: An introduction to the tourism of taste. In C. M. Hall, L. Sharples, R. Mitchell, N. Macionis, & B. Cambourne (Eds.), *Food tourism around the world: Development, management and markets* (pp. 1–25). London: Butterworth-Heinemann.

Heinz, B., & Lee, R. (1998). Getting down to the meat: The symbolic construction of meat consumption. *Communication Studies*, *49*(1), 86–99.

Hernández, F. (2007). *Proyectos productivos de la Región Mixteca: producción de leche de cabra y cabrito*. México: UNAM.

Hernández, Z. (2000). La caprinocultura en el marco de la ganadería poblana (México): Contribución de la especie caprina y sistemas de producción. *Archivos de zootecnia*, *49*(187), 341–352.

Hiernaux, D. (2002). Turismo e imaginarios. In C. Allen, D. Hieraux, & L. Van Duynen (Eds.), *Cuadernos de Ciencias Sociales* (Vol. 123, pp. 7–36). San José, CA: FLACSO.

Holloway, L., & Morris, C. (2007). Exploring biopower in the regulation of farm animal bodies: Genetic policy interventions in UK livestock. *Genomics, Society and Policy*, *3*(2), 1–17.

Hribal, J. (2003). Animals are part of the working class: A challenge to labor history. *Labor History*, *44*(4), 435–453.

Kellman, S. (2000). Fish, flesh, and foul: The anti-vegetarian animus. *The American Scholar*, *69*(4), 85–96.

Lázaro, A. (2015). *Guía para sacrificar cabritos* [video]. Retrieved September 16, 2016, from www.youtube.com /watch?v=OlKpNJg3X9M.

Lemle, R., & Mishkind, M. (1989). Alcohol and masculinity. *Journal of Substance Abuse Treatment*, *6*(4), 213–222.

Lewis, V. (2009). When "Macho" bodies fail: Spectacles of corporeality and the limits of the homosocial/sexual in Mexican cinema. In S. Fouz-Hernández (Ed.), *Mysterious skin: Male bodies in contemporary cinema* (pp. 177–192). London: IB Tauris.

Lima, J. (2010). Pífanos, Epifanía, Cabritos. *República de las Letras: Revista literaria de la Asociación Colegial de Escritores*, (118), 108.

Lira, I. (2016). Activistas piden protección legal para animales en la Constitución de la CDMX. *Sin Embargo* [online]. Retrieved September 18, 2016, from www.sinembargo.mx/05-09-2016/3088657

Lynn, W. (1998). Contested moralities: Animals and moral value in the dear/Symanski debate. *Ethics, Place and Environment*, *1*(2), 223–242.

México Desconocido. (2015). *15 Cosas que hacer en Monterrey* [online]. Retrieved September 16, 2016, from www.mexicodesconocido.com.mx/cosas-que-hacer-en-monterrey.html

Mkono, M. (2011). The othering of food in touristic eatertainment: A netnography. *Tourist Studies*, *11*(3), 253–270.

Murillo, K. (2016). 10 platillos que debes probar al viajar por México [online]. *About en Español*. Retrieved September 16, 2016, from http://enmexico.about.com/od/Cultura-en-movimiento/tp/Diez-Platillos-Imperdibles- Al-Viajar-Por-Mexico.htm

Napolitano, V. (2009). The virgin of Guadalupe: A nexus of affect. *Journal of the Royal Anthropological Institute*, *15*(1), 96–112.

Nield, K., Kozak, M., & LeGrys, G. (2000). The role of food service in tourist satisfaction. *International Journal of Hospitality Management*, *19*(4), 375–384.

Notimex. (2016). Festival del Cabrito llega a la Ciudad de México. *Chilango* [online]. Retrieved September 14, 2016, from www.chilango.com/restaurantes/nota/2016/06/30/festival-del-cabrito-llega-a-la-ciudad-de-mexico

Nussbaum, M., & Sunstein, C. (2004). *Animal rights*. New York: Oxford University Press.

Panorama agropecuario. (2015). La cabrita, Chapter 105 [video file]. Retrieved December 13, 2016, from www.youtube.com/watch?v=Ghg6X03I0Nk

Parrilleros Mamones. (2016). Facebook group site. Retrieved October 13, 2016, from www.facebook.com/Parrilleros Mamones/photos/pcb.1589076541396048/1589076411396061/?type=3&theater

Pawn, S. (2012). *Matando un cabrito* [video]. Retrieved September 16, 2016, from www.youtube.com/watch?v =_Z7RFTtsX5A

Plumwood, V. (2000). Integrating ethical frameworks for animals, humans, and nature: A critical feminist eco-socialist analysis. *Ethics and the Environment*, *5*(2), 285–322.

Pollicino, P., Gandini, M., Perona, G., Mattoni, M., & Farca, A. (2007). Use of elastrator? Rings to repair umbilical hernias in young swine. *Journal of Swine Health and Production*, *15*, 92–95.

Quan, S., & Wang, N. (2004). Towards a structural model of the tourist experience: An illustration from food experiences in tourism. *Tourism Management*, *25*(3), 297–305.

Quiroz, C., & Hernández, P. (2014). *Crianza artificial de cabritos y hembras de reemplazo con el uso de tinas amamantadoras*. Saltillo: Instituto Nacional de Investigaciones Forestales, Agrícolas y Pecuarias.

Regan, T. (1986). A case for animal rights. In M. W. Fox & L. D. Mickley (Eds.), *Advances in animal welfare science* 1986/87 (pp. 179–189). Washington, DC: The Humane Society of the United States.

Rinfret, S. (2009). Controlling animals: Power, Foucault, and species management. *Society and Natural Resources*, *22*(6), 571–578.

Rodríguez, J., & Cavazos, L. (1990). *Estudio del mercado del cabrito (Capra hircus) en el área Metropolitana de Monterrey*. Monterrey: ITESM.

Rollin, B. (2003). An ethicist's commentary on the elastrator for older bulls. *The Canadian Veterinary Journal*, *44*(8), 624.

Rothgerber, H. (2013). Real men don't eat (vegetable) quiche: Masculinity and the justification of meat consumption. *Psychology of Men & Masculinity*, *14*(4), 363.

Ruby, M., & Heine, S. (2011). Meat, morals, and masculinity. *Appetite*, *56*(2), 447–450.

Sahlins, M. (1997). *Cultura y razón práctica: Contra el utilitarismo en la teoría antropológica*. Barcelona: Gedisa.

Salinas, H., Moysen, E., de Santiago, M., Deras, F., Jáquez, J., Monroy, L., & Viramontes, U. (2016). Análisis descriptivo de unidades caprinas en el suroeste de la región lagunera, Coahuila, México. *Interciencia*, *41*(11), 763–768.

Sánchez, Á., López, A., & Propín, E. (2005). Estructura territorial del turismo en la Zona Metropolitana de Monterrey, México. *Investigaciones geográficas*, (58), 80–105.
Seto, K. (1999). Distinguishing metonymy from synecdoche. In K. Panther & G. Radden (Eds.), *Metonymy in language and thought* (pp. 91–120). Amsterdam: John Benjamins Publishing Company.
Sin Embargo. (2016). La guía de la parrillada norteña para principiantes. México [online]. Retrieved September 24, 2016, from www.sinembargo.mx/26-08-2016/3083137
Singer, P. (1975). *Animal liberation: A new ethics for our treatment of animals*. New York: Harper Collins.
Sobal, J. (2005). Men, meat, and marriage: Models of masculinity. *Food and Foodways*, *13*(1–2), 135–158.
Tapia, J. (2016). Celebran con feria gastronómica. *El Horizonte* [online]. Retrieved September 17, 2016, from http://elhorizonte.mx/monterrey/area-metropolitana/644464/celebran-con-feria-gastronomica
Terrazas, A., Serafin, N., Hernández, H., Nowak, R., & Poindron, P. (2003). Early recognition of newborn goat kids by their mother: II. Auditory recognition and evidence of an individual acoustic signature in the neonate. *Developmental Psychobiology*, *43*(4), 311–320.
Trauer, B., & Ryan, C. (2005). Destination image, romance and place experience: An application of intimacy theory in tourism. *Tourism Management*, *26*(4), 481–491.
Trip Advisor. (2016). Buena comida: Opinión sobre el Rey del Cabrito [online]. Retrieved September 17, 2016, from www.tripadvisor.com.mx/ShowUserReviews-g150782-d812560-r376563010-El_rey_del_cabrito-Monterrey_Northern_Mexico.html
UNESCO. (2010). *Traditional Mexican cuisine – ancestral, ongoing community culture, the Michoacán Paradigm* [online]. UNESCO. Retrieved September 13, 2016, from www.unesco.org/culture /ich/en/RL/traditional-mexican-cuisine-ancestral-ongoing-community-culture-the-michoacan-paradigm-00400
Webb, E., Casey, N., & Simela, L. (2005). Goat meat quality. *Small Ruminant Research*, *60*(1), 153–166.
Webster, A. (2001). Farm animal welfare: The five freedoms and the free market. *The Veterinary Journal*, *161*(3), 229–237.
Wilkinson, J., & Stara, B. (1998). *Producción comercial de cabras*. Madrid: Acribia.
Zafrilla, P. (2013). Implicaciones normativas de la psicología moral: Jonathan Haidt y el desconcierto moral. *Daimon, Revista internacional de filosofía*, (59), 9–25.

5 Provisioning in the animal tourism industry

Through the lens of the Amazon river dolphin

Cadi Y. Fung

Introduction

Animals play a prominent role in many of our lives, whether as family pets, happenstance encounters trekking through nature, or the nameless whales often set up as fundraisers in elementary school. My experiences working with captive bottlenose dolphins, North American river otters, domestic dogs and cats, binturongs, scarlet macaws, a wallaby – the list goes on – have taught me a lot about the human–animal relationship, public perceptions of animals, and a seemingly intense desire to have intimate connections with non-human animals.

As humans are increasingly disconnected from the natural world through urbanization and population growth, the desire to interact with nature grows (van den Berg, Hartig, & Staats, 2007). Nature-based tourism is the fastest growing sector of the tourism industry (Kuenzi & McNeely, 2008), and wildlife tourism, a niche within nature-based tourism, can be particularly attractive to tourists, especially given the opportunity to observe or interact with threatened, endangered, or rare animals (Ballantyne, Packer, & Hughes, 2009). Cetaceans in particular seem to have captured our attention and awe for millennia, and dolphins especially are universally beloved (Rauch, 2014). It comes as no surprise that cetacean-based tourism like whale watching tours have grown in popularity over the past few decades (O'Connor, Campbell, Cortez, & Knowles, 2009).

Whale and dolphin tourism (and wildlife tourism in general) exists in a variety of forms, ranging from very hands-on ("consumptive") activities like trainer-for-a-day programs to more hands-off ("non-consumptive") activities like whale-watching tours (Duffus & Dearden, 1990; Lovelock, 2008). While non-consumptive forms of wildlife tourism have traditionally been more attractive, Franklin (2008, p. 39) believes that "consumptive forms . . . may become more attractive because they offer a more embodied and intimate *relationship with* the natural world" (emphasis in original). This embodied turn in tourism can be seen in an increase in wild dolphin interaction programs (Peters, Parra, Skuza, & Möller, 2013) and the growth of fly fishing in North America (Franklin, 2008).

Across the spectrum, wildlife tourism activities have been steadily increasing in popularity worldwide (Poudel, Munn, & Henderson, 2016). Proponents of this kind of tourism tout benefits for mental health and wellbeing, particularly for the more hands-on activities like dolphin interaction programs (Curtin, 2006; Martinez, Orams, & Stockin, 2011), where participants feed, swim with, or otherwise interact in a hands-on way with a dolphin. Establishing an up-close interaction with a wild animal also helps reconnect or reestablish a connection with nature. There exists the belief that these kinds of interactions help foster empathy for the more-than-human, which in turn leads to actions and behaviors that further conservation efforts (Curtin, 2009).

Such tourism is not without critique. In the case of wild animals, there are important ecological and ethological impacts to consider. Behavioral changes in wild animal populations become a concern with increased human interaction (Christiansen et al., 2016; Lusseau & Higham, 2004); evidence shows clear behavioral pattern changes in wild dolphin pods who are frequently visited by humans (Baker, Perry, & Vequist, 1988; Blane & Jaakson, 1995; Constantine, 2001; Hazelkorn, Schulte, & Cox, 2016; MacGibbon, 1991; Nowacek & Wells, 2001; Peters et al., 2013; Williams, Trites, & Bain, 2002; Wursig, 1996). For animals in captivity, an entirely separate set of ethical questions comes into play concerning the welfare and treatment of captive animals, animal rights, and the ethics of captive animal tourism (Agoramoorthy, 2004; Hughes, 2001; Mason, 2000; Rose, Parsons, & Farinato, 2009).

Although the use of animals in tourism has been widely studied, little attention has been paid to the use of food animals in animal tourism, that is, using animals as food for other animals in order to provide a tourist experience. Given the popularity of zoos and aquariums, and dolphin interaction programs ("swim-with-dolphin" programs), it becomes important to consider the use of fish and other aquatic animals as food in the continuation of these activities.

The use of fish as a resource in animal tourism has not been well-studied. Most research pertaining to provisioning wild animals as a tourism activity focuses on the behavioral and ecological impacts of such an activity; little attention has been paid to just how much fish (and other animals) are used for the purposes of tourism. Given increased concern about global food security (especially in light of climate change, agricultural land availability and degradation, human population growth, and geopolitical conflicts) (Barrett, 2010), rising demand for fish and fish products (Kent, 1997; Thilsted et al., 2016), and issues of ethics in the use of animals in tourism and agriculture (Fennell, 2014; Thompson, 2015), it is important to recognize the extent to which non-human animals are dependent on the same resources of which humans are dependent, and to what degree we can consider the use of food animals in animal tourism an unnecessary luxury, or an excessive use of a dwindling resource.

In the case of the Amazon river dolphin, the species of focus for this chapter, the situation is complicated by a historically contentious relationship between people and the dolphin. Following this introduction, I describe the sociocultural history of the dolphin, the bourgeoning tourism industry centered on this dolphin species in the Brazilian Amazon, and the relevance of this industry to fish resources and the local subsistence fishing community. Finally, the chapter concludes by situating the case of the Amazon river dolphin within a global context of fish use in cetacean-based tourism. The purpose of this chapter is to illuminate and propose discussion about an issue in animal tourism that has been neglected – the use of food animals (in this case, fish) for animal-based tourism activities.

Human relations with the Amazon river dolphin

The Amazon river dolphin (*Inia geoffrensis*, locally known as the *boto vermelho* (red dolphin) or *boto cor-de-rosa* (pink dolphin), or simply the *boto*) is a freshwater dolphin species classified by the International Union for Conservation of Nature's (IUCN) Red List of Threatened Species as "data deficient" (Reeves et al., 2011). This classification means there is "inadequate information to make a direct, or indirect, assessment of its risk of extinction based on its distribution and/or population status" (IUCN, 2001, para. 47). However, the dolphin is also recognized as an ecological indicator species of the health of the Amazon region (Gomez-Salazar, Coll, & Whitehead, 2012), meaning that the condition of the species reflects the condition of the greater Amazonian ecosystem. As such, there has been a push by researchers to learn more about the *boto* and the myriad factors influencing the wellbeing of the species, to more effectively determine the greatest threats to the species and what, if any, conservation policies are needed to protect them (e.g., Martin & da Silva, 2004).

The relationship between humans and the *boto* has shifted over time from being a relationship based in fear to one rooted in contention, distrust, and anger. Historically, contact between the two groups was minimized because of fear founded upon local mythology. Traditional Amazonian folklore includes stories of the *boto* as a powerful, supernatural being, viewed as mischievous and tempestuous, with the ability to transform into a handsome Caucasian man skilled at dancing and seducing young women. Stories tell of dolphins entering boats and households at night to paralyze and rape their occupants (Gravena, Hrbek, da Silva, & Farias, 2008). Unexpected teenage pregnancies in this region of Brazil are often attributed to seduction by an enchanted *boto* (Cravalho, 1999), who is assumed to be the father of all children of unknown parentage (Câmara Cascudo, 1972). Because of the *boto*'s perceived sexual prowess, some dolphin body parts are thought to have magical properties (Cravalho, 1999).

Traditional belief in the legend of the *boto* centered on the fear of negative consequences of interacting with these supernatural creatures. When humans came in contact with an enchanted *boto*, the consequences were often catastrophic; people could become impregnated, insane, cursed, or lured to the bottom of the river to live in the *botos*' enchanted underwater city (Slater, 1994). Interactions with these powerful creatures were taboo, and the belief was that harming *botos* would result in a form of karmic punishment, sometimes resulting in death. Over time, however, these taboos and beliefs have degraded, and interactions between humans and *botos* have increased because of population growth, migration to urban areas, education, economic forces and pressures, and other development factors (da Silva & Best, 1996; da Silva, Martin, & do Carmo, 2011).

Moreover, conflicts between *botos* and fishers have increased over the past few decades, as *botos* are frequently seen as competition for resources and as disruptors of fishing operations (Loch, Marmontel, & Simões-Lopes, 2009). The animals are blamed for scaring fish away from sites, stealing fish from nets, and destroying the nets themselves, all of which are actions that cause great financial harm to the fishers (Mintzer et al., 2015). As these interactions increase, so too has the direct killing of *botos*. Most commonly, this practice occurs among the *piracatinga* fishing community. *Piracatinga* (*Calophysus macropterus*), also known as *mota*, *simi*, *zamurito*, or *mapurite*, is a species of catfish consumed primarily in and exported to Colombia, but also increasingly in Brazil (under the guise of *douradinha* or *dourada*). *Botos* are frequently slaughtered for use as *piracatinga* bait (da Silva, Martin, & do Carmo, 2011; Mintzer et al., 2013; Trujillo, Crespo, van Damme, & Usma, 2010); *boto* meat is allegedly a very effective form of bait because of its strong odor, and some fishers claim that one *boto* carcass can catch around 300 kg of *piracatinga* (Schelle, 2010). According to a superintendent with the Brazilian Institute of Environment and Renewable Natural Resources (IBAMA) (personal communication, 2013), market prices for *piracatinga* are also more consistent than the majority of fish consumed domestically, so although it may not necessarily be more lucrative than mainstream fish stocks, the demand is consistent enough to drive the desire to fish *piracatinga*.

Boto feeding tourism

In contrast to this sometimes lethal conflict, a new form of tourism centered on the *boto* has emerged over the past twenty years. Capitalizing on the legend of the *boto*, as well as international interest in the Amazon as a premier ecotourism destination, communities along the Rio Negro river near Manaus, the state capital of Amazonas in Brazil, have created a tourism industry called "*boto* feeding tourism" (Alves, Andriolo, Orams, & Azevedo, 2011). The activity involves proprietors who outfit a floating structure, or *flutuante* (referred to here as a *boto* interaction platform, or BIP), to act as a site where people can get in the water with *botos* while an employee (referred to here as an operator) attracts *botos* to the site by provisioning fish.

This activity reportedly creates economic growth opportunities for local townspeople, and in some cases, it represents the primary source of income for residents (Alves et al., 2013). Moreover, it is thought that *boto* tourism might act as a conservation education tool, with advocates of dolphin tourism claiming that tourist interaction with dolphins supposedly creates increased sympathy and support for *boto* survival among tourists (e.g., Alves et al., 2011). Additionally, if people are able to earn a living in dolphin tourism, there is the presumption that at least some individuals would consider subsisting off this activity, rather than profiting off dolphin slaughter, or engaging in other eco-harmful activities.

Despite the rosy outlook maintained by advocates of this activity as a positive force for *boto* conservation efforts, it is undecided how, if at all, *boto* tourism benefits *botos*. *Boto* feeding tourism is not formally regulated nor legislated, though there are ongoing attempts to establish legislation. While Brazil does not currently have any legislation in place that governs human–*boto* interactions (Alves et al., 2011), laws do exist that prohibit the appropriation of wild fauna and mandate that the use of wild fauna is subject to federal regulation (Federal Republic of Brazil, 1998).

Given that no such federal regulation yet exists, the legality of this activity rests in a liminal state. The lack of regulation, as well as a lack of specialized training for the people who run these interaction programs, has led to dangerous encounters between dolphins and humans (Trujillo et al., 2010). There are reports that people have been bitten and/or rammed by the *botos*, usually because of inappropriate behavior on the human's part (most commonly harassment of dolphins, including physically abusing them by punches to the head and inserting objects into the blowhole). *Boto* feeding tourism obviously involves feeding the dolphins, but the methods of preparation and quality of fish are unregulated; sometimes dolphins are fed fish that have been left on the ground or trampled on, and in some cases, dolphins have even swallowed the plastic bags used to hold fish (Alves et al., 2011).

Starting in 2010, collaborative efforts between environmental organizations and research institutions in the state of Amazonas began instituting what could be considered "informal" regulations of activities at these *boto* interaction platforms (BIPs). These regulations were proposed as a way to try to mitigate some of the problematic consequences of increased human–*boto* interactions described above. Among the rules implemented were restrictions on where visitors could touch a *boto* (avoid the blowhole, flukes, eyes, mouth), how many visitors could be in the water at one time (ten), and the quantity of fish to be fed per *boto* per day (2 kg).

My visits to these sites began in the summer of 2014, and formal data collection took place along a 100 km stretch of the Rio Negro in Amazonas, Brazil (Figure 5.1) from June through August 2016. As of then, some BIP operators told visitors they were not allowed to make physical contact with a *boto*, though based on my observations, visitors often did not adhere to this rule, nor was it strictly enforced. Likewise, informal regulation stipulates that up to ten visitors can enter the water at a time; while most tour guides and BIP operators made sure that groups did not exceed this number, it is possible that such behavior was influenced by my presence as a researcher. Field observations from the two previous summers indicated that visitor limits were hardly regulated, if at all. Regardless, it is evident that BIP operators are now aware of these rules, and are adhering to them at least some of the time. Formal enforcement of these rules does not exist, but a renowned *boto* researcher at the National Institute of Amazonian Research (INPA) works closely with BIP operators to work toward more responsible tourism practices.

Data described in this chapter were collected as part of a larger project through two primary means: (1) survey questionnaires and semi-structured interviews at seven tourism sites along the Rio Negro (a tributary of the Amazon River), and (2) an extensive review of existing literature on fish consumption and use, specific

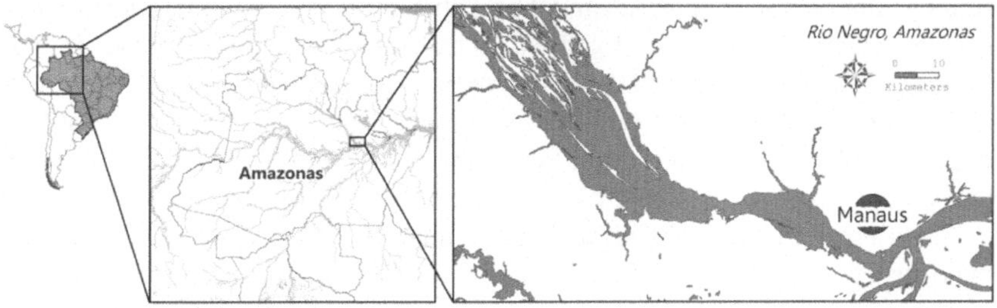

Figure 5.1 Study area. Map highlights the 100 km stretch of the Rio Negro, just outside Manaus, Amazonas, in which data collection took place

to animal tourism. Survey questionnaires were conducted with eleven tourism operators over the seven tourism sites, from June through August 2016. The questionnaires consisted of forty-one questions pertaining to household demographics, socioeconomic status, economic activities (alternative livelihoods), experiences and practices of their tourism operation, and cultural beliefs. Questionnaires were followed with a semi-structure interview, based off of an interview guide and expanding on some of the questionnaire responses. All individuals who participated were either the owner of a tourism operation (*flutuante*) or an employee who conducted tourist interactions with the river dolphins. On average, deploying questionnaires and conducting interviews lasted an hour total per respondent (excluding inevitable interruptions for business operations).

Fish as a resource

For the purposes of this chapter, the limitation on fish is the most pertinent informal regulation. Although these regulations were developed to be implemented at a specific BIP in Anavilhanas National Park (ICMBio, 2016), they were also introduced to and adopted by other BIPs in the region. Each BIP operator was aware of the rule that they are allowed to feed each *boto* a maximum of 2 kg of fish per day; some reported feeding between 1–3 kg of fish per *boto* per day, and others reported feeding between 5–10 individual units of fish per *boto* per day. Mondays and Wednesdays are designated "days off" for the *botos*; on these days, no one is allowed to feed the animals. This measure was implemented as an attempt to ensure that the *botos* will not become fully dependent on humans for food, and it is assumed that on their days off, they resume natural hunting behaviors.

Boto visitation varies from BIP to BIP. Reported numbers of *botos* at each site ranged from five to thirty, with a majority of respondents estimating between eight and fifteen. Taking the average of eight to fifteen *botos* (11.5), the 2-kg fish limitation, and the two days off for *botos* (approximately 260 total "working days" per year), I estimate that approximately 6,000 kg (or approximately 13,192 lbs.) of fish, annually, are fed to the *botos* at each site. That equates to 42,000 kg in total just for the seven sites I surveyed.

In reality, there is no way of knowing how much fish each *boto* is actually consuming. One reason behind the limitation of fish per day is to attempt to minimize *boto* dependency on humans for food, so that they continue to conduct natural foraging behaviors. The non-captive nature of *boto* feeding tourism, however, allows for the same *boto* to make rounds at each BIP every day, if he or she so chooses. Indeed, this is the exact behavior described by several BIP operators of the *botos*, whom they know by name. One *boto* in particular has been known to travel between two BIPs located approximately 75 km apart. Given that the majority of the BIPs along this stretch of the Rio Negro are located within a 13-km radius of each other, it is reasonable to assume high likelihood of some *botos* (particularly the larger, dominant males) visiting multiple BIPs in one day, and as such, consuming much more than the 2 kg/day limit.

While 42,000 kg of fish per year may seem like a relatively small figure, one study suggests that the average fisher along the Middle Rio Negro (approximately 350 km northwest from my study site) catches approximately 3,084 kg of fish per year (Sobreiro, 2015). In another study, researchers found that on average, an entire village of 170 individuals consumed approximately 13,578 kg of fish per year (Oliveira et al., 2010). Fish is also a staple in the diets of *ribeirinhos* (traditional communities who live along rivers); for some communities on the Rio Negro, fish comprised approximately 17% of their self-reported most frequently consumed food, and 70% of their total protein intake (da Silva & Begossi, 2009). Within the fishing communities I visited, which were generally located within a 5-km radius of the BIPs, individuals often responded that part of their catch was for subsistence, and the other part for commerce (usually local, within their communities), but the proportion of each varied throughout the year. Further, fishing activity is restricted by federal fishing ordinances as well as a fairly new moratorium established by the Brazilian government (Brasil, 2014).

In January 2015, as a response to the increasing incidence of *boto* mortality within the *piracatinga* industry, the Brazilian government enacted a five-year moratorium that prohibits the fishing and commercialization of *piracatinga* in Brazilian jurisdictional waters and throughout the national territory (Brasil, 2014). Exceptions exist for subsistence fishers; the capture and transport of up to 5 kg of *piracatinga*, for the sole purpose of the fisher and his/her family, is allowed.

Moreover, throughout Brazil, there is also a closed fishing period (*defeso*) to protect natural reproduction of fish species (IBAMA, 2007). In Amazonas state, the period begins November 15 and ends on March 15 the following year. Recognizing the economic blow many fishers would face because of this restriction, the government enacted a *seguro defeso* payment that would provide minimum wage salaries to fishers during the fishing prohibition. However, in October 2015, the government suspended these payments (Brasil, 2015), and as of November 11, 2017, they have not yet reinstated the program.

It is important to note that most of the BIP operators surveyed also fish for subsistence. For a majority of the tourism operations, the fish used to provision *botos* are acquired from both fish markets in a local municipality, and through subsistence fishing. The price and quantity of fish varies throughout the year, as the rainy and dry seasons dictate the availability of fish (more fish are caught in the dry season), and as an extension, the price of fish (fish are more expensive in the rainy season).

Given all of the above factors, the relationship between fishers, the *boto* tourism industry, and the *botos* themselves is complex. Complicating matters further, much of the study area falls within a protected area. Some of these protected areas are no-take zones, where fishing is prohibited (with the exception of subsistence fishing). Fishers who also fish for commerce sometimes travel hours away from their communities to find a spot suitable for fishing. On top of the prohibitions, population growth has crowded some fishers out as well; most fishers complained of a decrease in fish quantity over time, and they often blamed the growth of communities for causing the decline. Further, members of some communities have grievances with BIP tourism. While tourism has economically benefitted some individuals by bringing tourists to nearby communities, others complain that they have not seen any of the reported trickle-down benefits from increased tourism.

Similarly, some locals report that *boto* behavior has changed over time. In some cases these changes are friendly (e.g., their children enjoy seeing an increase of *botos* in the area); in other cases, the changes have been detrimental (e.g., acclimation to human proximity has made some *botos* more aggressive in their interactions). In terms of long-term behavioral changes, *botos* naturally follow their prey throughout the year. Under normal circumstances, during the rainy season when water levels are high, *botos* usually leave the main river channels and enter the flooded forests in search of food. In the dry season, as water levels fall, they return to the main channels. Given that fishing and fish availability is highly seasonal, but BIP tourism operates year-round, it can become a concern if BIP tourism artificially induces *botos* to remain along the main river channels during times of the year when they would normally be elsewhere.

Taking all of these considerations together, fish availability becomes an underlying concern. If fish are already a contested issue, with several stakeholders fighting for the same resource, what role does tourism play in mitigating or exacerbating conflicts that already exist? Policymakers and experts in the region have been working steadily toward finding solutions to the myriad of problems involving the human–*boto* relationship, particularly in light of increased BIPs. To that conversation, I offer the suggestion that we need to consider the sustainability of this activity in ways extending beyond what has already been proposed, to include the potential impacts of BIPs on fish populations and relations among human communities.

Fish in the global cetacean tourism industry

In contrast to the lack of regulation in fish feeding in BIP tourism, aquariums in the US have many regulations when it comes to feeding captive cetaceans. In working with dolphins and river otters, one thing I was struck by was how much fish would potentially go to waste. The standards of fish that could be fed to the mammals was such that any fish with a skin tear, bloody eye, or freezer burn was automatically thrown in the trash pile (in some cases, we could save the best of the unusable fish for the sea turtle department, who could feed some of our discarded fish to the turtles). Females with eggs were also discarded because of the extra caloric content.

Globally, approximately 30% of harvested food is never consumed by humans (KC, Haque, Legwegoh, & Fraser, 2016); fish waste accounts for approximately 35% of this wasted food (FAO, 2016a). These include losses from agricultural production (discards during fishing), post-harvest handling and storage ("spillage and degradation during icing, packaging, storage and transportation after landing"), processing (industrial processing like canning or smoking), distribution (within the market system), and consumption (FAO, 2011, p. 3).

When we think of food waste, we normally think of food wasted for human use. However, non-human animals, particularly those in human care, also require food inputs, and these numbers can quickly add up. For example, SeaWorld reports that on average, their bottlenose dolphins are fed between 25 and 35 pounds (11.3 and 15.9 kg, respectively) of fish per day (SeaWorld, 2016). It is estimated that at least 2,337 cetaceans (dolphins, beluga whales, orca, porpoises, and false killer whales) are held in captivity worldwide (BornFree, 2016). If we extend SeaWorld's reported bottlenose dolphin feeding standard to all captive cetaceans, keeping in mind that food consumption is a percentage of total bodyweight (therefore larger animals like orcas and belugas require more food than bottlenose dolphins), annual fish consumption by captive cetaceans could range between approximately 21.3–29.9 million pounds (9.7–13.5 million kg).

While the percentage of cetacean tourism consumption of fish is only a fraction of that consumed by humans (a staggering 140.8 billion kg per year) (FAO, 2016b), when taken into account with all the ethical, ecological, and behavioral implications of keeping cetaceans captive and provisioning wild cetaceans, this use of fish presents an additional factor to consider in the discussion of the ethics and environmental responsibility of such tourism activities. This does not take the needs of other, non-cetacean animals into consideration – in terms of marine mammals, for example, there are also pinnipeds (seals, sea lions, walruses), otters, and polar bears. When we consider *all* animals in captivity, the number grows even more.

If fish standards for captive cetaceans in the US are extended to all tourism operations that provision dolphins and whales, both captive and free, the quantity of fish required and potential for waste increases dramatically. In terms of animal welfare and human responsibility to those animals we interact with, it makes sense to argue for higher standards of treatment and welfare across the board. In doing so, however, one must consider the possible repercussions down the line and recognize that our good intentions may have wider negative social and ecological consequences. Extending from here, we must question what it is we value most in our relationships with cetaceans, and the myriad of ways in which they manifest.

Regarding the *boto* tourism industry specifically, whether or not this tourism activity inadvertently contributes to the controversy and conflicts that exist between humans and the *boto* remains to be seen. It is clear that fish are a much-desired resource and a foundation of the local economy, and while most BIP operators are arguably well-intentioned, the possibility remains that *boto*-feeding tourism is detrimental both to the population of fish in the region, as well as to *boto* and human communities. However, the activity has also contributed to a greater appreciation for *boto* and ecological conservation, both by BIP operators and visitors, and it has helped bring international attention to the plight of the *boto* and of the socio-environmental injustices occurring in the greater Amazonian region. Perhaps rather than increasing polarity between stakeholders, *boto*-feeding tourism could serve as a vehicle for opening communication channels among these stakeholders, and working toward an effective solution that simultaneously protects the interests of *botos*, fishers, BIP operators, and the Rio Negro ecosystem.

In order for this to be accomplished, conflicts among and within stakeholder groups need to be addressed. We need to identify, among all stakeholders, (1) their end goals (what are they trying to achieve, either personally or within their communities), (2) perceived barriers to meeting these goals, and (3) possible points or spaces of compromise. Without an in-depth understanding of the multiple and often conflicting viewpoints, progress cannot be made.

Similarly, hostility and animosity among individuals and groups must be identified and discussed in order to work toward an effective solution. For example, when asking a BIP operator about aggressive behavior from fishers toward the *botos*, he responded:

> It's not legal, and it's difficult for you to control a fisher so he doesn't hit and doesn't attack, because you talk with them so that they don't do it, and sometimes they even attack people. So you have to be cautious with them. "Oh, will you give me a gillnet if it rips?" That's all they talk about. And it's difficult, it's not easy. You have to make them aware that they can't attack, can't beat [the animal], but there isn't a way. It's not easy. And if you speak louder with them, they already want to set the platform [BIP] on fire, loosen the cables, all this, it's not easy. It's a war.
>
> (BIP operator 2016, personal communication, 12 July)

However, such interactions were rarely reported by other respondents. If conflicts like these do indeed exist – if there is, in fact, a "war" between fishers and BIP operators – this must be taken into consideration when determining the future of BIP tourism activities. Moreover, these conflicts need to be brought out into the open for discussion, without fear of immediate authoritative retaliation.

Taking all of these considerations together – the reliance on fish by all communities in the region, the heavy usage of fish for BIP operations, a lack of regulation of BIP activities, and potential harm to *botos* (both immediate and long-term) – the additional conflicts between fishers and BIP operators seems to tilt the scale in favor of regulating, minimizing, or even altogether eliminating BIP activities. A preliminary utilitarian view of the situation would suggest that the benefits do not outweigh the costs for a majority population (human and more-than-human); the immediate benefits seem to only apply to BIP operators and their families. However, the potential for BIP tourism to serve as a conservation education tool or alternative economic activity still holds some hope. More research is needed in order to assess the actual impacts of *boto* tourism and its role in enhancing or mitigating the conflicts that exist within and among human and more-than-human communities in the region.

Limitations and future directions

Amounts of fish reported by BIP operators were generally approximations. Based on my observations and data, fish are not weighed prior to each feeding activity; some BIP operators approximated amounts of fish based on numbers, rather than weight. Thus, estimations reported may not be accurate. Similarly, it is likely that many more BIPs exist than I am aware of, which would also affect estimations. I also did not include an estimation of fish used to provision wild cetaceans outside of this study. On a global scale, such provisioning activities would contribute significantly to the total amount of fish used in cetacean-based tourism.

Information about captive animals and the use of food animals in the upkeep of non-human animals in places like zoos and aquariums is difficult to find. The data described in the previous section could be a gross under- or over-estimation of how much fish is actually used in cetacean-based tourism; further research is needed to provide more accurate estimations. Additionally, the expansion of this topic to include other marine and terrestrial species would help illuminate the topic further, and demonstrate to a greater degree the extent to which animals are used as food in the animal tourism industry.

References

Agoramoorthy, G. (2004). Ethics and welfare in Southeast Asian zoos. *Journal of Applied Animal Welfare Science*, *7*(3), 189–195. doi:10.1207/s15327604jaws0703.

Alves, L. C. P. S., Andriolo, A., Orams, M. B., & Azevedo, A. de F. (2011). The growth of "botos feeding tourism", a new tourism industry based on the boto (Amazon river dolphin) Inia geoffrensis in the Amazonas State, Brazil. *Sitientibus serie Ciencias Biologicas*, *11*(1), 8–15.

Alves, L. C. P. S., Zappes, C. A., Oliveira, R. G., Andriolo, A., & Azevedo, A. de F. (2013). Perception of local inhabitants regarding the socioeconomic impact of tourism focused on provisioning wild dolphins in Novo Airao, Central Amazon, Brazil. *Anais da Academia Brasileira de Ciencias*, *85*(4), 1577–1591. doi:10.1590/0001-37652013108812.

Baker, C. S., Perry, A., & Vequist, G. (1988). Humpback whales of Glacier Bay, Alaska. *Whalewatcher*, *21*(2), 13–17.

Ballantyne, R., Packer, J., & Hughes, K. (2009). Tourists' support for conservation messages and sustainable management practices in wildlife tourism experiences. *Tourism Management*, *30*(5), 658–664. doi:10.1016/j.tourman.2008.11.003.

Barrett, C. B. (2010). Measuring food insecurity Christopher B. Barrett. *Science*, *327*(5967), 825–828. doi:10.1126/science.1182768.

Blane, J. M., & Jaakson, R. (1995). The impact of ecotourism boats on the Saint Lawrence beluga whales. *Environmental Conservation*, *21*(3), 267–269.

BornFree. (2016). *Captive whales and dolphins – global*. Retrieved November 2, 2016, from www.bornfree.org.uk/campaigns/zoo-check/captive-whales-dolphins/global/.

Brasil. (2014). *Instrução Normativa Interministerial nº 6, de 17 de julho de 2014*. Retrieved November 5, 2016, from http://pesquisa.in.gov.br/imprensa/servlet/INPDFViewer?jornal=1000&pagina=13&data=18/07/2014&captchafield=firistAccess

Brasil. (2015). *Portaria Interministerial nº 192, de 5 de outubro de 2015*. Retrieved November 5, 2016, from www.camara.gov.br/proposicoesWeb/prop_mostrarintegra?codteor=1398617

Câmara Cascudo, L. (1972). *Dicionário de folclore Brasileiro*. São Paulo: Edições Melhoramentos.

Christiansen, F., Mchugh, K. A., Bejder, L., Siegal, E. M., Lusseau, D., Mccabe, E. B., Lovewell, G., & Wells, R. S. (2016). Food provisioning increases the risk of injury in a long-lived marine top predator. *Royal Society Open Science*, *3*, 160560. doi:10.1098/rsos.160560.

Constantine, R. (2001). Increased avoidance of swimmers by wild bottlenose dolphins (Tursiops truncatus) due to long-term exposure to swim-with-dolphin tourism. *Marine Mammal Science*, *17*(4), 689–702.

Cravalho, M. A. (1999). Shameless creatures: An ethnozoology of the Amazon River dolphin. *Ethnology*, *38*(1), 47. doi:10.2307/3774086.

Curtin, S. (2006). Swimming with dolphins: A phenomenological exploration of tourist recollections. *International Journal of Tourism Research*, *8*, 301–315. doi:10.1002/jtr.577.

Curtin, S. (2009). Wildlife tourism: The intangible, psychological benefits of human – wildlife encounters. *Current Issues in Tourism*, *12*(5–6), 451–474. doi:10.1080/13683500903042857.

da Silva, A. L., & Begossi, A. (2009). Biodiversity, food consumption and ecological niche dimension: A study case of the riverine populations from the Rio Negro, Amazonia, Brazil. *Environment, Development and Sustainability*, *11*, 489–507. doi:10.1007/s10668-007-9126-z.

da Silva, V. M. F., & Best, R. C. (1996). Freshwater dolphin/fisheries interaction in the Central Amazon (Brazil). *Amazoniana*, *XIV*(1/2), 165–175.

da Silva, V. M. F., Martin, A. R., & do Carmo, N. A. S. (2011). Boto bait – Amazonian fisheries pose threat to elusive dolphin species. *IUCN Magazine of the Species Survival Commission*, *53*, 10–11.

Duffus, D. A., & Dearden, P. (1990). Non-consumptive wildlife-oriented recreation: A conceptual framework. *Biological Conservation*, *53*(3), 213–231. doi:10.1016/0006-3207(90)90087-6.

FAO. (2011). *Global food losses and food waste: Extent, causes and prevention*. Rome: FAO.

FAO. (2016a). *Key facts on food loss and waste you should know, SAVE FOOD: Global initiative on food loss and waste reduction*. Retrieved November 10, 2016, from www.fao.org/save-food/resources/keyfindings/en/

FAO. (2016b). *The state of world fisheries and aquaculture: Contributing to food security and nutrition for all*. Rome. Retrieved from www.fao.org/3/a-i3720e.pdf.

Federal Republic of Brazil. (1998). *Lei nº 9.605, de 12 de fevereiro de 1998*. Retrieved November 5, 2016, from www.planalto.gov.br/ccivil_03/leis/L9605.htm

Fennell, D. A. (2014). Exploring the boundaries of a new moral order for tourism's global code of ethics: An opinion piece on the position of animals in the tourism industry. *Journal of Sustainable Tourism*, *22*(7), 983–996. doi:10.1080/09669582.2014.918137.

Franklin, A. S. (2008). The "Animal Question" and the "consumption" of wildlife. In B. Lovelock (Ed.), *Tourism and the consumption of wildlife* (pp. 31–44). London: Routledge.

Gomez-Salazar, C., Coll, M., & Whitehead, H. (2012). River dolphins as indicators of ecosystem degradation in large tropical rivers. *Ecological Indicators*, *23*, 19–26. doi:10.1016/j.ecolind.2012.02.034.

Gravena, W., Hrbek, T., da Silva, V. M. F., & Farias, I. P. (2008). Amazon River dolphin love fetishes: From folklore to molecular forensics. *Marine Mammal Science*, *24*(4), 969–978. doi:10.1111/j.1748-7692.2008.00237.x.

Hazelkorn, R. A., Schulte, B. A., & Cox, T. M. (2016). Persistent effects of begging on common Bottlenose dolphin (Tursiops truncatus) behavior in an estuarine population. *Aquatic Mammals*, *42*(4), 531–541. doi:10.1578/AM.42.4.2016.531.

Hughes, P. (2001). Animals, values and tourism – structural shifts in UK dolphin tourism provision. *Tourism Management*, *22*(4), 321–329. doi:10.1016/S0261-5177(00)00070-4.

IBAMA. (2007). *Portaria nº 48, de 5 de novembro de 2007*.

ICMBio. (2016). *Turismo com botos vermelhos, Parque Nacional de Anavilhanas*.

IUCN. (2001). *Categories and criteria (version 3.1), the IUCN red list of threatened species*. Retrieved November 4, 2016, from www.iucnredlist.org/static/categories_criteria_3_1.

KC, K. B., Haque, I., Legwegoh, A. F., & Fraser, E. D. G. (2016). Strategies to reduce food loss in the global south. *Sustainability*, *8*(7), 1–13. doi:10.3390/su8070595.

Kent, G. (1997). Fisheries, food security, and the poor. *Food Policy*, *22*(5), 393–404. doi:10.1016/S0306–9192(97)00030-4.

Kuenzi, C., & McNeely, J. (2008). Nature-based tourism. In *Global risk governance* (pp. 155–178). Dordrecht, The Netherlands: Springer. doi:10.1007/978-1-4020-6799-0_8.

Loch, C., Marmontel, M., & Simões-Lopes, P. C. (2009). Conflicts with fisheries and intentional killing of freshwater dolphins (Cetacea: Odontoceti) in the Western Brazilian Amazon. *Biodiversity and Conservation*, *18*(14), 3979–3988. doi:10.1007/s10531-009-9693-4.

Lovelock, B. (2008). An introduction to consumptive wildlife tourism. In B. Lovelock (Ed.), *Tourism and the consumption of wildlife* (pp. 3–30). London: Routledge.

Lusseau, D., & Higham, J. E. S. (2004). Managing the impacts of dolphin-based tourism through the definition of critical habitats: The case of bottlenose dolphins (Tursiops spp.) in Doubtful Sound, New Zealand. *Tourism Management*, *25*(6), 657–667. doi:10.1016/j.tourman.2003.08.012.

MacGibbon, J. (1991). *Responses of sperm whales (Physeter macrocephalus) to commercial whale watching boats off the coast of Kaikoura*. Christchurch: Department of Conservation.

Martin, A. R., & da Silva, V. M. F. (2004). Number, seasonal movements, and residency characteristics of river dolphins in an Amazonian floodplain lake system. *Canadian Journal of Zoology*, *82*, 1307–1315. doi:10.1139/Z04-109.

Martinez, E., Orams, M. B., & Stockin, K. A. (2011). Swimming with an endemic and endangered species: Effects of tourism on Hector's dolphins in Akaroa Harbour, New Zealand. *Tourism Review International*, *14*(1–3), 99–115.

Mason, P. (2000). Zoo tourism: The need for more research. *Journal of Sustainable Tourism*, *8*(4), 333–339. doi:10.1080/09669580008667368.

Mintzer, V. J., Martin, A. R., da Silva, V. M. F., Barbour, A. B., Lorenzen, K., & Frazer, T. K. (2013). Effect of illegal harvest on apparent survival of Amazon River dolphins (Inia geoffrensis). *Biological Conservation*, *158*, 280–286. doi:10.1016/j.biocon.2012.10.006.

Mintzer, V. J., Schmink, M., Lorenzen, K., Frazer, T. K., Martin, A. R., & da Silva, V. M. F. (2015). Attitudes and behaviors toward Amazon River dolphins (Inia geoffrensis) in a sustainable use protected area. *Biodiversity and Conservation*, *24*(2), 247–269. doi:10.1007/s10531-014-0805-4.

Nowacek, S. M., & Wells, R. S. (2001). Short-term effects of boat traffic on bottlenose dolphins, Turciops truncatus, in Sarasota bay, Florida. *Marine Mammal Science*, *17*(4), 673–688. doi:10.1111/j.1748-7692.2001.tb01292.x.

O'Connor, S., Campbell, R., Cortez, H., & Knowles, T. (2009). *Whale watching worldwide: Tourism numbers, expenditures and expanding economic benefits, A special report from the International Fund for Animal Welfare*. Yarmouth: International Fund for Animal Welfare.

Oliveira, R. C., Dórea, J. G., Bernardi, J. V. E., Bastos, W. R., Almeida, R., & Manzatto, Â. G. (2010). Fish consumption by traditional subsistence villagers of the Rio Madeira (Amazon): Impact on hair mercury. *Annals of Human Biology*, *37*(5), 629–642. doi:10.3109/03014460903525177.

Peters, K. J., Parra, G. J., Skuza, P. P., & Möller, L. M. (2013). First insights into the effects of swim-with-dolphin tourism on the behavior, response, and group structure of southern Australian bottlenose dolphins. *Marine Mammal Science*, *29*(4), 484–497. doi:10.1111/mms.12003.

Poudel, J., Munn, I. A., & Henderson, J. E. (2016). Economic contributions of wildlife watching recreation expenditures (2006 & 2011) across the U.S. south: An input-output analysis. *Journal of Outdoor Recreation and Tourism*, (In Press, Corrected Proof), 1–7. doi:10.1016/j.jort.2016.09.008.

Rauch, A. (2014). *Dolphin*. London: Reaktion Books.

Reeves, R. R., Jefferson, T. A., Karczmarski, L., Laidre, K., O'Corry-Crowe, G., Rojas-Bracho, L., . . . Zhou, K. (2011). *Inia geoffrensis*. Retrieved January 19, 2017, from www.iucnredlist.org/details/10831/0

Rose, N. A., Parsons, E. C. M., & Farinato, R. (2009). *The case against marine mammals in captivity* (4th ed.). Washington, DC: The Humane Society of the United States and the World Society for the Protection of Animals.

Schelle, P. (2010). *River dolphins & people: Shared rivers, shared future*. Gland: World Wildlife Fund.

SeaWorld. (2016). *Frequently Asked Questions (FAQ's) – Ask Shamu, SeaWorld Parks & entertainment*. Retrieved October 4, 2016, from https://seaworld.org/en/animal-info/ask-shamu/faq/

Slater, C. (1994). *Dance of the dolphin: Transformation and disenchantment in the Amazonian imagination*. Chicago: University of Chicago Press.

Sobreiro, T. (2015). Urban-rural livelihoods, fishing conflicts and indigenous movements in the Middle Rio Negro region of the Brazilian Amazon. *Bulletin of Latin American Research*, *34*(1), 53–69.

Thilsted, S. H., Thorne-Lyman, A., Webb, P., Bogard, J. R., Subasinghe, R., Phillips, M. J., & Allison, E. H. (2016). Sustaining healthy diets: The role of capture fisheries and aquaculture for improving nutrition in the post-2015 era. *Food Policy*, *61*, 126–131. doi:10.1016/j.foodpol.2016.02.005.

Thompson, P. B. (2015). *From field to fork: Food ethics for everyone*. New York: Oxford University Press.

Trujillo, F., Crespo, E., van Damme, P. A., & Usma, J. S. (2010). *The action plan for South American River dolphins: 2010–2020*. Bogota: Union Grafica Ltda.

van den Berg, A. E., Hartig, T., & Staats, H. (2007). Preference for nature in urbanized societies: Stress, restoration, and the pursuit of sustainability. *Journal of Social Issues*, *63*(1), 79–96. doi:10.1111/j.1540-4560.2007.00497.x.
Williams, R., Trites, A. W., & Bain, D. E. (2002). Behavioural responses of killer whales (Orcinus orca) to whale-watching boats: Opportunistic observations and experimental approaches. *Journal of Zoology*, *256*(2), 255–270. doi:10.1017/S0952836902000298.
Wursig, B. (1996). Swim-with-dolphin activities in nature: Weighing the pros and cons. *Whalewatcher*, *30*(1), 11–15.

6 Animals off the menu

How animals enter the vegan food experience

Giovanna Bertella

Introduction

Vegan food experiences are food experiences characterized by the absence of animal-derived products (Fox & Ward, 2008). The choice of avoiding animal-derived foods can be explained in terms of lifestyle, understood here as a set of values, attitudes, and practices (Haenfler, Johnson, & Jones, 2012; Wahlen & Laamanen, 2015). In some cases, individuals following the vegan lifestyle are ethically motivated and hold the belief that any unnecessary form of oppression and violence toward animals is morally wrong and therefore should be avoided (Hamilton, 2000; Van der Kooi, 2010).

Partial veganism, also called vegetarianism, and veganism are fast-growing phenomena, and it is only recently that some scholars, including tourism scholars, have begun to focus their attention on such a trend, its understanding, and its implications (Ruby, 2012). Attempting to contribute to this under-researched field, this study explores veganism and focuses on vegan food experiences in the context of rural tourism.

The adopted perspective is inspired by the ecofeminist care tradition. Yudina and Fennel (2013) argue that the ethical position of ecofeminism can be particularly relevant in addressing concerns regarding human interactions with animals. The authors note that the most common interaction that tourists have with animals is when animal-derived products are presented as food on their plates. They suggest reflecting on the moral aspects of such animal encounters by adopting the ecofeminist philosophical perspective. This study accepts this suggestion and focuses on the absence of animal-derived food from tourists' plates and how such an absence can be understood from an ecofeminist perspective.

This chapter is organized as follows. First, the main tenets of ecofeminism and veganism are described. Second, the foodscape concept is presented. This concept permits the investigation of the complex settings in which food-related activities take place in the form of processes of relationalities concerning the materiality of food as well as its intangible dimensions (Mikkelsen, 2011). This aspect is particularly important in relation to the adoption of the ecofeminist perspective, as such a perspective emphasizes the relevance of our relations with the rest of the world and the context in which such relations develop. This study further develops the foodscape concept using the concepts of service- and experiencescape from the service and tourism literature to highlight the experiential aspect of vegan meals. After these theoretical considerations, this study's empirical part is presented. This concerns the vegan food experiences offered by two holiday country houses in the Parma area (Italy). The findings of this case are then discussed from an ecofeminist perspective using the foodscape concept.

Theoretical framework

Ecofeminism and veganism

The feminist care tradition in animal ethics has its origin in women's relational culture of caring and attentive love and its core tenets in a set of values that support the recognition and practice of dignity and respect toward animals (Donovan, 1983; Gruen, 2011). Such a position is part of a broader discourse concerning the interconnection among forms of oppression toward various actors, among which are animals and women (Gruen, 2007). In this sense the ecofeminist care tradition can be qualified as inclusive – it involves various "others" – and liberatory, whereby values and actions are viewed as inseparable. What is advocated is raising awareness of systematic oppression mechanisms in our society and performing actions that contribute to ending such mechanisms (Birkeland, 1983; Gruen, 1993). Moreover, it can be qualified as inclusive in relation to the inclusion of emotions as important factors for our moral positions, an aspect that is peculiar to ecofeminism in comparison with other animal liberation theories (Donovan, 1983; Slicer, 2007).

Ecofeminists recognize the oppression of animals by humans in several contexts; among these, the food context is the one in which such oppression is most evident. The origin of vegetarian ecofeminism can be related to the feminist activism of the 1960s, and the first articulated conceptualizations are from the 1990s (Gaard, 2002). Rejecting the dualistic view, according to which humans and animals differ in such a way that humans are superior and can exploit animals, ecofeminists view animals as individuals for whom humans have the moral obligation to care (Donovan & Adams, 2007).

In line with this consideration, several ecofeminists propose a position that, avoiding any form of universalism, takes into account the specific situation and the realism and feasibility of a vegetarian or vegan choice (Curtin, 1991; Twine, 2015). Some adopt an invitational approach, highlighting the opportunity to enlighten the people so that their food choices will become more conscious (Gruen, 2007). Here, vegetarianism and veganism are understood as moral choices that can come only "from within us," under the condition that we are genuinely interested in contributing to a better world. Such a position is also discussed in relation to the existence of social norms and traditions that tend to be accepted uncritically.

Carol Adams is among the ecofeminists who explore the practice of eating meat more deeply. She writes extensively about the similarities between the eating of meat and the oppression of women, noting that in both cases the body parts of the respective individuals are viewed as usable and disposable commodities (Adams,

1983). Adams also reflects on the ambiguity of the human practice of eating meat. For example, she observes how the use of the mass term "meat" acts as a distancing device that contributes to the conceptualization of the flesh of a once-alive someone into something edible (Adams, 1983).

Adams introduces the concept of "absent referents" to indicate that, when people eat animals, the animals are not perceived as present because they are dead (Adams, 1990; De Mello, 2012). However, the concept of "absent referents" can also be discussed in relation to vegetarian and vegan food experiences. During such experiences the animals are absent from the plates but present in the minds of those consuming plant-based food: the animals are present as absent, and their absence is celebrated through a vegetarian or vegan meal (Shapiro, 2015).

Posing the question regarding the ways in which animals enter the vegan tourism experience, this study aims to investigate whether and how the absence of animals from tourists' plates is highlighted by factors related to the food experience and its context. To achieve this, the concept of foodscape is developed.

The foodscape concept

The term "foodscape" highlights the relationship between food, the spatial context of its supply chain, and the subjects who engage in food-related activities (Mikkelsen, 2011). The foodscape concept concerns the physicality of the food environment as well as other elements and dimensions relevant to the involved subjects and significant terms of food production and consumption. Foodscapes can be described in terms of social, cultural, economic, political, and historical factors (Adema, 2006; Johnston & Baumann, 2014).

The foodscape concept is applied in the tourism context as part of the recent reflections about the new role of gastronomy (Richards, 2015). In the post-modern society, food-related practices are important to individuals' meaning making, identity development and affirmation. Food can be viewed as an identity marker and as the basis for forming and communicating a specific lifestyle. Moreover, food and the values attached to it are strictly connected to the locality where food-related activities are performed and therefore can assume an important role in tourism (Yeoman, McMahon-Beattie, Fields, Albrecht, & Meethan, 2015). This is particularly true for those foods promoted as traditional, which thus assume a central role in experiencing a destination in a multi-sensorial way that highlights the authenticity and uniqueness of the specific place (Bessière, 1998; Lee & Arcadia, 2011; Lin, Pearson, & Cai, 2011). This is often the case of rural tourists searching for distinctive food experiences to achieve a sort of "full immersion" in the local context (Quan & Wang, 2004; Sidali, Kastenholz, & Bianchi, 2015).

To explore better the experiential aspect of food consumption in the tourism context, the foodscape concept can be developed further using the concepts of service- and experiencescape. Such concepts focus on the service encounter and the related experience value. The servicescape concept indicates the context in which the service encounter takes place (Bitner, 1992; Ezeh & Harris, 2007; Rosenbaum & Massiah, 2011). Here, the following factors are identified: (1)

the environmental factors, including both artificial and natural elements, such as space, objects and ambient conditions, (2) the social factors, including the contact with local people, personnel and other tourists, and (3) the symbolic factors, including signs and artifacts to which particular values and meanings are attached.

Similarly, the tourist experiencescape is described as a scape consisting of various factors, including personnel, tourists, objects, and the physical environment (Mossberg, 2007). In addition to this, the concept highlights these factors' synergetic effect in contributing to a main theme that acts as the story that the tourists live when away from their ordinary lives.

Based on such considerations, the conceptualization of the foodscape adopted in this study is illustrated in Figure 6.1.

The ethical aspect of the foodscape

As foodscapes include meanings and values attached to food-related processes, the concept can be applied to investigate the ethical aspect of food-related activities (Adema, 2006; Panelli & Tipa, 2009; Mikkelsen, 2011; Johnston & Goodman, 2015). Thus, foodscapes can be viewed as places where specific ideologies are more or less explicitly advanced, discussed, and promoted. This can occur in line with different ethical approaches so that foodscapes can host food-related contestations and resistances. This can be the case for ideologies such as vegetarianism and veganism.

Recognizing that food has a central role in the way in which we care for others and ourselves, Morgan (2010) proposes viewing foodscapes in terms of the ecofeminist ethics of care. This study adopts this perspective and applies the foodscape concept to describe and understand vegan food experiences in rural tourism.

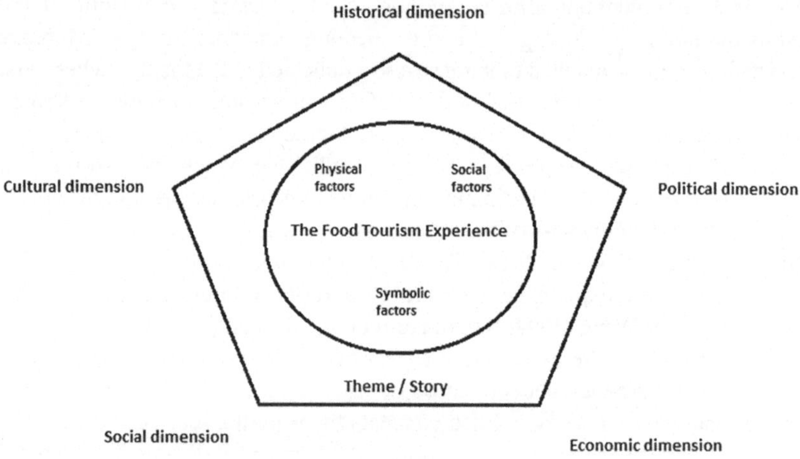

Figure 6.1 The conceptual model of the foodscape

Case study: vegan food experiences in the Parma area

Aiming to generate context-based knowledge that can improve our understanding of the specific phenomenon of vegan food experiences in tourism, a case study strategy was adopted (Yin, 2003; Flyvbjerg, 2006). The investigated case concerns vegan food experiences in hospitality facilities located in the rural area surrounding the town of Parma (Italy). The rural Parma area is selected as particularly relevant due to the dominant presence of traditional animal-derived food products. Secondary data concerning the local gastronomy are collected by consulting the official tourism agency webpage and the 2014–2017 marketing plan of Parma Municipality. In addition, an internet search was conducted to identify local animal-derived, food-based businesses, such as animal farms and meat and dairy production plants.

Through an initial internet search and the application of a snowball method, five country houses for holidays that profile themselves as vegetarian are identified. Among these, two are vegan. The study focuses on these, as they represent an extreme case in which all animal-derived food is eliminated from the menu.

The perspective reflected is that of the hosts'. The data collection is based on interviews with the owners and managers of the two farmhouses along with observations. The interviews are performed in two rounds: first by video Skype call and then face-to-face while visiting the facilities. The first round of interviews is semi-structured. During the interviews the business owners are probed to provide examples that could illustrate the various dimensions and factors of the foodscape. For example, to investigate the social dimension, the respondents are asked to describe their relations with the local community, while, for the cultural dimension, they are asked to comment on the local cultural activities concerning animals and food. In addition to being discussed during the interviews, some aspects, such as the physical factors of the vegan food experience, are observed during the field observation. During the fieldwork, a second round of interviews is performed and supplemented with several spontaneous conversations.

The gastronomic panorama of the Parma area

The Parma area is known as the "Italian food valley" due to the presence of a network of several institutional and commercial actors focused on the production and promotion of food and wine. Two examples are the Alma International School of Italian Cuisine and the Academia Barilla.

The Parma province hosts numerous dairy factories and, through the Parmigiano Reggiano consortium, many of these organize guided tours for various target groups, including families, foodies, schools, food trades, restaurants, tour operators, journalists, and bloggers. The local slaughterhouses promote themselves on the Internet, referring to their historical background, professionalism, and size. For example, a slaughterhouse reports its origin back to 1898 and illustrates it with old family pictures of the owner. This is also the case of a more recent group of eight companies, of which two are located in the Parma province. The group operates along the different phases of pork meat production and is presented on the Internet as follows: "[The owner's] experience has its roots deeply imbedded in the farming tradition. When the hog raised with care by the farmer was ready, grandfather Geminiano and his sons were called to perform the slaughtering rite" (Martelli, n.d.).

Similarly, another group formed by two companies, both located in the Parma area, presents itself by referring to its historical background as a small family business in the 1970s, its focus on quality and technology, and its capacity, around 5,000,000 slaughtered pigs per year.

Parma is part of the UNESCO (United Nations Educational, Scientific and Cultural Organization) network of creative cities of gastronomy. The official tourist information office of the province of Parma dedicates several sections of its website to gastronomy. The following quotation illustrates well the core products of the area and the pride with which they are presented: "A celebration of taste for any food lover: pork products and cheese are the best contributions of Parma to world cuisine" (turismo.comune.parma.it, n.d.) The majority of the foods and recipes described on this website concern animal-derived products. Among the traditional products, the *prosciutto crudo di Parma* (Parma ham) and the *salame di Felino* (salami) have a central role in the presentation, together with *Parmigiano Reggiano* (Parmesan cheese). These products are described quite extensively in relation to their origins, production processes, and quality. A network of six museums dedicated to food and wine, including two vegan products (tomatoes and pasta), is presented in relation to the possibility for tourists to experience and learn about the local traditions. The website presents some vegetarian and vegan foods, such as truffles and *porcino* mushrooms. Some recipes are described by referring to the meals prepared by the *rezdore* – the local housewives – often in relation to special occasions. Eight main course recipes are presented: five are based on meat, such as *punta di vitello* (stuffed veal), and three are vegetarian, such as *tortelli d'erbetta* (thin pasta filled with spinach and ricotta cheese). The other recipes listed on the website are for desserts and include eight vegetarian recipes for cakes and cookies and a vegan recipe.

A list of restaurants and cafés is provided with no specification about the presence of any vegetarian- or vegan-friendly places. The website also presents several food festivals. An example is the *November Porc*, described as "the most yummy event in Italy, 4 villages in 4 weekends and a star: the pork" (turismo.comune.parma.it, 2017a). Among the festivals indicated by the website as being "multiple," an event relevant to vegetarianism and veganism is listed. This is the *Parma Etica Festival*, described as the biggest ethical festival in Europe, which aims to promote a lifestyle that is "respectful of all the living beings and sustainable" (turismo.comune.parma.it, 2017b). It arranges various activities for adults and children and includes a vegetarian restaurant and vegetarian stands. In the marketing plan of the Parma Municipality, gastronomy is recognized as a strength of the area. Here, vegetarian and vegan foods are indicated as being potentially relevant to a niche market to which the priority is not given but that is recognized as being important for the completeness of the food offer.

Vegan holiday country houses

The two vegan country houses investigated are the agritourism business Borgo di Tara and the bed and breakfast Brugnola 1932, located 60 and 80 km from Parma respectively. This area is characterized by hills, mountains, valleys, rivers, and forests, which host a variety of wild animals. This nature, together with the presence of several small historical villages, makes the area attractive from a tourist point of view, although it is not particularly well known, especially at the international level. Both businesses opened quite recently (2011 and 2013) and are owned and run by two couples who are not originally from the local area.

Borgo di Tara offers accommodation and meals. The owners have renovated the house using eco-friendly methods and vegan material. This aspect is described on the business website as being in line with the owners' " 'cruelty-free' philosophy and lifestyle choice" (agriturismovegan.it, n.d.). During the interviews the owners noted that some guests show an interest in, and sometimes surprise concerning, this aspect. An example is the case of tourists who are uninformed about the common use of animal-derived products for building materials. The rooms are provided with cruelty-free and eco-friendly shampoo and soaps. In addition, the products used for cleaning the house are of the same type.

The second business, Brugnola 1932, is a bed and breakfast in a small village. The owners are now also considering opening a restaurant to serve meals to the guests and other possible customers. This aspect was stated during the interviews, suggesting that this could encourage guests to sleep at the bed and breakfast because there are no restaurants nearby, and, in any case, it is not particularly easy to find restaurants with vegan options in the area. Such difficulties were also mentioned by the agritourism business and stated in the following way: "They (the local people in general and the ones working in the hospitality in particular) put lard everywhere, also in the bread. I guess that it might be because they have so much of it, considering the amount of pork meat they produce."

As the above quotation illustrates, when asked to describe the context in which the country houses are located and their relationship with the local community, the comments were often about "we" (the couples) and "they" (the local community). As mentioned above, in both cases the owners are not originally from the local community, and their presence is quite recent. Such a lack of common roots was mentioned openly during the interviews, and it seems to be perceived quite strongly, with some exceptions concerning a few local people with whom the couples have managed to develop friendship relations. Although this is not unusual for outsiders, the data suggest that such a division could also be caused by the couples' alternative lifestyle. This aspect was noted in relation to the couples' failed attempts to arrange meetings for the local communities, inviting experts and focusing on food or on animal-related issues that are particularly relevant to the area, such as the debate about the presence of wolves. Only recently has one of the couples come closer to the local community, being invited to the local kindergarten that their son attends to talk about veganism to the children's parents.

At the Borgo di Tara property, books and leaflets are displayed in the area close to some of the bedrooms and on the way to the room where the meals are served.

Some contain tourist information, such as maps, and some concern vegan food and veganism. The latter materials present the choice of not consuming animal products as part of a broader opposition to any form of discrimination, including but not limited to the use of animals as food.

When asked whether and to what extent animal ethics are discussed with the guests, the owners of both businesses said that it happens quite often and that it is always the guests who initiate such conversations. Several tourists are couples in which at least one person is vegan or vegetarian. These are the cases in which, as a respondent said, the communication is easy, and conversations can be very pleasant and concern animal issues as well as environmental and social justice issues. In some cases, the discrimination and oppression mechanisms in today's society are also discussed. Quite often, the guests ask about the recipe for the food that they are eating, and sometimes they start talking about animal ethics and veganism. Commenting on this, one owner said:

> Sometimes people ask directly about veganism and our choice. Then we talk and explain our point of view. We are usually better informed than they are, as we have been vegetarian first and then vegan for many, many years. We are confident about our choice and we don't feel threatened in any way. We don't preach, we just tell them our point of view. The guests tend to listen and show curiosity. I remember only one case when this conversation ended in a sort of discussion, a conflict . . . but it was not a matter of agreeing or disagreeing, it was more a matter of respect.

At Brugnola 1932 some literature is also displayed in the room used for breakfast. This includes leaflets from an animal rights association concerning the boycott of *foie gras* and books about dog training, plants and herbs and the village history. With regard to discussing veganism with the guests, this couple had similar experiences to the one reported by the owners of the other holiday house. They added some comments about the meaning that eating meat might have for the local population, which has a historic background of emigration and poverty, possibly rendering the consumption of animal-derived products as a status symbol. They also highlighted that some vegans tend to use strong images of suffering animals to communicate their point of view. These images were described as "inconvenient truths" that might be counterproductive from the perspective of promoting a change in lifestyle. According to them, a softer approach could be more effective, avoiding triggering shame or a self-defense mechanism in people.

The animals at the vegan holiday country houses

Both houses host some animals, including dogs, cats, horses, hens, rabbits, and donkeys. Based on their health conditions and safety, the animals enjoy considerable freedom of movement. All these animals are mentioned and sometimes presented with their names and pictures on the houses' websites. In the case of Brugnola 1932, the vast majority of the posts on the blog concern the animals. In one of the houses, a portrait of the couple's dog, which recently passed away, is displayed in the room used for serving the meals.

In one of the houses, all the animals have a past of abuse or neglect. An example is the rabbits, which were adopted through a project that aims to relocate lab animals after they have been used in experiments. This was mentioned, highlighting the importance of giving these animals a nice life after the time they had spent in the labs and the importance for this to be undertaken legally, in collaboration with the labs, and not, as some animal activists do, by breaking into the labs and taking the animals.

Among the dogs living at Brugnola 1932, one moves around using a wheeled trolley, as she lost the use of her back paws due to a car accident. The owner commented on several guests liking this dog particularly, due to her sweet temperament and the way that she seems to enjoy life despite her disability. Another dog has a challenging temperament caused by some traumatic past experiences. The comments on his re-education by one of the owners, who is also a dog trainer, led to some considerations of animals in general:

> I have attended some courses and I can handle difficult situations with dogs. Considering this and our interest for animals, some animal associations asked us to become a sanctuary. But I'm not interested in becoming a sort of hospital for animals. This is not really what we want to do. We want to live in the countryside, work in the fields and, in this context, we might have some animals helping us. In my opinion animals, when living in contact with us, have to be given a role. I could say a sort of job, always in line with their natural instinct and also individual peculiarities. I don't want to take a shepherd dog if I don't have sheep: I couldn't offer much to this dog. I know many vegans would not agree with me, but in my opinion in the countryside the dogs, and also other animals, should be first of all co-workers.

In addition to the animals living at the houses, both businesses welcome pets, with Brugnola 1932 also offering fodder for horses and arranging courses and workshops for dog training. Finally, wild animals populate the surroundings; among these are wolves and easily observable deer. Hunting wildlife (deer, hares, birds) is a common leisure activity among the local people, and this was mentioned by the Borgo di Tara owners with regard to their dog. This dog came to their house after being abandoned by his previous owner, a hunter. According to the respondents, the practice of "getting rid" of dogs that for any reason can't be used for hunting is relatively common so that stray dogs can occasionally be found in the countryside.

The food at the vegan farmhouses

Being a bed and breakfast, Brugnola 1932 offers only breakfast. This, in addition to coffee, tea, and fruit juices, consists of vegan cereals, milk, and homemade cakes. Some homemade food products, jams, and sauces are for sale. When talking about their plan to serve other meals, the owners appeared to be confident in the quality that they can provide, based on their long-time experience with veganism as individuals and in the role as parents.

The food served at Borgo di Tara is homemade and includes a broad variety of ingredients, both traditional, from the Italian and Mediterranean cuisine, and international. On the business website, the food is qualified as bio-vegan (organic vegan food) and illustrated with several pictures. The owners are particularly interested in homemade food production, for example jams, bread, and flour, with one of them having attended several courses. The *porcino* mushroom festival in Borgotaro, a nearby village, is also promoted on the company website.

Discussion

The main findings of the case study are discussed in this section by applying the foodscape concept as shown in Figure 6.2.

Figure 6.2 shows that the story related to vegan food experience in rural Parma is supported by the factors indicated within the circle and develops in contrast to the elements of the context along the five foodscape dimensions. The findings show that along these dimensions only a minority of elements can be qualified as being in line with the vegan food experience: those relative to some vegan local products and recipes and the *Parma Etica Festival*. These elements are not illustrated in Figure 6.2.

The data suggest that vegan food experiences can be viewed as experiences related to a specific lifestyle: veganism. As suggested by Adams (1990) with the metaphor of the "absent referent" and by Shapiro (2015), a vegan meal can be viewed as the tangible expression of an ethical position centered on the recognition of the moral relevance of animals and the practice of respect toward them.

It can be argued that the story that frames the vegan food experience is about living in the countryside in harmony with the natural environment and viewing animals as companions (domesticated animals) and fellow earthlings (wild animals). This is illustrated in Figure 6.2, in which the story is related to veganism as a moral choice and the practice of harmony, care, and respect. This story is reinforced by the social, physical, and symbolic factors of the service encounter, as shown in Figure 6.2 by the examples reported within the circle. In addition to the presence of exclusively plant-based food on the tourists' plates, the physical factors related to this are the various objects that can appeal to the curiosity of the tourists and that are relevant to the vegan cause, such as the books and leaflets concerning veganism, animals, and animal ethics issues. Another example is the cruelty-free washing products used by the tourists in their private rooms and eventually taken home as souvenirs. These objects also become symbols of the respect paid to animals in the everyday routine.

The social factors of the service encounter are manifested in the conversations sometimes taking place among the guests and between the guests and the hosts. As exposed above, these can concern vegan food and recipes as well as the ideas underpinning veganism as a lifestyle. In this context, direct contact with the hosts is particularly important. The data suggest that such conversations are usually not

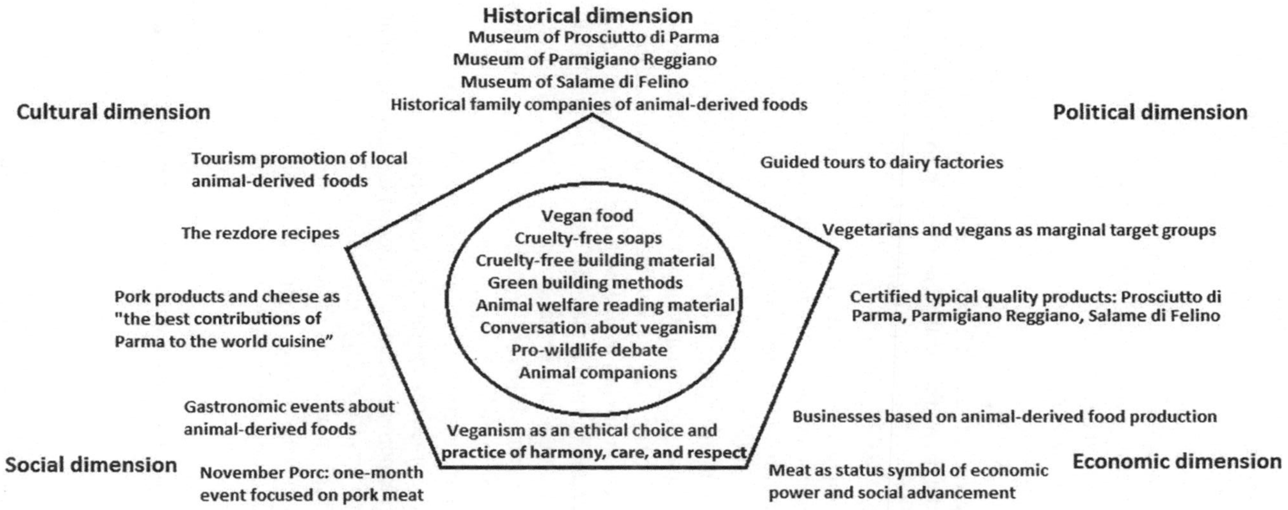

Figure 6.2 The foodscape concept applied to the Parma case study

initiated by the hosts and in their view never aim to affirm a form of universal veganism but instead resemble the invitation format described by some ecofeminists (Curtin, 1991; Gruen, 2007; Twine, 2015).

Still as part of the service encounter, located between the physical and the social factors, the animals living at the houses and nearby enter the story of the vegan food experience as an expression of the possible harmonious way in which humans and animals can coexist. Their presence is in the form of pictures and their physical presence, which can act as a marker of the practices in line with the vegan thought concerning the respect and care that should be paid to animals. The tourists can interact with the animals, such as the dogs, and come into contact with situations that can be far from their ordinary reality. These are the cases of the rabbits from the labs and the disabled dog, illustrating well the care with which animals can be treated. Another form of respect and care that can be conceptualized as a sort of giving voice to animals concerns wild animals. This is the case of the wolves and the attempt by the hosts to use experts to inform the local population about the challenges and solutions regarding human–wolf interactions and possible co-existence. Also relevant to the presence of animals around the vegan food experience is the dignity of recognizing the domestic animals in relation to their freedom of movement and their role as family members and co-workers.

The data suggest that the experience of living at these vegan houses is about living in harmony not only with animals but also with the natural environment. The care in relation to this aspect is observable in the use of eco-friendly products and the eco-sustainable architecture employed in one of the investigated houses.

Broadening the focus of the discussion, it can be argued that the investigated vegan food experiences are not in line with the mainstream trend dominating the gastronomic panorama of the Parma area. This is illustrated in Figure 6.2 by the examples reported around the pentagon. Most of the culturally appreciated and promoted foods are animal-derived, and these are also particularly present in the political plan for the region. The respondents explain the prevalence of non-vegan food with both socio-historical and economic reasons. Moreover, such a contrast with the dominating practices seems to be viewed as a barrier to social integration.

The vegan food experiences can be viewed as the manifestations of the feasibility of an alternative way to conceptualize animals and practice food-related activities. Such an alternative practice is primarily expressed through actions – first, the establishment and management of vegan businesses. This practical approach is in line with the position of the care tradition. Also in line with this tradition is the way in which care is viewed as emerging both from emotions, such as the ones openly expressed toward the domestic animals, and from rationality, as shown in the discussions around veganism and the challenges in relation to the local community.

Conclusion

This study argues that animals have an important role in the vegan food experience. To understand such a role better, a model has been developed and applied to the case of two vegan holiday country houses. The investigated vegan experiences are in clear conflict with the dominant contextual view of animals. The vegan business owners understand and explain this conflict by referring to the area's socio-historical and economic aspects as well as viewing it as a political and cultural choice by the local population. The absence of animals from the menu is a marker of the ethical position of the hosts and, often, also of the guests. This is highlighted by several factors of the service encounter, with many objects, cues, and situations emphasizing the role of animals in human life as companions and fellow earthlings.

The data suggest that, from the hosts' perspective, animals have an important role in the vegan food experience. Still, all the hosts argued for a broader view of veganism, such as that in relation to environmentalism, practiced by the adoption of eco-friendly products and methods. It can thus be concluded that the vegan food experience is about veganism as a lifestyle reflecting on the human role in the world.

From a tourism development perspective, the data might suggest that the vegan food experience does not have an important role in place branding and destination distinctiveness. On the other hand, this is not necessarily true. Although this did not emerge from the case study, it can be argued that many food traditions are based on "poor" ingredients that, in some geographical areas, coincide with plant-based food. The critical point here is whether the food traditions promoted and used in the tourist context are, historically speaking, those of the elite and special occasions or those of the ordinary life of the peasant families.

This study suggests that vegan food experiences and non-vegan food experiences could be discussed further in terms of the values that they promote and encourage. This could include an empirical investigation of the tourists' perspective. If we accept, as this study indicates, that tourism experiences that embrace the vegan lifestyle promote and reinforce values such as care and respect, which values do tourism food experiences that reject or ignore veganism promote and encourage? Considering the potential educational role of tourism, it could be fruitful to reflect on this question. This is particularly true in light of the recent information diffusion and advancements in knowledge about the environment and social justice-related aspects concerning industrial food production, as well as human health and animals.

References

Adams, C. J. (1983). The feminist traffic in animals. In G. Gaard (Ed.), *Ecofeminism: Women, animals, nature* (pp. 195–218). Philadelphia, PA: Temple University Press.

Adams, C. J. (1990). *The sexual politics of meat*. London, Bloomsbury.

Adema, P. (2006). Foodscape: An emulsion of food and landscape. In P. Adema (Ed.), *Festive foodscapes*. Dissertation, Doctor of Philosophy, The University of Texas at Austin.

agriturismovegan.it. (n.d.). *L'agriturismo*. Retrieved November 15, 2017, from http://www.agriturismovegan.it/web/lagriturismo/

Bessière, J. (1998). Local development and heritage: Traditional food and cuisine as tourist attractions in rural areas. *Sociologia Ruralis*, *38*(1), 21–34.

Birkeland, J. (1983). Ecofeminism: Linking theory and practice. In G. Gaard (Ed.), *Ecofeminism: Women, animals, nature* (pp. 13–59). Philadelphia, PA: Temple University Press.

Bitner, M. J. (1992). Servicescapes: The impact of physical surroundings on customers and employees. *Journal of Marketing*, *56*(2), 57–71.

Curtin, D. (1991). Toward an ecological ethic of care. *Hypatia*, *6*(1), 60–74.

De Mello, M. (2012). *Animals & society. An introduction to human – animal studies*. New York: Columbia University Press.

Donovan, J. (1983). Animal rights and feminist theory. In G. Gaard (Ed.), *Ecofeminism: Women, animals, nature* (pp. 167–194). Philadelphia, PA: Temple University Press.

Donovan, J., & Adams, C. J. (2007). *The feminist care tradition in animal ethics*. New York: Columbia University Press.

Ezeh, C., & Harris, L. C. (2007). Servicescape research: A review and a research agenda. *Marketing Review*, *7*(1), 59–78.

Flyvbjerg, B. (2006). Five misunderstandings about case-study research. *Qualitative Inquiry*, *12*(2), 219–245.

Fox, N., & Ward, K. (2008). Health, ethics and environment: A qualitative study of vegetarian motivations. *Appetite*, *50*(2–3), 422–429.

Gaard, G. (2002). Vegetarian ecofeminism: A review essay. *Frontiers: A Journal of Women Studies*, *23*(3), 117–146.

Gruen, L. (1993). Dismantling oppression: An analysis of the connection between women and animals. In G. Gaard (Ed.), *Ecofeminism: Women, animals, nature* (pp. 60–90). Philadelphia, PA: Temple University Press.

Gruen, L. (2007). Empathy and vegetarian commitments. In J. Donavan & C. J. Adams (Eds.), *The feminist care tradition in animal ethics* (pp. 333–341). New York: Columbia University Press.

Gruen, L. (2011). *Ethics and animals: An introduction*. Cambridge: Cambridge University Press.

Haenfler, R., Johnson, B., & Jones, E. (2012). Lifestyle movements: Exploring the intersection of lifestyle and social movements. *Social Movement Studies: Journal of Social, Cultural and Political Protest*, *11*(1), 1–20.

Hamilton, M. (2000). Eating ethically: "Spiritual" and "quasi-religious" aspects of vegetarianism. *Journal of Contemporary Religion*, *15*(1), 65–83.

Johnston, J., & Baumann, S. (2014). Entering the delicious world of foodies. In J. Johnston & S. Baumann (Eds.), *Foodies: Democracy and distinction in the gourmet foodscape* (pp. 1–29). New York: Routledge.

Johnston, J., & Goodman, M. K. (2015). Spectacular foodscapes. *Food, Culture & Society*, *18*(2), 205–222.

Lee, I., & Arcadia, C. (2011). The role of regional food festivals for destination branding. *International Journal of Tourism Research*, *13*(4), 355–367.

Lin, Y.-C., Pearson, T. E., & Cai, L. A. (2011). Food as a form of destination identity: A tourism destination brand perspective. *Tourism and Hospitality Research*, *11*(1), 30–48.

Martelli. (n.d.). *Our roots*. Retrieved November 11, 2017, from http://www.martelli.com/en/pages/storia

Mikkelsen, B. E. (2011). Images of foodscapes: Introduction to foodscape studies and their application in the study of healthy eating out-of-home environments. *Perspectives in Public Health*, *131*(15), 209–216.

Morgan, K. (2010). Local and green, global and fair: The ethical foodscape and the politics of care. *Environment and Planning A*, *42*, 1852–1867.

Mossberg, L. (2007). A marketing approach to the tourist experience. *Scandinavian Journal of Hospitality and Tourism*, *7*(1), 59–74.

Panelli, R., & Tipa, G. (2009). Beyond foodscapes: Considering geographies of indigenous well-being. *Health and Place, 19*, 455–465.

Quan, S., & Wang, N. (2004). Towards a structural model of the tourist experience: An illustration from food experiences in tourism. *Tourism Management, 25*, 297–305.

Richards, G. (2015). Evolving gastronomic experiences: From food to foodies to foodscapes. *Tourism and Gastronomy, 1*, 5–17.

Rosenbaum, M. S., & Massiah, C. (2011). An expanded servicescape perspective. *Journal of Service Management, 22*(4), 471–490.

Ruby, M. B. (2012). Vegetarianism: A blossoming field of study. *Appetite, 58*, 141–150.

Shapiro, J. K. (2015). "I am a vegetarian": Reflections on a way of being. *Society and Animals, 23*(2), 128–147.

Sidali, K. L., Kastenholz, E., & Bianchi, R. (2015). Food tourism, niche markets and products in rural tourism: Combining the intimacy model and the experience economy as a rural development strategy. *Journal of Sustainable Tourism, 23*(2/8), 1179–1197.

Slicer, D. (2007). Your daughter or your dog? A feminist assessment of the animal research issue. In J. Donavan & C. J. Adams (Eds.), *The feminist care tradition in animal ethics* (pp. 105–134). New York: Columbia University Press.

turismo.comune.parma.it. (2017a). *November porc: the taste of pork in the Bassa Parmense*. Retrieved November 15, 2017, from http://turismo.comune.parma.it/en/thematic-channels/events/events-and-initiatives/folklore-and-festivals/november-porc-the-taste-of-pork-in-the-bassa-parmense

turismo.comune.parma.it. (2017b). *Parma etica festival*. Retrieved October 30, 2017, from http://www.turismo.comune.parma.it/en/thematic-channels/events/events-and-initiatives/multiple-events/parma-etica-festival

turismo.comune.parma.it. (n.d.). *Typical products*. Retrieved November 15, 2017, from http://www.turismo.comune.parma.it/en/thematic-channels/flavors/typical-products

Twine, R. (2015). Ecofeminsim and veganism: Revisiting the question of universalism. In C. J. Adams & L. Gruen (Eds.), *Ecofeminism: Feminist Intersections with other animals & the earth* (pp. 191–208). New York: Bloomsbury.

Van der Kooi, M. (2010). The inconsistent vegetarian. *Society and Animals, 18*, 291–305.

Wahlen, S., & Laamanen, M. (2015). Consumption, lifestyle and social movements. *International Journal of Consumer Studies, 39*, 397–403.

Yeoman, I., McMahon-Beattie, U., Fields, K., Albrecht, J., & Meethan, K. (2015). *The future of food tourism: Foodies, experiences, exclusivity, visions and political capital*. Bristol: Channel View Publications.

Yin, R. K. (2003). *Case study research: Design and methods*. London: Sage.

Yudina, O., & Fennel, D. (2013). Ecofeminism in the tourism context: A discussion of the use of other-than-human animals as food in tourism. *Tourism Recreation Research, 38*(1), 55–69.

7 The cow goes "moo"

Farm animal and tourist interactions on Long Island's North Fork

Rose Sayre and Kent Henderson

Introduction

In 2009, the USDA launched a local food campaign called the "Know Your Farmer, Know Your Food" initiative. In a kickoff video posted to the USDA's YouTube channel, Agriculture Secretary Tom Vilsack describes the goals of the campaign as "support[ing] the development of local and regional food systems," and "reconnecting consumers with local producers" (USDA, 2009). This initiative followed on the heels of a number of high-profile movies, books, and news reports that called into question the environmental viability and health benefits of the mass-scale, global production system for food, and emphasized the benefits of local, organic, and sustainable sources of food. Couched in the very language of the campaign is the evocation of a desirable intimacy between the farmer and consumer, and a nostalgia for the past when such a relationship could be taken for granted. It is not enough to simply buy from local growers, the consumer must *know* them. The campaign speaks to an emerging wariness of greenwashing, and a belief that personally knowing and seeing the source of consumer products can help avoid such a pitfall of ethical consumption (Goodwin & Francis, 2003). These narratives of "knowing" and authenticity in the producer–consumer relationship have spread into "foodie" culture: the first book on Amazon's current list of bestsellers in their "Cookbooks, Food & Wine" category (that is not a cookbook or diet book) is Larry Olmsted's 2016 book entitled *Real Food, Fake Food: Why You Don't Know What You're Eating and What You Can Do About It* (Amazon, 2017).

For urban and suburban consumers, however, there are typically scant opportunities to personally know the farmers they are buying from, even for those who regularly shop at farmers' markets or those who are CSA members. For producers, responsibilities in the field compete with attendance at multiple farmers' markets, coordinating multiple CSA share drop-off sites, and managing customer service for hundreds of CSA members, at times, resorting to middle-men to help unburden their load (Moskin, 2016). Being personally present to interact with their consumers is often not possible. Agritourism offers visitors the opportunity to know the farm, even if the farmer is absent. There are a number of proxies for one-on-one interaction between farmer and visitor that convey a sense of "knowing" for visitors: farm tours or other opportunities to observe the farm, U-pick, and contact with farm animals. The purpose of this study is to explore the extent to which visitor interaction with farm animals at publicly accessible farms is associated with a positive impression of a farm by fostering a sense of authenticity and familiarity that is often absent from other producer–consumer interactions.

Agritourism and ethical consumption

Agritourism is an umbrella term used to describe a wide range of activities. The term itself has only recently emerged as dominant from a host of other near, or exact, synonyms (Phillip, Hunter, & Blackstock, 2010). Definitions vary over which activities should, or should not, be included. Phillip et al. (2010) have created a typology of activities ranging from stays in former farm houses on non-working farms to direct participation on working farms (2010). This study looks to Barbieri and Mshenga's sufficiently broad definition to guide our case selection: "a working farm with the purpose of attracting visitors" (2008, p. 168). Our sample includes Long Island's working farms that engage in direct sales on-site, some of which have no other tourist attractions. Farms without tourist attractions are intentionally included because they may still be considered tourist destinations regardless of the farmer's intentions; tourists may still choose to visit a farm to purchase goods as a tourist activity even if the purveyor does not recognize it as such.

We investigate ethical consumption in agritourism and begin with the idea that consumption is an act of identity-construction whereby consumers routinely make choices that reinforce their understanding of themselves and the world (Gregson & Crewe, 2003). Environmental issues, which we focus on here, include organic agriculture, sustainable/conservation agriculture, and local production. The growing significance of ethical consumption has been documented across many studies and disciplines (Berry & McEachern, 2005). Despite this growth in ethical consumption, there remains an "Ethical Purchasing Gap," wherein the ethical values and preferences of the consumer vastly outweigh their actual purchasing habits (Nicholls & Lee, 2006). Bray et al. (2011) cite a number of factors that impede ethical consumption, including the issue of cynicism on the part of consumers: "[Focus group] participants expressed cynicism about retailers' ethical claims to justify their reluctance to purchase on a more ethical basis. There was a feeling that ethical claims were just another marketing ploy, commanding higher prices by taking advantage of consumer goodwill" (p. 603). A recurring dilemma for ethical consumption advocates is that "distance leads to indifference" (Smith, 2000, p. 93). The goal, therefore, of local producers and locavore advocates is "reconnecting the separated moments of production, distribution, and consumption [intended] to restore to view a previously hidden chain of commitments and responsibilities" (Barnett, Cafaro, & Newholm, 2005, p. 3).

Studies of ethical consumption in agritourism are still nascent, and scant data exists to connect the motivations of agritourists to ethical consumption. Kline, Knollenberg, and Deale note that, despite their "interdependence and obvious philosophical agreement," ethical food systems and ethical tourism have few linkages in the existing literature (2014, p. 104). In this chapter, we contend that these linkages exist as an intersection between ethical choices in tourism and the desired authenticity of direct agricultural marketing, where there are no middlemen in the interaction between producers and consumers. These connections, or social ties, offer a solution to consumers seeking to "know" their farmers and their food in a more intimate capacity. Social ties are especially important in local food systems that conscientiously promote personal relationships between consumers and producers. This has been demonstrated most frequently in the farmers' market setting (see Hinrichs, 2000; Garner, 2015), but it can be extended to include visits to farms for farm stand purchases, U-pick, and most CSA-related activities. Ethical consumption advocates, especially locavores, utilize these narratives of connection and authenticity that overlap with the expectations of agritourists seeking authentic experiences. Whether or not the tourists themselves make ethical choices is difficult to pinpoint without survey data, however agritourists may have been exposed to, or are familiar with, these narratives and draw on them to describe and frame their experiences. This perspective of agritourism brings to bear MacCannell's conception of tourism as analogous to the religious pilgrimage, where modern tourists seek authenticity outside of their daily lives in romanticized notions of other cultures and time periods that they believe offer "purer, simpler life-styles" (MacCannell, 1973, p. 593). Contributing to this search for authenticity is the "romantic gaze," in which the tourist seeks "solitude, privacy and a personal, semi-spiritual relationship with the object of the gaze" (Urry, 1990, p. 25). As Trauer and Ryan (2005) point out, the gaze itself is a socially constructed understanding of place that draws on cultural images, personal experiences, and marketed expectations. It should be noted that the tourist destination, which in this study is the agritourism farm, plays a role in manipulating the visitor's experience and "staging" the image of a bucolic agricultural scene that attempts to match visitor expectations (MacCannell, 1973).

Our position is that agritourism is, to a certain extent, an act of ethical consumption, regardless of the motivations of the consumer, if it supports a business engaging in (1) organic agriculture, (2) sustainable production techniques, (3) local food distribution, (4) ethical animal treatment, or (5) any combination of the above. In the absence of survey data to directly establish the ethical concerns of agritourists, we argue that by visiting and purchasing from a farm that engages in one or more ethical practices, tourists are supporting ethical production, whether or not it is an individual motivating concern.

Data and methodology

This article is based on a study of ten different farms on Long Island's North Fork that are open to the public and have animals on location as an attraction, for production, or both. Descriptive information about the farms was obtained through a series of visits during the spring, summer, and fall of 2016 during which detailed notes were taken to create a typology of visitor access to animals. The typology is meant to indicate different levels of "staging" (MacCannell, 1973) that the farms engage in: having animals on site expressly for tourists, having them on site as work animals but facilitating tourist interactions with some or all of them, or having them on site as work animals only while tourist interactions are not facilitated in any obvious way. We include this as a potential correlate to visitors' perceptions of authenticity. The researcher visits attempted to mimic what an agritourist would see and experience and therefore included observing the spaces open to the public, and on regularly scheduled tours but excluded tours that required advance scheduling or a special request. Each visit varied in duration depending on the area accessible to the public, from ten minutes to over thirty minutes. We took note of the planned activities available to the public, the types of animals to interact with, any other animals on location that the public did not have access to, and the products on sale. We also visited the website of each farm, if they had one, and included any activities or products advertised there that were "off-season" on the farm at the time of our visit. Wineries were excluded from our case selection; while they fit our definition of agritourism, and at least two have animals on-site, the Yelp reviews are dominated by oenophiles focused primarily on describing details about the wine.

The experience of agritourists to Long Island's North Fork were collected using Yelp review data. Yelp has been in operation since 2005, and there are almost 108 million business reviews on the site (Yelp, 2016). Users may create an account and leave a review for a business, which includes a quantitative component (star-ratings of only whole numbers between one and five) and a qualitative component (the user's evaluation in text form with no character limits). Yelp was chosen over other comparable online check-in and review sites because it has a high number of users, and users must actively engage with the website or app. To collect our reviews, a series of searches were performed on Yelp with "farm" as a keyword for all zip codes on Long Island's North Fork, which included all businesses within a five-mile radius of the zip code center. Farmers' markets, restaurants that contained the word "farm" anywhere in their name or description, farms on the South Fork, and farms not open to the public were excluded from our cases. Reviews were coded for mentions of experiences that stood out to reviewers. Our final set of cases included twenty-two farms, ten of which have animals on location.

Weaknesses of the data

Yelp review data has, at times, been called into question due to possibility of fraudulent reviews. Yelp filters approximately 16% of reviews on the basis of suspected fraud, but their algorithm is imperfect resulting in both "false positives" (legitimate reviews that get removed as suspicious), and "false negatives" (illegitimate reviews that are not caught) (Luca & Zervas, 2016). Luca and Zervas find that high levels of competition and a decline in rating are motivating factors for businesses who create fraudulent reviews. Given our obvious limitations in ascertaining whether any particular review is fraudulent or not, we rely on Yelp's filtering algorithm to identify possibly fraudulent reviews.

Another consideration is the "warm-start bias" identified by Potamias (2012). There is a tendency for initial reviews to be inspired by a positive experience at a particular business, resulting in an average of 4.1 stars for first reviews across all businesses on Yelp. Less positive reviews increase in frequency afterwards, resulting in an average of 3.7 for the twentieth review. The review average essentially stabilizes after the twentieth review, while the steepest decline is observed between the first (average 4.1 stars) and the third (average 3.9 stars) reviews. Additionally, Yelp reports that 67% of all reviews are four or five stars, while only 22% are one or two stars (Yelp, 2016). Only three of the ten most reviewed farms in our sample attracted more than twenty reviews. We therefore chose a minimum of three reviews as a threshold to counter the most extreme effects of the "warm-start bias" while still retaining as much content as possible.

Third, there is a degree of self-selection bias in all of Yelp's reviewers, as well as for the reviewers who chose to review the farms in our sample of cases. Yelp reports that their users are predominantly White (69%), female (63%), young (41% in the 18–34-year-old category), educated (78% with a college education or higher), and middle-income (44% in the $0–$50k income bracket, 30% in the $50–$100k bracket). African Americans and Hispanics are underrepresented relative to national demographics (9% and 11% respectively on Yelp), while Asians are overrepresented (9% on Yelp) (Yelp, 2016). Demographic data is only attainable in aggregate, therefore there is no reported demographic information on the reviewers in our sample. However, the gender of the reviewers in our sample were coded based on name and the gender-presentation in the user's profile picture. The gender of 192 out of 197 reviewers was coded, and we found that 65% of the reviewers in our sample were women.

Finally, the issue of what constitutes ethical conduct for researchers using data posted online by individuals must be addressed – specifically with regard to obtaining informed consent. If communication is assumed to be private or semi-private, the researcher is under an ethical obligation to obtain informed consent of subjects; however, if the post is explicitly public and performative, such an obligation is not required (Association of Internet Researchers, 2002). Holmes (2009) suggests that most online research involves minimal risks to participants beyond three potential sources: (1) a strong emotional response to prompts or posts, (2) breaches of confidentiality, and (3) when the welfare of the online group is damaged. Because Yelp posts are public and reviewers are not associated with any vulnerable groups via their Yelp profile, we did not seek the informed consent of reviewers to utilize their posts in this research. However, in order to protect the identity of reviewers, no direct quotes that could be attributed back to any one particular user will be used. Instead, review content was compiled and coded, and only paraphrasing of reviews and aggregate data will be presented. In terms of the farms used in the study, businesses' names are not used, and descriptions of the businesses are relegated to information and areas that are publicly accessible.

Findings and discussion

Agriculture and agritourism in Suffolk County

Long Island begins at the border of Brooklyn and Queens in New York City and extends over 100 miles to the easternmost point of New York State. Its widest point is no more than 23 miles, and it includes two counties of mostly densely populated suburbs. Suffolk County, which comprises the entire eastern half of the island, has a population of 1.5 million people (US Census, 2015). The eastern tip of the island is bifurcated by the Peconic Bay, creating northern and southern peninsulas known as the North Fork and South Fork. The South Fork, the locale of the Hamptons, is dominated by luxury summer homes, and housing has pushed out most of the preexisting agricultural production. The North Fork, which we have chosen as our focus, is slightly shorter than the South, extending approximately 30 miles, and is dominated by agriculture. The geography is ideal for agritourism because of its proximity to New York City and because of the corridor of farmland created by the peninsula through which almost all of the region's farms are accessible via one of two main roads.

Despite their small size (the average farm size in Suffolk is 60 acres, while the US average farm size is 434 acres), Suffolk's farmers generate a large portion of the state's agricultural sales and Suffolk is consistently one of New York's most lucrative agricultural regions (National Agricultural Statistics Service, 2014). Agritourism has become more important to farmers as a source of additional income in Suffolk County and throughout New York. Partially owing to the new state funds and newly formed interest groups, the state increased income from agricultural tourism by 74% between 2007 and 2012. New York now ranks third in agritourism in the country (behind Texas and California) with $31.3 million in income from agritourism (National Agricultural Statistics Service, 2014). In Suffolk County, agritourism generated $4.3 million, or 14.5% of all income for farmers in 2012 (National Agricultural Statistics Service, 2014).

Overview of cases

As stated previously, farms were identified based on their number of reviews on Yelp. Table 7.1 provides basic information about the attributes, number of reviews, and star-ratings of our included cases. It should be noted that of the twenty-two total farms, all of them had direct retail operations/farm stands, but the combination of other attractions they offered varied a great deal. Therefore, the number cases offering each of the attractions listed do not add up to the total number of cases.

Table 7.1 Overview of attractions for all cases

Farm Attractions	*Number of Cases*	*Number of Reviews*	*Star Rating*
Farm Stand/Retail	22	515	4.43
U-Pick	12	401	4.65
Seasonal Attractions	7	246	4.21
CSA	3	52	4.50

Among the farms in our sample, twelve of them had no access to animals, while the remaining ten had access to chickens, cows, llamas, ducks, or some other farm animals. Overall, farms without animals had more reviews per farm than those with animals (25.1 and 21.4 respectively; see Table 7.2), but farms with animals had slightly higher average reviews (4.65) than farms without animals (4.21).

Reviews were coded for mention of interactions with animals, whether the reviewer explicitly identified the farm as local, organic, or sustainable, and for reported interactions with the farmer (or owner) in person. Reviews were also coded for whether the reviewer identified a farm as inauthentic, by describing it as "touristy," "corporate," "too crowded," or "too expensive." We used this coding schema to establish linkages between a positive rating and an impression of authenticity, an appreciation of ethical production habits, and/or an appreciation of animal interactions. Those with animals on the premises are categorized into one of the three types described in the typology we outline in Table 7.3.

Table 7.2 Comparison of farms with and without animals accessible to visitors

Type	*Number of Cases*	*Number of Reviews*	*Number of Reviews per Farm*	*Star Rating*
No Animals	12	301	25.08	4.21
Farm Stand Only	3	20	6.67	4.33
Animals	10	214	21.40	4.65
Farm Stand Only	5	51	10.20	4.70

Table 7.3 Typology of animal use

Use Type	*Use Description*	*Number of Farms*	*Types of Animals*
Attraction Only	Animals are kept in an area specifically for viewing and interaction with visitors. While some of these may be working animals, animal products from the farm are not sold to the public. Includes pony rides.	Three: Cases 1A, 2A, 3A	Horses, Ponies, Goats, Chickens, Rabbits, Pigs
Attraction and Work	Some animals are kept in an area where visitors may view and interact with them, but visitor access is limited seasonally to certain animals and/or by the size of the paddock. Farm sells animal products.	Three: Cases 1AW, 2AW, 3AW	Alpaca, Cows, Goats, Sheep, Rabbits, Pigs Guinea Hens, Chickens, Turkeys
Work Only	Animals may be visible, but they are removed from direct interaction with visitors, or interaction is incidental. Farm sells animal products.	Four: Cases 1W, 2W, 3W, 4W	Cows, Goats, Sheep, Pigs, Chickens, Ducks, Turkeys

Table 7.4 shows the proportion of mentions for each coding categories within each star-rating level. As can be seen in the table, animals play a more prominent role in five-star reviews than either farmers or ethical considerations. The ethical practices we include are "local," "organic," and "sustainable." Other ethical considerations exist, of course, such as labor rights, fair trade, and many others. Below, we describe how these interactions are facilitated or discouraged by producers and experienced by consumers in the three types of farms we identified: (1) ones who use animals as an attraction, (2) ones who use them for work and production, and (3) ones who use them for both. Those with animals on the premises are categorized into one of the three types described in the typology we outline in Table 7.3.

Attraction only animals (Cases 1A, 2A, 3A)

"Attraction only" farms use animals solely as an attraction whereby visitors have the ability to see and interact with animals, but animal products are not sold by the farm. This category included three farms, with a combined 119 reviewers, all of which marketed their animals on their websites. In cases 2A and 3A, a small number of farm animals are kept in paddocks that visitors have access to, although access is limited by the relatively large size of the enclosures. In both of these cases, other tourist attractions are available; however, these activities are seasonal and modest in comparison to case 1A discussed below. The farm stand/retail area for these farms is fairly small, and they attracted a combined ten reviews. Three reviewers mentioned that the owner was present during their visit, although there was no description of a personal interaction. Three reviewers also commented on the opportunity to interact with the animals as a benefit to visiting the farm, and an additional three posted pictures of the animals to Yelp. Given that access to the animals is fairly limited, it is remarkable that a majority of reviewers chose to mention or include pictures of the animals. Animals did not appear to be staged for the benefit of visitors in any obvious way on-site, and this conveyed a sense of authenticity to visitors who reviewed the farms. Four of the ten expressed an

Table 7.4 Number of mentions by star rating for each coding category

	Animals		*Farmers*		*Ethics*		*Expensive*		*Inauthentic/ Crowded*	
Star Rating	*Mention (1)*	*No Mention (0)*	*1*	*0*	*1*	*0*	*1*	*0*	*1*	*0*
1	0	15	1	14	0	15	9	6	7	8
2	1	6	0	7	0	7	4	3	3	4
3	3	14	0	17	0	17	5	12	2	15
4	28	37	5	60	12	53	7	58	11	54
5	46	64	24	86	35	75	0	110	2	108
Total	**214**		**214**		**214**		**214**		**214**	

Note: Coding of 0 = no mention; coding of 1 = mention

appreciation that the businesses are local, and that they experienced a sense of "hominess."

For the remaining case (1A), the animals in question were explicitly used as an attraction. This particular farm caters extensively to tourists by offering a wide variety of attractions, especially during the fall season, including pick-your-own orchards and pumpkin patches, corn mazes, hay rides, live music, various games like bean-bag toss, wine tasting, and "farm style" prepared foods like roasted corn and apple-cider donuts. Animals are one element of a long list of activities, and little of the actual working farm is available, or even visible, to tourists. A farm stand selling produce grown on the farm is available, but it is dwarfed by the many other activities being offered during the fall season. This particular farm attracted the most visitors of any in our sample with animals on the premises, and during visits in the fall by the investigators, it was clear that the 109 posted Yelp reviews were a small fraction of the total number of visitors the farm hosts. It also had the lowest overall star-rating (3.85) of any of the ten cases in our study. A proportion of visitors, 28% of the Yelp reviews, mentioned the animals, but almost exclusively in reference to being a kid-friendly attraction (and not in description of a personal interaction with the animals) or in list-form among other attractions to demonstrate the variety and quantity of attractions that the farm offers. Positive reviews for this farm most often mentioned the farm-style food and the family-friendly activities, while only a small handful of reviews mentioned the owners or that the farm was a local business. This particular farm was the only one of any in our sample that attracted negative reviews (14%) citing particular characteristics of the farm itself (instead of a negative interaction with staff), specifically the large crowds and the "corporate" and "touristy" atmosphere. These results suggest that about a third of reviewers made note of the presences of farm animals, but that the perception that these interactions – as well as other activities on the farm – were staged detracted from the overall rating of the farm. (Cohen, 1985).

Work only animals (Cases 1W, 2W, 3W, 4W)

Farms coded to this category included those whose farm animals may be visible to visitors, but any direct contact with visitors is incidental and not obviously staged or designed in such a way that the animals could be considered an attraction used to draw in tourists. All four of these farms sell animal products from the animals they raise; however there is a high level of heterogeneity within this group in terms of the layout, online presence, and products sold. Most of these farms attract much fewer visitors from in-person observations compared to farms in the other two categories, although the reviews they do receive are almost exclusively positive. These farms attracted 33 reviewers and an overall average star-rating of 4.89. While none of the farms are certified organic, two of the farms (1W and 2W) explicitly emphasize that they practice sustainable farming and that their animals are pasture-raised and hormone free.

The first and second cases (1W and 2W) sell a variety of meat products. The first (1W) primarily sells whole poultry, while the other (2W) sells poultry, ham, lamb, and mutton, as well as some processed meat products, like sausage and bacon. Access to both farms is limited to a view from the parking lot, with one (2W) offering tours to visitors upon request (although this offering is not immediately obvious to visitors). Of the combined seventeen reviews of these two farms, seven mentioned positive, in-person interactions with the owners themselves, and an appreciation that the business was small, local, and (in the case of one of them) practiced sustainable agriculture. Many reviewers extolled the excellence of the animal products at these farms: one reviewer described the meat products as "superb," while another claimed they could "taste the difference." Another reported that the pork they bought tasted "real," and not like the "flavorless" products they purchase at the store. Animals themselves were not mentioned by reviewers except in reference to the animal products. In this case, the animals affect the gaze of the tourists as a component of the scenery and an impression of authenticity about the farm, but did not otherwise make an impression on reviewers. This suggests that in situations where the animals are explicitly used for meat, farmers are less likely to stage the animals for the benefit of visitors, and visitors are reflexively detached from them (Wilkie, 2005). One reviewer anticipated that other customers might be "squeamish" about freshly slaughtered farm animals and warned them away.

The third case (3W) is a dairy farm that produces mostly milk and eggs, with small amounts of vegetables. The farm does little to actively attract agritourists, having no real website to speak of, only small, hand-painted signs marking the entrance. However, according to their Yelp reviewers, their products are highly sought after and sell out daily. Despite their lack of marketing, of the ten reviews they have received, six are from different parts of New York City, with two mentioning that they made the trip to the North Fork specifically for this farm. Reviewers commented on the ' "nostalgic" charm of the farm and also made a point of mentioning the quality of the dairy and eggs. One reviewer claimed the milk was "so much more flavorful" than anything they had tasted from the supermarket, and that the eggs were the best they had tasted "In [My] LIFE!" (Emphasis in original.) The dairy cows, chickens, and ducks on the property are minimally staged for visitors, who are free to walk the portion of the grounds that is adjacent to their fields and enclosures. This provides much more access than the previous two cases. Six of the ten reviews mentioned the animals: feeding and petting goats and viewing the cows, llamas and other herd animals nearby. Of the twenty-six photos posted by users, ten featured their various farm animals. However, just as many reviewers mentioned interactions and familiarity with the farm owners. In this case, interactions with animals act in conjunction with interaction between visitor and owner to create the sense of intimacy and authenticity expressed by reviewers (the overall star-rating is 4.7).

In the final case (4W), the site is primarily a vegetable farm. Chickens are kept for egg production, and a number of other farm animals are present on site although no other animal products are sold. Like the first two cases in this category, the animals were visible, but access was limited by tall fencing and warnings not to put hands or fingers inside enclosures. Only one of a total six reviews mentioned the animals. In this instance, positive reviewers mentioned interaction with the owner (four of six), the benefit of being small-scale, local, and not "corporate" (four of six), and an element of nostalgia for the "honor system" in payment and experience of being in the fields (three of six), since the farm offers U-pick. This farm's overall rating is five stars.

Attraction and work animals (Cases 1AW, 2AW, 3AW)

The farms in this category have working animals used for animal products sold by the farm, but the farms are engaged in soliciting agritourists to a greater degree than farms in the previous category of working animals only. These farms cater to tourists by providing access to certain farms animals, and encourage interaction with them. They have a larger number of reviews (sixty-two total) and a considerable web presence.

The first case (1AW) is the only certified organic farm in our set of cases. It is primarily a vegetable farm and offers a CSA. They also produce eggs, and, periodically, organic and pasture-raised poultry. Most of the meat and egg-laying birds are not accessible to visitors. Instead, visitors have access to a small herd of sheep, an alpaca, and a smaller flock of chickens and guinea hens that are not used for animal products. The pens are set up to maximize visitor access to the animals, and they are located near a play area for children. This farm also hosts a number of festivals throughout the year, as well as special attractions in the fall. Like cases 2A and 3A, this farm (while still fairly small) caters to tourists with many types of activities meant to appeal to visitors. This case had a number of poor reviews, however, with a star-rating of 3.87, barely higher than the festival-type farm (case 1A). Most negative reviews (19% giving one or two stars) focused on unpleasant interactions with staff members and, in one instance, the owner. Their posts expressed an alienation (rather than an intimacy with) the farm, due to the treatment they described. Other negative reviews felt the quality of produce to be poor and therefore not worth the cost. While mentions of their animal products were small in number (it is not the main focus of the farm), they were all positive. One reviewer thought that it was "cool" when a fellow customer picked out a chicken to be bought and butchered, but continued that they didn't want to "look it in the eyes." Another stated that the eggs are the "best on earth." Mention of animals were fairly high (37%) while interaction with owners was much less frequently mentioned than for work-animal farms. Overall on this farm, animals played a significant role for visitors who had a positive experience; for example, one visitor describes an experience with multiple animals as especially adoring: "[t]here was also a separate room in the barn that held the cutest chicks [. . . but] [w]hat got us really excited was the baby lamb in the small pen. It was so sweet and the little baa noise literally melted your heart."

The last two cases, (2AW and 3AW) are both primarily dairy farms, one of which offers cheese, milk, and eggs, while the other offers only cheese. Both have enclosures with baby goats, sheep, and cows, and visitors are encouraged to feed them. The enclosures have low barriers, making it easy to touch the animals. Case

3AW also offers meat products, but only to customers who order online, and visitors stopping at the farm stand exclusively would not necessarily be aware that any animals on the farm were used for meat. Additionally, meat animals (primarily hogs) are kept in areas out of sight to visitors. Multiple reviewers mentioned the freshness of the products, including one who identified as a "cheesemonger." Another claimed the cheese was superior to the "processed products in supermarkets." A large majority of reviews in both cases focused on their interactions with the farm animals (90% and 78% respectively), many describing these interactions in detail. There was only one review, of a combined twenty-nine, that made mention of interacting with an owner, and the single mention was in the context of a tour and not a one-on-one interaction. Further, the dairy goats are not pasture-raised or organic at either location (although the dairy cows are pasture-raised). Neither the lack of farmer interaction, or the fact that (most) of the products sold are not explicitly sustainable, organic, or pasture-raised seemed to negatively impact visitor's perception of the farms. The access to animals was not, for the most part, perceived as staged or inauthentic, perhaps because the "attraction animals" are used for production as adults. 30% of reviewers also mentioned that these are local businesses, described in such a way that the reader assumes the benefits of buying local to be self-evident.

Conclusions

The purpose of this study has been to explore the extent to which visitor interaction with farm animals is associated with a positive impression of a farm, ostensibly by fostering a sense of authenticity and a more than superficial knowledge about the farm, a type of consumer–producer relationship that is increasingly sought after for ethical consumers (Barnett et al., 2005; Hinrichs, 2000; Smith, 2000). While ethical concerns, including the farmer–client relationship sought after in locavorism, may or may not be important to the reviewers in our study, the values and narratives espoused by ethical consumers contribute to the socially constructed understanding of a place (Trauer & Ryan, 2005) and therefore inform their review as a positive component or, at the very least, one they would mention in case it was of concern to other potential visitors reading their review. We see repeated mention of "realness" and "authenticity," as well as "local" as an attribute with self-evident virtues. Given that our data is based on reviews, and not interviews, we cannot provide direct evidence that interaction with farm animals provided visitors with a sense of connection to the farm, but we can compare the mention of farms animals to the mention of meeting the farmer in person and to mentions of ethical practices, and note the correlation of these mentions with an overall positive rating of the farm. We found a large degree of heterogeneity regarding the ways in which farms manage visitors in general, and visitor interaction with their farm animals specifically. These different strategies were associated with different consequences in terms of how reviewers perceived the farm as a whole, and the farm animals themselves.

The strategy for which interactions with animals elicited the most positive and enthusiastic responses, were in cases where the operation was too large for one-on-one interactions between owner and visitor to be very frequent or consistent, and access to animals is fostered in some way, but not read as staged solely for the benefit of visitors. Farms with this set-up associated with a high proportion of reviews that mentioned the animals in a positive light. These farms were, overall, typically read as local, authentic, and fostering of a personal connection with the visitor, with the exception of one case where negative interactions with staff diminished the sense of intimacy that visitors expected. In cases where the access to animals was read as staged, the farm animals did not feature prominently in positive reviews and reviewers did not report a sense of intimacy with the farm, although intimacy did not appear to be expected for most reviewers regarding the particular farm in question. In cases where access to animals was available, but not facilitated by the owners, intimacy was established via one-on-one interactions between visitors and owners and the perception that the farm was "secret" to most other tourists. Animals were superfluous in such cases. Certain types of animals, namely cows, horses, donkeys, sheep, and goats, appealed more to visitors than chickens, ducks, turkeys, and pigs. While some visitors mentioned an appreciation for organic, sustainable, and pasture-raised products for the places that advertised these features, none mentioned the lack of being organic, sustainable, or pasture-raised as a drawback. Negative reviews centered solely around a perceived corporate mentality, a "touristy" experience, or unpleasant interactions with staff.

We conclude with a few practical suggestions for farm owners and operators. They may consider utilizing pictures of visitors enjoying these animals on social media or on their farm's website. Low fencing that allows easy access to animals, rather than high fences that can block tourists' views, can offer visitors a better connection with the animals on location. Finally, some animals tended to appeal more to visitors than others (horses, cows, donkeys, and sheep/goats). Operators may want to feature these animals more prominently both at their farms and as part of their social media/internet presence.

References

Amazon. (2017). *Bestsellers in cookbooks, food & wine*. Retrieved January 15, 2017, from www.amazon.com/Best-Sellers-Books-Cookbooks-Food-Wine/zgbs/books/6

Association of Internet Researchers. (2002). *Ethical decision making and internet research: Recommendations from the AoIR*. Ethics Working Committee. Retrieved September 2, 2016, from www.aoir.org/reports/ethics.pdf

Barbieri, C., & Mshenga, P. (2008). The role of the firm and owner characteristics on the performance of agritourism farms. *Sociologia Ruralis*, *48*, 166–183.

Barnett, C., Cafaro, P., & Newholm, T. (2005). Philosophy and ethical consumption. In T. Newholm, D. Shaw, & R. Harrison (Eds.), *The ethical consumer* (pp. 11–24). London: SAGE.

Berry, H., & McEachern, M. G. (2005). Informing ethical consumers. In R. Harrison, T. Newholm, & D. Shaw (Eds.), *The ethical consumer* (pp. 69–88). London: SAGE.

Bray, J., Johns, N., & Kilburn, D. (2011). An exploratory study into the factors impeding ethical consumption. *Journal of Business Ethics*, *98*(4), 597–608.

Census of Agriculture. (2012). *Income from farm-related sources: 2012 and 2007*. Retrieved September 2, 2016, from www.agcensus.usda.gov/Publications/2002/Volume_1,_Chapter_2_US_State_Level/st99_2_006_006.pdf

Cohen, E. (1985). The tourist guide: The origins, structure and dynamics of a role. *Annals of Tourism Research*, *12*(1), 5–29.

Garner, B. (2015). Communication at farmers' markets: Commodifying relationships, community, and morality. *Journal of Creative Communications*, *10*(2), 186–198.

Goodwin, H., & Francis, J. (2003). Ethical and responsible tourism: Consumer trends in the UK. *Journal of Vacation Marketing*, *9*(3), 271–284.

Gregson, N., & Crewe, L. (2003). *Second-hand cultures*. New York: Berg Publishers.

Hinrichs, C. (2000). Embeddedness and local food systems: Notes on two types of direct agricultural market. *Journal of Rural Studies*, *16*(3), 295–303.

Holmes, S. (2009). Methodological and ethical considerations in designing an internet study of quality of life: A discussion paper. *International Journal of Nursing Studies*, *46*(3), 394–405.

Kline, C., Knollenberg, W., & Deale, C. (2014). Tourism's relationship with ethical food systems. In C. Weeden & C. Boluk (Eds.), *Managing ethical consumption in tourism* (pp. 104–121). New York: Routledge.

Luca, M., & Zervas, G. (2016). Fake it till you make it: Reputation, competition, and Yelp review fraud. *Management Science*. Retrieved September 15, 2016, from https://dash.harvard.edu/bitstream/handle/1/22836596/luca%2czervas_fake-it-till-you-make-it.pdf?sequence=1

MacCannell, D. (1973). Staged authenticity: Arrangements of social space in tourist settings. *American Journal of Sociology*, *79*(3), 589–603.

Moskin, J. (2016, July 29). When community supported agriculture is not what it seems. *New York Times*, D1.

National Agriculture Statistics Service, United States Department of Agriculture. (2014). *2012 Census of agriculture – state and county data, New York*. Retrieved September 5, 2016, from www.agcensus.usda.gov/Publications/2012/Full_Report/Volume_1,_Chapter_1_State_Level/New_York/

Nicholls, A., & Lee, N. (2006). Purchase decision-making in fair trade and the ethical purchase 'gap': Is there a fair trade 'Twix'? *Journal of Strategic Marketing*, *14*(4), 369–386.

Phillip, S., Hunter, C., & Blackstock, K. (2010). A typology for defining agritourism. *Tourism Management*, *31*(2010), 754–758.

Potamias, M. (2012). The warm-start bias of yelp ratings. *Groupon*. Retrieved September 15, 2016, from arXiv preprint arXiv:1202.5713

Smith, D. (2000). *Moral geographies: Ethics in a world of difference*. Edinburgh: Edinburgh University Press.

Trauer, B., & Ryan, C. (2005). Destination image, romance and place experience: An application of intimacy theory in tourism. *Tourism Management*, *26*(4), 481–491.

US Census. (2015). *Quickfacts for Suffolk county*. Retrieved September 25, 2016, from www.census.gov/quickfacts/table/RHI105210/36103

USDA. (2009). Know your farmer, know your food. *YouTube*. Retrieved September 2, 2016, from www.youtube.com/watch?v=Tms8ye8mw_k

Urry, J. (1990). The consumption of tourism. *Sociology*, *24*(1), 23–35.

Wilkie, R. (2005). Sentient commodities and productive paradoxes: the ambiguous nature of human-livestock relations in Northeast Scotland. *Journal of Rural Studies*, *21*(2), 213–230.

Yelp. (2016). *Factsheet*. Retrieved September 5, 2016, from www.yelp.com/factsheet

8 Feed thy tourist well

CAFOs or cooperatives?

Kelly Bricker and Leah Joyner

Introduction

America hosts the largest feed cattle industry in the world (Lowe & Gary, 2009), dominated by four major firms which collectively control over 80 percent of all the cattle slaughtered in the U.S. (Ostlind, 2011). These firms supply meat products through the leading food distributors in the nation, including those that serve tourism and hospitality industry sectors (Jackson & Singh, 2015). Sustainable tourism at its core is based on the premise that tourism should provide positive outcomes for communities and minimize negative impacts to the environment through economically sustainable models. In this chapter we discuss the flawed economic systems that support the CAFO industry, detail expansive negative impacts to the environment from CAFO pollution, and present evidence that CAFOs harm the communities in which they operate. As demand for locally and humanely produced meat increases (Animal Welfare Institute, 2016a; Consumer Reports, 2015; Dunning, Blacklin, & McKissick, 2013) sustainable farmers are developing unique business models to supply the growing market. Alternatives to factory farms do exist and should be incorporated into food supply chains for tourism to be considered sustainable both operationally and at the destination level. Our hope in uncovering the unsustainable forms of meat production in the U.S. is that we raise awareness and heighten the concern for alternative meat production strategies in working toward sustainable tourism. The structure we use to frame our discussion is the Global Sustainable Tourism Criteria.

Defining sustainable tourism: Global Sustainable Tourism Criteria

The Global Sustainable Tourism Council (GSTC) was created to assist the industry with a common understanding of sustainability in tourism around the world. Sanctioned and supported by the United Nations World Tourism Organization (UNWTO), the Criteria are the "minimum that any tourism business should aspire to reach" (GSTC, n.d., p. 1). The Criteria are organized around four pillars, designed to raise the industry to practices that ensure destinations, accommodations, and tour operations contribute to a sustainable future. While the

Criteria suggest what steps the industry should take, the performance indicators and associated tools indicate how the Criteria might be applied to a given business or destination in tourism. Because the provision of food is a significant part of any tourism experience and host tourism destination, we explore the impact of unsustainable food production, which is largely ignored in tourism operations and destination landscapes, and thus detracts significantly from the environmental and social sustainability of sustainable tourism and development goals.

Linkages to Global Sustainable Tourism Criteria

The first pillar of the Criteria, *demonstrate effective sustainable management*, focuses on long-term sustainability management systems that address environmental, social, cultural, economic, quality, human rights, health, safety, and risk management. The second pillar proposes *maximizing social and economic benefits to the local community and minimizing negative impacts*. Criteria relative to sustainable food production and consumption include supporting local purchasing. The third pillar addresses *cultural heritage* and is likely the least directly relevant to sustainable food production, yet conceptually, sustainable food production can be a cultural and community focused activity, supporting local cuisine and traditions. The fourth pillar, *maximizing benefits to the environment and minimizing negative impacts*, has the most significant implication to sustainable food production overall. For the purposes of understanding CAFOs and sustainable tourism, we focus on three concepts within the Criteria, which address sustainable food production and consumption: (1) sustainable management, (2) social and economic considerations, and (3) environmental sustainability.

GSTC criteria and CAFOs

According to the GSTC, the first pillar is the *sustainable management* of tourism enterprises, which includes a wide range of planning and supply chain concepts. To ensure progress toward sustainability, tourism enterprises are to develop a long-term sustainability management system to address "environmental, social, cultural, economic, quality, human rights, health, safety, risk and crisis management issues and drives continuous improvement" (GSTC, n.d., p. 1). Further, sustainably run tourism enterprises ensure that they comply with various regulations relevant to their locale and are transparent in their reporting of sustainability policies. This includes mechanisms for staff to be fully engaged in the delivery of sustainable management, and ultimately increasing the satisfaction of their customers.

Several issues within the operation of CAFOs are in conflict with the GSTC pillars of sustainable management and environmental sustainability including:

- Mismanagement of the agricultural system through toxic storage 'lagoons' and spray field applications on land to address excessive waste, processes that have moved into fossil-fueled mechanics relying on chemical fertilizers (Environmental Protection Agency [EPA], 2009; EPA, n.d.; Thorton, 2010);

- Excessive size and density, which impair the environment's ability to absorb pollutants and impact water quality (Centner, 2006; Mallin & Cahoon, 2003);
- Disregard for soil and water quality, in part due to excessive size, use of chemicals, and lack of environmental protection laws (Centner, 2006; Mallin & Cahoon, 2003);
- Air pollution, greenhouse gas emissions through methane and other gases from waste (Burns et al., 2007; EPA, n.d.; Massey & Ulmer, 2008; Merkel, 2002);
- Disregard for animal welfare from living conditions, transport, and slaughter (Animal Welfare Institute, 2016b; Webster, 2001); and
- Reliance on chemicals, medicine, and hormones (Waters et al., 2011; Harrison, 2006, 2008; Food and Drug Administration and Center for Veterinary Medicine, 2014; Waters et al., 2011).

And based on the GSTC pillar – *maximizing social and economic benefits to the local community and minimizing negative impacts* – social issues include:

- Socially irresponsible corporate ownership, plagued by low-wage hazardous work environments, economic outsourcing, and declining property values (Herriges, Secchi, & Babcock, 2005; Purdue Extension, 2008; Weida, 2004).

As noted, many negative impacts of unsustainable food production cut across social, ecological, and economic impacts. The Criteria asks of sustainable tourism to "implement a long-term sustainability management system that is suitable to its size and scope, addresses environmental, social, cultural, economic, quality, human rights, health, safety, risk and crisis management issues and drives continuous improvement" (GSTC, n.d., p. 1). Communities and the types of industries within them are complex systems of social–ecological relationships. For the purposes of this chapter, we present detailed examples and highlight concepts relative to specific Criteria, yet acknowledge the inter-relationships between each of the impacts considered (i.e., social, economic, and ecological).

Sustainable management and the environment

The Criteria specifically address conserving resources, reducing pollution, conserving biodiversity, ecosystems, and landscapes. Within the Criteria associated with conserving resources, environmentally preferable purchasing directly relates to a sustainable industry favoring sustainable food production. In addition, it asks that energy and water conservation practices are in place. Mekonnen and Hoekstra (2010) documented the enormous water footprint of animal production, with the water footprint per gram of protein for dairy and chicken (approximately 1.5 times) and beef production (6 times larger) significantly larger than protein from crop production. Significant issues surround pollution. The Criteria for sustainable operations address transport, wastewater, solid waste, harmful substances, and efforts to minimize pollution. Some of the challenges relative to pollution, specific to CAFOs, are discussed.

Water pollution from manure

Human waste gets treated immensely, while animal waste does not get treated at all (Cassuto, 2013). Nutrient pollution is one of America's "most widespread, costly and challenging environmental problems" (EPA, 2016a, p. 1). Agriculture is one of the largest sources of nutrient pollution in the country (EPA, 2016b). As a result, there are several implications for the sustainability of communities in and around CAFOs. For example, infants are particularly susceptible to high nitrate levels in drinking water and may develop fatal blood disorders (EPA, 2016a). And, too much of these nutrients can kill fish and other aquatic organisms, devastating the entire aquatic food chain. Unfortunately, mismanagement during food production has the potential to contribute other pollutants such as pathogens (e.g., giardia, cryptosporidium), heavy metals, hormones, and antibiotics in the waters we use for drinking, swimming, and fishing (EPA, 2016a). To provide some indication of the "downstream" impact of agricultural pollutants, 44%of rivers and streams assessed in 2004 were not "clean enough to support their designated uses, such as fishing and swimming" (EPA, 2016c, p. 1).

Nitrates are one of the most destructive pollutants resulting from CAFOs. Nitrates are notably related to human health and can be especially harmful and possibly fatal to infants. Low blood oxygen levels in adults caused by nitrates in drinking water can also lead to birth defects, miscarriages, higher rates of stomach and esophageal cancer, and poor general health (Bowman, Mueller, & Smith, 2000; Hribar, 2010).

Further, because food production is the leading source of water quality impacts on surveyed rivers and streams (EPA, 2016d), it is important to understand the high costs associated with remediation. For example, in Kansas remediation relative to leaching from dairy and hog CAFOs was projected costing taxpayers $56 million – noting Kansas is not one of the top producers in these areas (UCS, 2008). The estimated total cost of cleaning up the soil from U.S. hog and dairy production is nearly $4.1 billion dollars (UCS, 2008). The true costs of CAFOs are likely under-reported, lacking a holistic accountability at community and state levels. The Union of Concerned Scientists estimates that compliance with Clean Water Act rules and standards with respect to manure specifically could comprise between 43 and 49%of overall net returns on the 100 billion+ livestock and poultry generate annually (USDAERS, n.d.; UCS, 2008).

Air pollution

The primary issues with air pollution stem from the way in which untreated manure is addressed. Because ground application of untreated manure is the least expensive, it is widely used. Other types of manure management strategies include spraying it onto fields, trucking it off-site, or storing it until it can be used or treated (Hribar, 2010; UCS, 2008). "While CAFOs are required to have permits that limit the levels of manure discharge, handling the large amounts of manure inevitably causes accidental releases which have the ability to potentially impact humans" (Hribar, 2010, p. 3). Hence, the two most common methods of addressing massive production of untreated waste cause a range of issues and are counter to sustainable management. Spraying liquid manure onto croplands and fields risks the spread of harmful gases, viruses, pathogens, and antibiotics transfer, and metals that run off the land, contaminate the groundwater, travel through subterranean field drains (tiles), and pollute the atmosphere (EPA, 2009; EPA, n.d.; Hribar, 2010; Thorton, 2010; CAFOthebook, 2016, p. 1), all which eventually enter back into ecosystems through groundwater, rivers, and streams causing algal blooms and fish kills (Moses & Tomaselli, 2017).

Mismanagement of the agricultural system

A *sustainable* agricultural system renews itself. Animal waste is integrated back to soils to replenish and balance nutrients utilized by crops which feed the animals. Therefore, disrupting natural processes is a clear negative impact of CAFOs and counter to a sustainable food production system (PEW, 2016; Owen, Chiras, & Reganold, 1998). By separating these systems, soils are depleted and wastes accumulate to toxic levels (Owen et al., 1998). As identified, several aspects of CAFOs contradict sustainable operations. Systematically, the Criteria relative to management and ecological systems are disrupted. Next, we consider the impacts of CAFOs to social and economic factors relative to sustainable development.

Social and economic sustainability

Beyond the development of a sustainable management plan for operations, the Criteria specifically asks that tourism operations maximize social and economic benefits to local communities and minimize negative ones. Several issues with CAFOs are highlighted with respect to employment, exploitation and harassment, decent work, and not adversely affecting access to livelihoods and access to land and aquatic resources.

CAFOs and subsidies

With an array of U.S. Farm Bill program subsidies in place, farmers using alternatives to CAFOs end up on the short end of support with continued leanings for support by government for the industrial and large scale farming models that rely on CAFOs for production (Wender, 2011; Windham, 2007). One example of this is the Environmental Quality Incentives Program (EQIP), designed to help smaller farming operations with pollution prevention programs, which now also includes CAFOs (Ribaudo, Cattaneo, & Agapoff, 2004). The Union of Concerned Scientists (UCS) sees the criteria used to determine subsidies as favoring CAFOs. For example, in some states, such as California, where the state spends over $10 million USD to address dairy manure issues alone, and Georgia, a state with the most broiler chicken production in the US, EQIP funds are used to transport chicken manure to other areas; the distance of transportation would not be economically feasible without substantial subsidies (UCS, 2008). Ultimately, these government subsidies present disincentives for sustainable producers, lacking access to the ample funding provided to CAFOs.

CAFOs and local communities

While sustainable management and environmental issues directly affect the quality of life and wellbeing of community members, specific ideas surrounding mechanisms to enhance local employment, education, training, health and sanitation related to climate change, labor rights, a safe and secure work environment, and livelihoods are important to these set of Criteria for sustainable development (GSTC, n.d.). The increase in CAFOs and the clustering that occurs of these types of farms is causing a tremendous impact on communities located in and near these establishments (Donham et al., 2007; Wilson & Serre, 2007). Aside from several associated negative health impacts, when odors, insects, and water quality become issues in local communities, there are corresponding decreases in property values, and ultimately a decrease in tax base (Purdue Extension, 2008; UCS, 2008; PEW, 2008) as well as hazardous work environments (Ikerd, 2017). Eastern North Carolina is one of the most CAFO dense areas of the nation (Nicole, 2013; Kelly-Reif & Wing, 2016). CAFOs there are clustered around low income and minority communities (Nicole, 2013), garnering accusations of environmental racism and injustice (Wing & Johnston, 2014). The Criteria address ensuring a "safe and secure working environment" where employees are paid at least a "living wage" (GSTC, n.d., p. 6). Research into CAFO's once again can be counter to sustainability Criteria.

Low-wage, low opportunity for farmers

The design of CAFOs is such that production is industrialized, and operations use as little labor as possible. The jobs created are low paying (e.g., $7.50 per hour), and limited. For example, the University of Missouri estimated eight full-time jobs were supported by a 600-sow hog operation (Ikerd, 2011). Further, trends indicate that

> corporately controlled CAFOs, will result in even fewer people controlling agriculture and even fewer real farmers. CAFOs may employ a few local farm workers, but all of the important decisions, and profits, will be made by people in corporate headquarters, not by farmers. CAFOs will not save farmers or local farm economies.
>
> (Ikerd, 2011, p. 3)

Hazardous work environment

In poultry and hog production, high endotoxin, ammonia, and dust levels contribute to respiratory conditions such as bronchitis and asthma exacerbation (Von

Essen & Romberger, 2003). Findings suggest that workers in hog production are at risk of hydrogen sulfide poisoning (Von Essen & Romberger, 2003), and the repeated motions poultry workers engage in can cause chronic nerve and muscle damage (Ramsey, Musolin, & Meuller, 2015). Workers also report detrimental emotional and physical stressors resulting from the work environment and conditions (Herriges, Secchi, & Babcock, 2005; Purdue Extension, 2008; Weida, 2004).

Vertical integration and supplier selection

CAFOs consistently demonstrate a vertical integration and externalization of production costs (Ashwood, Diamond, & Thu, 2014; Walker & Lawrence, 2004). They own the hatcheries, feed mills, and production and slaughter facilities; they purchase goods and supplies within the organization rather than through local community providers; "building materials, equipment, feed, and feeder animals are from the cheapest outside suppliers" rather than purchased locally (CAFOthebook.org, 2016, p. 1). Hence, the multiplier effect of CAFOs appears to be minimal, which has little to no positive economic impacts on local communities.

Declining tax and property values

Based on the extensive impacts of CAFOs within communities, it is not surprising that evidence exists regarding negative impacts on property values (Kim & Goldsmith, 2009; Isakson & Ecker, 2008). Reasons include "the fear of loss of amenities, the risk of air or water pollution, and the increased possibility of nuisance related to odors and insects" (Ickerd, 2011, p. 11).

The previous examples demonstrate under many GSTC Criteria, CAFOs do not meet sustainable criteria related to sustainable tourism, nor of those economic conditions necessary to support long-term sustainable development.

Animal welfare

Sustainable tourism cannot ignore animal welfare, including within food industries. The ethical ramifications and implications of factory farming to fulfill the promise toward a sustainable tourism industry are tremendous, as they have removed any consideration of humane treatment and care of animals raised for food. While this chapter attempts to link sustainability to food production, the authors believe sustainable production and consumption patterns must be humane, and they shed light on inhumane conditions and treatment identified by CAFOs for production efficiencies.

As Cassuto (2013) stated, "They [animals] are the environment. This is an ethical issue because not only are they the environment, but they are living, sentient, feeling beings who are experiencing what it's like to be in those cages" (p. 582). Cassuto goes on to explain that CAFOs espouse a "deliberate indifference to life" (p. 582), pointing out that the Humane Slaughter Act, which provides protections to animals during slaughter, does not apply to poultry, which comprise 98% of the animals slaughtered for food in the U.S. (Cassuto, 2013). And although we have anti-cruelty laws in all fifty states, for the majority of states, these laws exclude "generally accepted agricultural practices," which are set by industrial farms (Cassuto, 2013, p. 582). Laws that do exist are inadequate to provide any level of decent care and husbandry. To date, there are no federal laws that set humane care standards for animals in factory farms (NHES, 2016; Cassuto, 2013). Physical and mental suffering of animals is given no consideration beyond its impact on the economic bottom line (WSPA, 2012).

Sustainable tourism enterprises should and can be congruent with international standards for animal welfare. The World Organization for Animal Health (OIE) is an intergovernmental organization responsible for improving animal health worldwide (OIE, 2017a, p. 1). The OIE is the World Trade Organization's (WTO) "reference organization for standards relating to animal health and zoonoses" (OIE, 2017b, p. 1). They publish both terrestrial and aquatic animal health codes to "assure the sanitary safety of international trade in terrestrial and aquatic animals, and their products" (OIE, 2017b, p. 1). With respect to animal welfare, they support the following principles:

1 There is a critical relationship between animal health and animal welfare. Animal Welfare refers to how an animal is coping with the conditions in which it lives. According to the OIE, an *animal* is in a good state of *welfare* if (as indicated by scientific evidence) it is healthy, comfortable, well nourished, safe, able to express innate behavior, and if it is not suffering from unpleasant states such as pain, fear, and distress. Good *animal welfare* requires *disease* prevention and veterinary treatment, appropriate shelter, management, nutrition, humane handling, and humane *slaughter/killing* (OIE, 2017c, p. 1).
2 The internationally recognized "five freedoms" (freedom from hunger, thirst and malnutrition; freedom from fear and distress; freedom from physical and thermal discomfort; freedom from pain, injury, and disease; and freedom to express normal patterns of behavior) provide valuable guidance in animal welfare.
3 The internationally recognized "three Rs" (reduction in numbers of animals, refinement of experimental methods, and replacement of animals with non-animal techniques) provide valuable guidance for the use of animals in science.
4 The scientific assessment of animal welfare involves diverse elements which need to be considered together, and selecting and weighing these elements often involves value-based assumptions which should be made as explicit as possible.
5 The use of animals in agriculture, education, and research, and for companionship, recreation, and entertainment, makes a major contribution to the wellbeing of people.
6 The use of animals carries with it an ethical responsibility to ensure the welfare of such animals to the greatest extent practicable.
7 Improvements in farm animal welfare can often improve productivity and food safety, and hence lead to economic benefits.

8 Equivalent outcomes based on performance criteria, rather than identical systems based on design criteria, should be the basis for comparison of animal welfare standards and recommendations (OIE, 2017d, p. 1).

Unfortunately, the laws that are in place do not support these principles and clearly do not support the protection for food production animals specifically within the United States. The National Humane Education Society and many others reveal inhumane treatment of animals and the limitations of the applicable/associated laws:

- The Humane Methods of Livestock Slaughter Act is designed to protect food animals just prior to and during their moment of slaughter. Yet animals slaughtered according to religious rituals and all poultry and all other birds and fish are excluded from the provisions of the act. The methods for humane slaughter include the use of stunning knives, electric baths, killing sticks, and captive bolt guns.
- The Federal Meat Inspection Act allows, among other provisions, licensed meat inspectors to enforce the HSA (USDA Food Safety and Inspection Service, n.d.).

Additionally, the accuracy rate of many forms of stunning the animals prior to slaughter is moderate at best, hence leaving this too inhumane at times. Without a coherent set of protections, such as those principles identified by the OIE, which address humane treatment of livestock, sustainable concepts within CAFOs do not exist. The basic conditions for livestock raised in factory farms are devoid of access to the outdoors, fresh air, or natural light. Even though nine states have banned the use of gestation crates (Ikerd, 2011), a majority of animals spend the majority of their life in confined crates, where animals are unable to stand up, turn around, or extend wings or limbs (PEW, 2008). These conditions are not only inhumane, but they also increase potential for disease. In addition, many livestock breeds are bred to specific production traits, resulting in abnormal growth patterns, structural deformities, susceptibility to infection, and metabolic issues (Gregor, 2010). Numerous drugs are utilized to increase growth rates, often causing severe side effects, stress, and untimely death. These drugs (e.g., Zilimax, Ractopamine, etc.) have increased aggressive behaviors in pigs and cows, causing difficulties during transport, increased response aggression by handlers, as well as injuries to both (Food & Water Watch, 2015). All of the above practices are in conflict with GSTC Criteria that explicitly outline criteria regarding animal welfare:

> D3.5 Animal welfare
>
> No species of wild animal is acquired, bred or held captive, except by authorized and suitably equipped persons and for properly regulated activities in compliance with local and international law. Housing, care and handling of all wild and domestic animals meets the highest standards of animal welfare.
>
> (GSTC, n.d., p. 10)

Fortunately, there are financially viable alternative systems for raising animals with respect to environmental and social-economic impacts and animal welfare principles. The following case study presents an example of a sustainable food production cooperative that is enhancing and supporting the growing local food tourism industry in North Carolina.

Case study: scaling up pasture-raised pork in North Carolina

The State of North Carolina is home to an estimated 6,500 hog and chicken CAFOs which produce nearly 10 million gallons of feces and urine per year, or "enough to fill 15,000 Olympic size swimming pools" (Environmental Working Group, 2016, p. 4). Much of this pork is produced for Smithfield Foods Company, a subsidiary of the Chinese corporation, WH Group. Through its other subsidiary holdings, including Murphy Brown LLC, WH Group owns most of the hogs in North Carolina's CAFOs, contributing to dense pockets of animal production especially in the ten counties in North Carolina that house the highest density of swine produced in the U.S. and three counties that host the highest density of turkeys in the nation (Kelly-Reif & Wing, 2016). While factory farms dominate the agricultural landscape of North Carolina, the state is also home to a flourishing network of local farmers, food system advocates, and food entrepreneurs. Many farmers in the state have opted to raise animals humanely, on pasture with plenty of access to fresh water and sunlight, allowing them to exhibit their natural behaviors.

Across the state farmers have bound together through membership and collaborative organizations such as The Carolina Farm Stewardship Association, Piedmont Grown, Appalachian Sustainable Agriculture Project, Blue Ridge Women in Agriculture, NC Choices, and the Center for Environmental Farming Systems. One such group, the North Carolina Natural Hog Growers Association (NCNHGA) is a grower cooperative group of pasture-based hog farmers who collectively market their products to wholesale buyers. The group consists of about twenty-five independently owned and operated member farms, and adherence to Animal Welfare Approved (AWA) third party certification is a requirement of membership. AWA is a USDA-approved third-party certification label which is offered free of charge to participating farmers who raise their animals in accordance with the highest welfare standards, outdoors, on pasture or range. AWA certification prohibits beak trimming of poultry, tail docking of pigs and cattle, and generally requires pain relief for removal of horn buds of cattle. AWA Standards also stipulate humane practices for the treatment of breeding, transporting, and slaughtering animals (Animal Welfare Institute, 2016a).

NCNHGA founder and president Jeremiah Jones operates GrassRoots Pork, a pasture-based farm in Duplin County. Duplin County is the heart of North Carolina's factory farming landscape and houses more pigs than any other county in the United States with over two million hogs being raised in CAFO's (Animal Welfare Institute, 2011). Through the NCNHGA, GrassRoots Pork has distinguished its place in the niche, humane meat market and partners with like-minded farmers to collectively provide pasture-raised meat products for wholesale customers like Firsthand Foods. Firsthand Foods, based in Durham, is an aggregator and distributor of meat from farms in North Carolina who raise animals humanely, on pasture, and without the use of sub-therapeutic antibiotics or animal by-products. The company purchases whole animals from farmers, handles all the processing, storage, and distribution, and provides a range of meat options to restaurants, grocers, and through a subscription-based M(eat) Local box program delivered directly to consumers. Firsthand Foods pasture-raised beef, lamb, and pork products are sold at a variety of retail outlets and to institutions and restaurants in North Carolina. Durham is cultivating a tourism reputation based on food, and it has been dubbed the Foodie Capital of the South by the *New York Post*, America's Tastiest Town by *Southern Living*, and America's Foodiest Small Town by *Bon Appetit* magazine (Durham CVB, 2012). The city boasts a long list of leading farm-to-table chefs and restaurants, many of which proudly offer Firsthand Foods meat products on their seasonally inspired menus. As an aggregator, Firsthand Foods is able to operate on a level of scale that chefs and wholesalers seek out, for both quality and consistency. This allows farm partners to focus on raising animals sustainably, outsourcing much of the marketing and logistics work load. Firsthand Foods is in its seventh year of business, grosses over $1 million in sales annually, and began operating at a net profit after their fifth year of operation. Their producer network now includes over sixty farms, and as the company continues to grow they are cultivating plans to expand into additional geographic markets (Quanbeck, 2014; Bridges, 2017).

Firsthand Foods also plays a critical role in supporting the burgeoning sustainable agriculture and food tourism industry of North Carolina by supplying local, pasture-raised meat for several industry conferences in the state. For example, the Carolina Meat Conference, an annual event hosted by NC Choices and an initiative of the Center for Environmental Farming Systems, sources much of the meat served to conference attendees from Firsthand Foods. The Carolina Meat Conference attracts more than 400 farmers, producers, butchers, and chefs from over twenty-five different states each year and brings together meat distributors and producers to help build capacity for local supply chains (NC Growing Together, 2013). Similarly, Firsthand Foods is also a leading supplier of humanely raised meat for The Carolina Farm Stewardship Association Annual Sustainable Agriculture Conference in Durham. The conference sources over 80% of food served at the event locally, and hosts over 1500 farmers, gardeners, concerned consumers, educators, and activists from across the Southeast annually.

The partnerships between the NCNHGA, Firsthand Foods, and the many other stakeholders in food and agricultural tourism in North Carolina provide a positive example of the economic opportunities in sustainable, humane animal production value chains. Adherence to a third-party certification standard ensures the transparency of the responsible farming practices that all growers in this supply chain follow. Unfortunately, the lack of regulation regarding unverified and misleading marketing claims contributes consumer confusion. Terms such as cage free, free range, natural, and vegetarian-fed have begun to saturate the market, yet are not regulated by the USDA and are often touted on meat labels from companies with weak standards for animal welfare. While new regulations have been proposed to include animal welfare standards in the regulation requirements for USDA Certified Organic meat products, at the time of this publication new rules that would regulate the handling, transport, and slaughter of animals remain postponed (USDA AMS, 2017). While AWA certification is arguably one of the most stringent programs to ensure animal welfare (Leigh, 2015, p. 40), other certification labels that encourage improved treatment of animals include American Grassfed Certified, Certified Humane, American Humane Certified, Food Alliance Certified, and Global Animal Partnership Certified (Animal Welfare Institute, 2016b).

Conclusions

As a significant element of the tourism product, sustainable food production must be considered in sustainable tourism development. Sustainable tourism's contribution where food is sourced has the potential to hail significant to sustainable development and ultimately to the health of the planet and its inhabitants (Schwab, Dustin, & Bricker, 2009). In a world of dwindling resources, destinations and individual tourism operations must examine the valuation of ecosystem services because inherent in the promise of sustainable tourism as David Orr (1994) suggests is consideration of the way in which we "do" business. He affirms our obligation to learn "how to build local prosperity without ruining some other place. . . . And, to revitalize an ecological concept of citizenship rooted in the understanding that activities that waste resources, pollute, destroy biological diversity, and degrade the beauty and the integrity of the landscape are forms of theft from common wealth" (p. 168). Further, according to the World Health Organization, approximately one-quarter of the global disease burden and over 80%of the diseases and injuries they monitor are affected by modifiable environmental factors, and such factors are related primarily to environmental degradation. CAFOs impact the environment, society, and the health and wellbeing of living creatures.

Alternatives to CAFOs that include consideration of increased animal welfare and environmental stewardship must be employed in order to give sustainable tourism a realistic chance for success. The hidden costs of animal food production by CAFOs are enormous, largely unaccounted economically, and cause negative impacts through extensive pollution, economic challenges to communities, threats to human health, subjects animals to unethical treatment, and reflects a challenge to sustainable tourism operators to responsibly meet food sourcing demands of increased tourism.

The North Carolina case study outlined in this chapter, however, presents opportunities and strategies for stakeholders to consider in the pursuit of responsible food sourcing for sustainable tourism destinations. Environmentally sound and economically viable methods of raising food animals humanely are possible, and they must be pursued as divergent strategies from current detrimental factory farming practices.

References

Animal Welfare Institute. (2011). *In NC, raising pigs right means keeping up with the Joneses*. Retrieved from https://awionline.org/awi-quarterly/2011-spring/nc-raising-pigs-right-means-keeping-joneses

Animal Welfare Institute. (2016a). *Consumer perceptions of farm animal welfare*. Retrieved from https://awionline.org/sites/default/files/uploads/documents/fa-consumer_perceptionsoffarmwelfare_-112511.pdf

Animal Welfare Institute. (2016b). *A consumer's guide to food label's and animal welfare* [Web Report]. Retrieved from https://awionline.org/sites/default/files/products/FA-AWI-FoodLabelGuide-Web.pdf

Ashwood, L., Diamond, D., & Thu, K. (2014). Where's the farmer? Limiting liability in midwestern industrial hog production. *Rural Sociology*, 79, 2–27. doi:10.1111/ruso.12026

Bowman, A., Mueller, K., & Smith, M. (2000). *Increased animal waste production from concentrated animal feeding operations (CAFOs): Potential implications for public and environmental health*. Nebraska Center for Rural Health Research. Retrieved from www.unmc.edu/rural/ documents/cafo-report.pdf

Bridges, V. (2017). Durham food hub feeds local market as it navigates way to sustainability. *News and Observer*. Retrieved June 7, 2017, from www.newsobserver.com/news/local/community/durham-news/article27448969.html

Burns, R., Xin, H., Gates, R., Li, H., Hoff, S., Moody, L., et al. (2007). *Tyson broiler ammonia emission monitoring project: Final report*. Retrieved from www.sierraclub.org/environmentallaw/ lawsuits/docs/ky-tysonreport.pdf

CAFOthebook.org. (2016). Retrieved December 21, 2016, from www.cafothebook.org/thebook_myths.htm

Cassuto, D. N. (2013). Environment, ethics, and the factory farm. *South Texas Law Review*, *54*(579). Retrieved from http://digitalcommons.pace.edu/lawfaculty/969/

Centner, T. J. (2006). Governmental oversight of discharges from concentrated animal feeding operations. *Environmental Management*, *37*(6), 745.

Consumer Reports® National Research Center Survey Research Report. (2015). *Natural food labels survey*. Retrieved from http://article.images.consumerreports.org/prod/content/dam/cro/magazine-articles/2016/March/Consumer_Reports_Natural_Food_Labels_Survey_2015.pdf

Donham, K., Wing, S., Osterberg, D., Flora, J., Hodne, C. Thu, K., & Thome, P. (2007). Community health and socioeconomic issues surrounding concentrated animal feeding operations. *Environmental Health Perspectives*, *115*(2), 317–320. Retrieved from www.jstor.org/stable/4133137

Dunning, R., Blacklin, S., & McKissick, C. (2013). *North Carolina Niche meat producers survey 2013*. Raleigh, NC: Center for Environmental Farming Systems, North Carolina State University. Retrieved from www.cefs.ncsu.edu/ncgt/niche-meat-survey.pdf

Durham Convention and Visitors Bureau. (2012). *Official Durham meeting & event planners guide*. Retrieved from www.dcvb-nc.com/sales/MPG2012.pdf

Environmental Protection Agency. (2009). *National water quality inventory: Report to congress: 2004 reporting cycle*. Retrieved from www.epa.gov/sites/production/files/2015-09/documents/2009_01_22_305b_2004report_2004_305breport.pdf

Environmental Protection Agency (EPA). (2016a). Retrieved August 15, 2016, from www.epa.gov/nutrientpollution/problem

Environmental Protection Agency (EPA). (2016b). Retrieved August 15, 2016, from www.epa.gov/nutrientpollution/sources-and-solution

Environmental Protection Agency (EPA). (2016c). Retrieved August 15, 2016, from www.epa.gov/sites/production/files/2015-09/documents/2009_01_22_305b_2004report_2004_305breport.pdf

Environmental Protection Agency (EPA). (2016d). Retrieved August 15, 2016, from www.epa.gov/nps/nonpoint-source-agriculture

Environmental Protection Agency. (n.d.). *Animal feeding operations*. Retrieved from www.epa.gov/global-mitigation-non-co2-greenhouse-gases/global-mitigation-non-co2-greenhouse-gases-livestock

Environmental Working Group. (2016). *Exposing fields of filth* [Web Report]. Retrieved from www.ewg.org/research/exposing-fields-filth.

Food & Water Watch. (2015). *Factory Farm Nation: 2015 Edition* [Web Report]. Retrieved from https://www.scribd.com/document/266806632/Factory-Farm-Nation-2015-Edition.

Food and Drug Administration Department of Health and Human Services and Center for Veterinary Medicine. (2014, September). *Summary report on antimicrobials sold or distributed for use in food-producing animals*. Retrieved from www.fda.gov/downloads/ForIndustry/UserFees/AnimalDrugUserFeeActADUFA/UCM231851.pdf

Global Sustainable Tourism Council (GSTC). (n.d.). *The criteria*. Retrieved from www.gstcouncil.org/en/gstc-criteria-hotels-tour-operators-destinations/sustainable-tourism-gstc-criteria.html

Gregor, M. (2010, May 30). Transgenesis in animal agriculture: Addressing animal health and welfare concerns. *Journal of Agricultural and Environmental Ethics*.

Harrison, J. (2006). Accidents" and invisibilities: Scaled discourses and the naturalization of regulatory neglect in California's pesticide drift conflict. *Political Geography*, *25*, 506–529.

Harrison, J. (2008). Abandoned bodies and spaces of sacrifice: Pesticide drift activism and the contestation of neoliberal environmental politics in California. *Geoforum*, *39*, 1197–1214.

Herriges, J. A., Secchi, S., & Babcock, B. A. (2005). Living with hogs in Iowa: The impact of livestock facilities on rural residential property values. *Land Economics*, *81*(4), 530–545.

Hribar, C. (2010). *Understanding concentrated animal feeding operations and their impact on communities*. Ohio: National Association of Local Boards of Health, Bowling Green.

Ikerd, J. (2011). *Corporate agriculture versus family farms: A battle for hearts and minds*. Retrieved, December 1, 2017, from web.missouri.edu/~ikerdj/papers/NorthDakotaCorpAgvsFamilyFarms.pdf

Ikerd, J. (2017). *Corporate agriculture versus family farms: A battle for hearts and minds*. Socially Responsible Agriculture Project (SRAP). Retrieved January 2, 2017, from www.sraproject.org/factory-farms-destroy-communities/

Isakson, H. R., & Ecker, M. D. (2008). An analysis of the impact of swine CAFOs on the value of nearby houses. *Agricultural Economics*, *39*, 365–372. doi:10.1111/j.1574-0862.2008.00339.x

Jackson, L. A., & Singh, D. (2015). Environmental rankings and financial performance: An analysis of firms in the US food and beverage supply chain. *Tourism Management Perspectives*, *14*, 25–33.

Kelly-Reif, K., & Wing, S. (2016). Urban-rural exploitation: An underappreciated dimension of environmental injustice. *Journal of Rural Studies*, *47*, 350–358.

Kim, J., & Goldsmith, P. (2009). A spatial hedonic approach to assess the impact of swine production on residential property values. *Environmental and Resource Economics*, *42*, 509. doi:10.1007/s10640-008-9221-0

Leigh, M. (2015). *The ethical meat handbook: Complete home butchery, charcuterie and cooking for the conscious omnivore*. Gabriola Island, Canada: New Society Publishers.

Lowe, M., & Gary, G. (2009). *A value chain analysis of the US Beef and Dairy Industries*. Duke University Center on Globalization, Governance and Competitiveness, Duke University. Retrieved from www.cggc.duke.edu/environment/valuechainanalysis/CGGC_BeefDairyReport_2-16-09.pdf

Mallin, M. A., & Cahoon, L. B. (2003). Industrialized animal production – a major source of nutrient and microbial pollution to aquatic ecosystems. *Population and Environment*, *24*(5), 369.

Massey, R., & Ulmer, A. (2008). *Agriculture and greenhouse gas emission*. University of Missouri Extension. Retrieved from http://extension.missouri.edu/publications/DisplayPub.aspx?P=G310

Mekonnen, M. M., & Hoekstra, A. Y. (2010). *The green, blue, and grey water footprint of farm animals and animal products*. Value of Water Research Report Series No. 48, UNESC-IHE. Retrieved from http://waterfootprint.org/media/downloads/Report-48-WaterFootprint-AnimalProducts-Vol1_1.pdf

Merkel, M. (2002). *Raising a stink: Air emissions from factory farms*. Environmental Integrity Project. Retrieved from www.environmentalintegrity.org/pdf/publications/CAFOAirEmissions_ white_paper.pdf

Moses, A., & Tomaselli, P. (2017). Industrial animal agriculture in the United States: Concentrated Animal Feeding Operations (CAFOs). In *International farm animal, wildlife and food safety law* (pp. 185–214). New York: Springer International Publishing.

National Humane Education Society (NHES). (2016). *Government Regulation of Factory Farms*. Retrieved from: https://nhes.org/3372-2/

NC Growing Together. (2013). *Niche meat producers connecting to mainstream markets*. Retrieved from www.ncgrowingtogether.org/stories/meat-and-greet/.

Nicole, W. (2013). CAFOs and environmental justice: The case of North Carolina. *Environmental Health Perspectives*, *121*(6), a182–a189. Retrieved from http://doi.org/10.1289/ehp.121-a182

Orr, D. W. (1994). *Earth in mind: On education, environment, and the human prospect*. Washington, DC: Island Press.

Ostlind, E. (2011). The big four meatpackers. *High Country News*, 43(5). Retrieved from www.hcn.org/issues/43.5/cattlemen-struggle-against-giant-meatpackers-and-economic-squeezes/the-big-four-meatpackers-1.

Owen, O. S., Chiras, D. D., & Reganold, J. P. (1998). *Natural resource conservation: Management for a sustainable future*. Upper Saddle River, NJ: Prentice Hall.

PEW Charitable Trust Fund (PEW). (2008). *Putting meat on the table: Industrial farm animal production in America* [Web Report]. Retrieved from www.pewtrusts.org/~/media/legacy/uploadedfiles/peg/publications/report/pcifapfinalpdf.pdf

PEW Charitable Trust Fund (PEW). (2016). *Major food companies committed to reducing antibiotic use* [Web Report]. Retrieved from www.pewtrusts.org/en/multimedia/data-visualizations/2016/major-food-companies-committed-to-reducing-antibiotic-use

Purdue Extension. (2008). *Community impacts of CAFOs: Property value*. Retrieved December 10, 2016, from www.ces. purdue.edu/extmedia/ID/ID-363-W.pdf

Quanbeck, K. (2014). Firsthand foods: Bringing North Carolina farmers and markets together. *Cooperative Extension Website*. Retrieved from http://articles.extension.org/pages/71823/firsthand-foods:-bringing-north-carolina-farmers-and-markets-together.

Ramsey, J., Musolin, K., & Meuller, C. (2015). *Health hazard evaluation report: Evaluation of carpal tunnel syndrome and other musculoskeletal disorders among employees at a poultry processing plant*. Cincinnati, OH: US Department of Health and Human Services, Centers for Disease Control and Prevention, National Institute for Occupational Safety and Health, NIOSH HHE Report No. 2014-0040-3232.

Ribaudo, M., Cattaneo, A., & Agapoff, J. (2004). Cost of meeting manure nutrient application standards in hog production: The roles of EQIP and fertilizer offsets. *Review of Agricultural Economics*, *26*(4), 430–444. Retrieved from www.jstor.org/stable/3700790

Schwab, K., Dustin, D., & Bricker, K. (2009). Parks, recreation, and tourism's contributions to Utah's health: An ecologic perspective. *UTAH Leisure Insights*, *29*(1), 12–14.

Thorton, P. K. (2010). Livestock production: Recent trends, future prospects. *Philosophical Transactions of the Royal Society B*, *365*(1554), 2853–2867.

Union of Concerned Scientists (UCS). (2008). *CAFOs uncovered: The untold costs of confined animal feeding operations*. Retrieved from www.ucsusa.org/sites/default/files/legacy/assets/documents/food_and_agriculture/cafos-uncovered.pdf

United States Department of Agriculture (USDA). (n.d.). *Humane Slaughter Act*. Retrieved from www.nal.usda.gov/awic/humane-methods-slaughter-act

United States Department of Agriculture Agricultural Marketing Service (USDA AMS). (2017). *Organic livestock and poultry practices*. Federal Register. Retrieved from www.federalregister.gov/documents/2017/05/10/2017-09409/national-organic-program-nop-organic-livestock-and-poultry-practices

United States Department of Agriculture Economic Research Service (USDAERS). (n.d.). Retrieved from www.ers.usda.gov/topics/animal-products/

United States Department of Agriculture Food Safety and Inspection Service (n.d.). *Federal Meat Inspection Act*. Retrieved from www.fsis.usda.gov/wps/portal/fsis/topics/rulemaking/federal-meat-inspection-act

Von Essen, S., & Romberger, D. (2003). The respiratory inflammatory response to the swine confinement building environment: The adaptation to respiratory exposures in the chronically exposed worker. *Journal of Agricultural Safety and Health*, *9*(3), 185–196.

Walker, P., & Lawrence, S. (2004). American meat: A threat to your health and to the environment. *Yale Journal of Health Policy, Law, and Ethics*, *4*(1), Article 12. Retrieved from http://digitalcommons.law.yale.edu/yjhple/vol4/iss1/12

Waters, A. E., Contente-Cuomo, T., Buchhagen, J., Liu, C. M., Watson, L., Pearce, K., & Price, L. B. (2011). Multidrug-resistant *Staphylococcus aureus* in US meat and poultry. *Clinical Infectious Diseases: An Official Publication of the Infectious Diseases Society of America*, *52*(10), 1227–1230.

Webster, A. J. F. (2001). Farm animal welfare: The five freedoms and the free market. *The Veterinary Journal Volume*, *161*(3), 229–237.

Weida, W. J. (2004). *Considering the rationales for factory farming*. Environmental Health Impacts of CAFOs: Anticipating Hazards – Searching for Solutions. Retrieved May 21, 2017, from www.sraproject.org/wp-content/uploads/2007/12/foundationsofsand.pdf

Wender, M. (2011). Goodbye family farms and hello agribusiness: The story of how agricultural policy is destroying the family farm and the environment. *Villanova Environmental Law Journal*, *22*, 141. Retrieved from http://digitalcommons.law.villanova.edu/elj/vol22/iss1/6

Wilson, S., & Serre, M. (2007, July). Examination of atmospheric ammonia levels near hog CAFOs, homes, and schools in Eastern North Carolina. *Atmospheric Environment*, *41*(23), 4977–4987. ISSN: 1352-2310. Retrieved from https://doi.org/10.1016/j.atmosenv.2006.12.055.

Windham, J. (2007). Putting your money where your mouth is: Perverse food subsidies, social responsibility & America's 2007 farm bill. *Environmental Law and Policy Journal University of California, Davis*, *31*(1).

Wing, S., & Johnston, J. (2014). Industrial hog operations in North Carolina disproportionately impact African-Americans, Hispanics and American Indians. *North Carolina*

Policy Watch. Retrieved from www.ncpolicywatch.com/wp-content/uploads/2014/09/UNC-Report.pdf.

World Organization for Animal Health (OIE). (2017a). *About us*. Retrieved January 5, 2017, from www.oie.int/en/about-us/

World Organization for Animal Health (OIE). (2017b). *International standards*. Retrieved January 5, 2017, from www.oie.int/en/international-standard-setting/overview/

World Organization for Animal Health (OIE). (2017c). *Glossary of terms*. Retrieved January 5, 2017, from www.oie.int/index.php?id=169&L=0&htmfile=glossaire.htm#terme_bien_etre_animal

World Organization for Animal Health (OIE). (2017d). *Principles of animal welfare*. Retrieved January 5, 2017, from www.oie.int/index.php?id=169&L=0&htmfile=chapitre_aw_introduction.htm

World Society for Protection of Animals (WSPA). (2012). *What's on your plate? The hidden costs of industrial animal agriculture in Canada*. Retrieved from http://richarddagan.com/cafo-ilo/WSPA_WhatsonYourPlate_FullReport.pdf

9 A life worth living

Reindeer in Nordic tourism experiences

Hin Hoarau-Heemstra

Introduction

> I have a coat from fox fur that I got from hunters here on the island. I could never think myself to have fur from an animal in a cage. It is disgusting; I get so sad when I think about those poor animals.
>
> (Laila Inga, 2016)

Laila Inga is the owner of Inga Sami Siida, a Sami tourism company offering reindeer experiences in Northern Norway. She has lived and worked with reindeer all her life and her relationship with animals is tightly connected to her Sami heritage. The quote illustrates the idea that it can be ethically right to use and kill animals but that they should have had a life worth living. The fox, the dogs, and reindeer . . . they should be able to develop their full potential without suffering. Over the last decade, the life of (some) reindeer has changed due to the introduction of a new role: the entertainer of tourists. Tourism activities and experiences are a relatively novel aspect in the life of reindeer and reindeer herders and this chapter discusses the animal–ethical challenges that the company Inga Sami Siida faces in their recently developed tourism operations.

Animals can be a very significant aspect of tourism experiences. They are the main focus of certain activities such as safari tourism. Specific species, for example whales and dolphins, are key tourism attractions and have generated dedicated tourist activities and tourism businesses (Markwell, 2015). Not only are wild animals the key players in many tourism experiences, but to a larger extent, domestic animals are as well – i.e.- dogsledding, horse tracking, and cow-cart adventure tours. Reindeer can be added to the list of species working for tourism, as the use of reindeer is increasingly common in Sami tourism (Pettersson, 2004). Reindeer rides (on sleighs) and encounters with reindeer in their natural environment can be seen as a mix between adventure tourism and indigenous tourism. The Adventure Travel Trade Association (ATTA) defines adventure tourism as a trip that includes at least two of the following three elements: physical activity, natural environment, and cultural immersion. Indigenous tourism has been defined as “tourism activity in which indigenous people are directly involved either through control and/or by having their culture serve as the essence of the attraction" (Butler, 1996, p. 9). Hence, indigenous adventure tourism would be a tourism activity that is physical, takes place in the natural environment, and is immersed in indigenous culture that is the essence of the attraction.

The lifestyle that comes with being a reindeer owner is an important part of Sami identity and cultural heritage. The Sami are the indigenous people of Northern Europe, and they can be found in sub-Arctic and Arctic parts of northern Norway, Sweden, Finland and the Kola Peninsula in Russia (Gáldu, n.d.). In Norway and Sweden, the Sami are the only ones allowed to own reindeer. The reindeer and their cycles are deeply interwoven with Sami culture, who are traditionally a nomadic people. Reindeer have roamed free in the mountains and forests of Northern Europe, with their human guardians protecting them from predators. In exchange, the Sami have used the reindeer for food, clothes, and other products made from their bones and skin. With climate and social change, the lifeworld of Sami people is rapidly shifting, after being the same for many, many generations. With the arrival of tourism and the experience economy, the Sami started using another aspect of the reindeer: their ability to entertain paying customers. In a way, the reindeer tourism experience is a form of cultural tourism, and the future development of Sami tourism is tightly connected to the development of reindeer herding, since many Sami tourism entrepreneurs are considering reindeer herding as their primary economy (Müller, Saarinen, & Hall, 2009). Hence, the roles of reindeer in Sami society have expanded from being food and an expression of culture to key players in tourism experiences. The remainder of this chapter presents Sami tourism as an example of indigenous adventure tourism and discusses two trends that are changing the roles of reindeer in the livelihood of Sami-people: climate change and the emergence of the experience economy. The case of Inga Sami Siida (Inga is the family name of the business owners; Sami refers to their ethnical and cultural background, and Siida means herders in Sami-language) will be presented to illustrate how reindeer are used in the co-creation of tourism experiences. The case is unique in that it involves a scenario where animals have value to the "owners" both when alive and when dead; but as opposed to similar scenarios related to livestock, the reindeer are left in their natural habitat, and the owners adjust their lifestyle to accommodate that. The case elaborates on some of the ethical challenges in the relationship between business, animals, and tourists.

Indigenous tourism, Sami, and reindeer

There are many different types of indigenous people in the world, and the Sami of Northern Europe are one of them. Indigenous people form non-dominant but distinctive groups of peoples in society. According to the United Nations Permanent Forum on Indigenous Issues (2009, p. 4), the term indigenous entails:

- Self-identification as indigenous peoples
- Historical continuity
- Strong link to territories and surrounding natural resources

- Distinct social, economic or political systems
- Distinct language, culture and beliefs.

Sami can be found in sub-Arctic and Arctic parts of northern Norway, Sweden, Finland and the Kola Peninsula in Russia, and they refer to their territory as *Sapmi*, in English known as Lapland. The Sami have a strong link to these northern territories and natural resources that have served as the core of their subsistence for thousands of years. The total number of Sami in the four countries is approximately 80,000 (United Nations Regional Information Centre for Western Europe [UNRIC], n.d.). In Norway, the Sami have their own parliament, which promotes political initiatives and manages missions and laws delegated to them by national authorities. Reindeer husbandry has been and still is an important aspect of Sami culture. Today in Norway and Sweden, reindeer husbandry is legally protected as an exclusive Sami livelihood, such that only persons of Sami descent with a linkage to a reindeer herding family can own, and hence make a living off of, reindeer. Climate change (making it harder for reindeer to find food in winter), ongoing cutbacks in pasturelands, and conflict with predators are considered major threats to the Sami, as are the impacts of globalization, increasing competition in the venison market, and a blurring of cultural differences from rest of the Scandinavian society (UNRIC, n.d.). In addition to these threats, opportunities present themselves with the rise of the experience economy and globalization. Experience offers great value to people who demand it and who are willing to pay a high price for experience-stimulating business activities (Sundbo & Darmer, 2013). Experience is a mental phenomenon, which means that it does not concern physical needs (as goods do) or solving material or intellectual problems (as services do) (Sundbo & Darmer, 2013). Pine and Gilmore (1998, p. 98) have defined "experiences" as occurring when a company intentionally uses services as the stage, and goods as props, to engage individual customers in a way that creates a memorable event. Since Pine and Gilmore´s well-known contribution, many authors have embraced the concept of the experience economy. The emerging tradition, or paradigm, of experience economy studies examines the formal economic activities related to experiences and how they can be managed and developed (Sundbo & Darmer, 2013). A shift has occurred from the company to the customer in understanding who is responsible for creating experiences. The company is only able to make a value-proposition, while the actual value is co-created with all stakeholders involved in the experience (Boswijk, Peelen, & Olthof, 2012).

Tourist travel has always been motivated by a desire to meet other people and experience other cultures. With the globalization of tourism, even the remotest areas and their indigenous peoples can now be visited (Müller & Pettersson, 2001). There is an increased interest in indigenous tourism as a form of cultural tourism fueled by a need for meaningful experiences and transformation through experience and knowledge. The touristic consumption of culture is not only about the physical visits to touristic sites, it is also about encounters between tourists with various cultural backgrounds and the cultural expression at issue, producing diverging meanings and experiences (Müller et al., 2009; Therkelsen, 2003). In a study by

Müller and Huuva (2009), tourism entrepreneurs considered tourism to be a good complement to reindeer herding, and tourism development is seen as a potential solution to problems troubling the Sami society, offering increased employment, income, a broader economic base, decreased antagonism (by increased transfer of knowledge), and improved infrastructure and tourism control (Müller et al., 2009). However, the combination is rather hard to develop, considering the small scale of many companies and the natural cycles of the reindeer (Müller & Huuva, 2009). Additionally, problems related to the commodification and commercialization of the Sami have been identified, for example in relation to the representations available at the Santa Claus Tourist Center in Rovaniemi, Finland. Here, Sami culture is mixed with Anglo-American Christmas traditions, leading to a representation Sami people might find insulting (Müller et al., 2009).

Although it seems that the reindeer-owning Sami are presented with an entrepreneurial opportunity right now, indigenous tourism is not a new phenomenon. Weaver (2010) proposes a model to understand the evolution of the relationship between indigenous people and tourism. The model consists of the following six stages: (1) pre-European *in situ* control, characterized by high local control and indigenous theme; (2) *in situ* exposure occurs in the early stages of colonialism and is followed by (3) *ex situ* exhibitionism and exploitation, as native artifacts are displayed in museums and exhibitions. The opening of remnant indigenous space to tourist visits marks (4) *in situ* exhibitionism and exploitation, which represents the nadir of indigenous control but fosters strategies of resistance. Reassertions of indigenous control give rise to (5) *in situ* quasi-empowerment, while the extension of this control to previously occupied territory characterizes (6) *ex situ* quasi-empowerment and the presence of "shadow indigenous tourism." Weaver (2010) argues that it is possible to identify activities among indigenous people in the era prior to European colonization that qualify as "tourism" under this definition, even though these activities have not yet been investigated as such by tourism academics.

The Sami people have co-existed with other Europeans for a long time, but they have been mainly physically separated. The Norwegians inhabited the islands and coastal areas in order to trade with European partners, while the Sami lived more inlands. Their nomadic lifestyle followed the cycle of the reindeer. Fonneland (2013) presents an overview of how the Sami people have been in contact with other people and cultures through trade, colonization, and tourism. With the colonization of the north of Scandinavia by other European cultures and groups, the Sami gradually lost control over their lands and lifestyle. At the same time, this opened up Sami culture by the traveling and exchange that is documented since the Viking era. Due to a growing interest in exotic cultures, a period of exhibitionism and exploitation of Northern Scandinavian indigenous people started in the nineteenth century. Representations and displays of Sami people and culture through varying forms and with shifting purposes have taken place over a long time span. In 1822, one of the first known exhibitions of Sami culture was arranged in the Egyptian Hall in Piccadilly, London (Fonneland, 2013). In the course of the 1800s more such exhibitions were established and all achieved great popularity and interest (Baglo, 2008). These *ex-situ* exhibitions woke the curiosity of travelers and during the 1900s and the Sami culture was made available for both cruise and road travelers (Fonneland, 2013). In today's experience economy, the Sami have gained back control of their cultural resources and can invite guests on their own premises. Sami nature- and culture- based tourism is now seen as a promising starting point for entrepreneurship, as well as for the development of both ecologically and culturally sustainable new industries in Sami communities (Kramvig, 2011). Entrepreneurship and tourism developed from Sami culture and lifestyle is often evolving around reindeer, as they are the most important and characteristic assets of the Sami people. It is about people meeting reindeer and getting to know the Sami culture and lifestyle through their interactions and meetings with reindeer and their human keepers.

Human–reindeer interaction: the case of Inga Sami Siida

The data for this case was gathered in March 2013 and January 2016. In 2013, the author participated in the reindeer experience of Inga Sami Siida, and in 2016 the author revisited the company for another observation of the experience and an interview with the owner Laila Inga. In addition, field notes and pictures were taken during the tourism experience that lasted about three hours. The interview lasted approximately one hour, was audio recorded, and transcribed verbatim. The interview was semi-structured with a set of topics but allowed the informant to speak freely about the topics addressed by the interviewer. Based on the tourism and animal ethics literature (Bulbeck, 2005; Fennell, 2012; Hughes, 2001), a "start list" of codes was created prior to performing the fieldwork. These codes functioned as a list of topics for the interviews. Examples of the codes are as follows: entrepreneurial history, Sami culture, tourism experience product, relationship with animals, communication with customers; customer satisfaction; customer expectations; responsibility toward others; and motivations for change and innovation. During the interview, the informant was asked to provide examples and discuss her experience with the concepts that were introduced.

The interview

Laila Inga sips her coffee at her kitchen table while talking about her eight years of experience running a tourism company, and her lifelong experience of owning a reindeer herd. It is January, one of the coldest and darkest months in Northern Norway, but nevertheless the number of tourists coming to Northern Norway in this season is growing.

Laila and her husband are reindeer owners on Hinnøya, the biggest island in Vesterålen. Lofoten-Vesterålen is a popular destination in Northern Norway, famous for its dramatic landscapes and unspoiled nature. In 2008 it was listed as a top destination by *National Geographic*, and people from all over the world travel to this archipelago to see wildlife and get to know Norwegian coastal culture. Since 2009 it has become possible to encounter Sami culture in Vesterålen as well.

In Norway, the Sami are the only ones with the right to own reindeer and let them roam free in the mountains. No reindeer owner will tell you how many reindeer he or she owns because they represent value for the Sami people. It is equated to sharing your bank account or retirement account balance. The reindeer are wild animals, roaming free in the mountains. They are earmarked by their owners and herded in for slaughter in the autumn. The Sami use everything from these animals: their meat, skins, and bones. The Sami traditional lifestyle has allowed them to survive in extreme arctic circumstances for thousands of years. Famous polar explorers like Roald Amundsun used Sami-technology to survive the cold, harsh poles. For example, shoes from reindeer skin are waterproof, warm, and you can attach them to cross-country skis.

Sami follow their reindeer; traditionally they are a nomadic people. Laila shares with a group of tourists that, for her, there are eight seasons connected to the cycles of her reindeer. She explains:

> The Reindeer define our year. I follow them; they do not follow me. The eight seasons depend on the reindeer cycles that repeat themselves every year; they have not changed for hundreds of thousands of years. It is very important to understand so we do not disturb them, let them be free. It is always their life that matters.

Hence, the reindeer define the life of their people, not the other way around. Quite recently, tourism has come into the picture as an alternative use of reindeer. This has had a profound consequence on the life of reindeer, the Sami, and the local communities they are living in. However, tourism was not a first choice for the Inga family. Climate change has caused harsher circumstances for the reindeer to survive in this part of Norway. The winters are different, with less snow and more ice, which made it more difficult for the reindeer to reach their food. In addition, the risk of avalanches has increased, killing more reindeer every winter. Laila and her husband had to bring the reindeer down from the mountains for a longer period and feed them extra so they would survive the winter.

> We started to build the fences to bring home parts of the herd during the hard winter. Especially the end of the winter; February, March, April. It is very important to help them to survive because when there is a lot of ice on the ground, the calves are starving and will die. So that was the beginning of the company. It was made for the reindeer, not for the tourists.
>
> (Laila Inga)

In order to cover the extra costs of food, the family started a tourism business in 2008. Since Laila and her husband started inviting tourists to their farm, the numbers of visitors in both winter and summer season have been growing steadily. Where first people passing by would stop for a visit, now entire busses drive three hours from neighboring Lofoten to see reindeer. Tourists come from all over the world, but recently there has been an increase in visitors from Asian countries.

The tourism experience offered at the farm is educational in nature. Laila explains "Tourists don't want just information – [they] also [want] education about our life, about the Sami people."

When you arrive to the Inga family's farm, you are welcomed by Laila in her traditional Sami-dress. The traditional clothes of Sami are very distinctive (e.g. a green woolen dress decorated with colorful bands). Laila never goes without her Sami-knife hanging on her hip. She wears boots, mittens, and a hat made from reindeer skin. Her husband wears a traditional hat that can be transformed into a comfortable pillow when sleeping outside herding reindeer. Laila drives a quad to the *Lavo* (traditional Sami tent, much like the ones from the indigenous people of the United States) and picks one lucky tourist who can join her ride up the hill. She is carrying the coffee, soup, and other gear while the rest of the groups walk to enjoy the landscape. This hike up in the snow is not easy for everybody, and Laila comments during the interview that some guests simply do not have the fitness to walk five minutes in the snow anymore.

Once the guests have reached the *Lavo*, they sit down in a circle. The tent can host up to forty people, and there is an open fireplace in the middle. There are oil lamps on the wall and reindeer skins to sit on, a comfortable and cozy change from the cold whiteness outside. Laila welcomes her guests with a traditional Sami *joik* (form of song) and speaks a few words of welcome in her own language. She is not worried that Sami culture is disappearing, but she does worry about the survival of the Sami language that kids have to learn after long days at school. Norwegian has taken over in many Sami households, and the indigenous

Figure 9.1 Laila driving her quad up to the *Lavo*

Sami-languages are severely threatened. Laila wants to share her culture with her visitors and tells them about the reindeer and their Sami herders.

> This [the tourism business] is not just to earn money. Of course, this is my work, but it is also very important for me to tell the right story about the Sami. So that we do not become like the Finnish tourism industry that tell jokes and lies to people. That is also the reason that people can ask me what they are wondering about. I tell them about the slaughter, the bad things that happen. We don't want to hide anything.

The reindeer are the only livestock that are still earmarked with a knife. Every Sami reindeer owner has its own mark that is unique for him or her. When the calves are born, the Sami go up in the mountain to herd them and mark the calves. This is a bloody activity that is carried out with a traditional Sami knife. Laila explains that her 11-year-old son has been doing this since he was 5 years old. He is interested in life as a reindeer owner and has therefore been taught the trade from an early age. When the season of marking approaches, the family practices the marks again on the skin of oranges. Apparently, they are very similar in consistency as the ears of newborn reindeer. Laila further explains to her customers that when the little boy wanted a game-computer he had to pay for it with his own reindeer. He could buy what he wanted but he had to slaughter some of his own animals for it. Value is expressed in life, and children are taught that everything has a price. Laila uses the anecdotes of her family when she entertains the tourists in the *Lavo*. For example, her children are worried when they see reindeer meat on their pizza, in their tacos and soups, and they ask if they had been from their herd or, hopefully, their father´s. The reindeer are slaughtered in a slaughterhouse that belongs to a few reindeer-owning families. Each family is allowed to kill a certain number of animals outside the slaughterhouse as well, in order to eat them or to help them when they are wounded or in pain. The main reason to keep reindeer is for their meat. Laila explains:

> They are there for meat. They are our income. When you slaughter them, we slaughter 80 of them before Christmas, it is just a grey mass of herd. But sometimes when we have to slaughter the animals we are close to, when we see them in the slaughterhouse, it can be difficult. But that is not often. Now I have a big male, my best ever. However, I have not seen him for two years. He is dead out in nature. I know that nature gives and nature takes but I want to know what happened to him. I think about him; where is he, where did he die; did he break a leg; was it an avalanche of snow or stones; what happened? They live in a big area, it is impossible to know for us what happened.

So, although the reindeer are livestock and their owners depend on them for their livelihood, meat production is artisanal and has a relatively small scale. Laila and her family care about their reindeer and their wellbeing. However, the life of reindeer is not easy, and every year as much as 5 % of the herd never returns from the mountains. They are taken by avalanches of snow or stones, attacked by eagles or lynx, or they are just unlucky in the steep terrain. They have to find their own food of lichens and mosses and are continuously on the move in search of food. A reindeer can smell moss through a meter of snow, so they are even out looking for food during the harsh, cold, and dark winter of Northern Norway. However, for a few years some animals of the herd are allowed to camp near the farm for when tourists come to see them. Laila comments:

> It is very important to always think about the reindeers' welfare. All these reindeer that are back home right now will be set free again in April . . . I change them each and every year. You cannot use the same animals within the fence all the time; it is against nature.

After Laila´s story in the *Lavo*, the group of tourists are allowed in the reindeer herd that is fenced in on the farm. These reindeer eat pebbles specially made from wild grasses and mosses. They love to be hand fed by tourists, and they all come to get their treats. The tourists have to be careful not to get their scarves entangled in large antlers, and the reindeer are happy to nibble and cuddle. However, it requires selection of the right individuals that can be used for tourists. Laila explains that she chooses the ones that are tamer and not afraid of people.

> Today there was a small black calf who was very tame, he has only been home five or six weeks but is already good with people. Him I should use. I will set him free and he will come back next year when he has grown. But I will recognize him. He will eat from people's hand.

Although a good nature helps, it requires also nurturing from Laila to tame the tourism-herd. It is an investment in the tourism experience product:

> I use a lot of time on the animals I keep here. When this herd came back before Christmas, the calves had never seen people, besides the earmarking. And that was not a good experience, so they are very afraid of people. I use a lot of time together with them to make them tame. I take my morning coffee and go out there and sit down with them. Just to be there so they can handle to see me. Then I start to walk slowly and try to make them get used but it takes some weeks. But it takes them not much time to understand that they see me, it means they get something to eat. That is how we tame them, with something to eat. But it takes a lot of time. It is important to take care of them, to follow them and to have a tame herd.

Most people check out their earmarks and look at the animals' legs to imagine a pair of Sami shoes. Laila has explained that the best parts of the animal for making shoes are the lower legs and face. Laila knows all animals within the fence and they all have their unique personalities, names, and stories. Some have lived wild for many years before they made the switch to tourism reindeer. Others were born with such charming personalities that they are kept for interaction with tourists

Figure 9.2 Tourists interacting with reindeer at Inga Sami Siida

from a young age. Laila uses the reindeer's uniqueness and personalities to get her guests immersed in the experience:

> The reindeer have personalities and I often use examples and tell the tourists about it; why does Little Brother has that name? Why has Maggi that name? Why is there one called Kompis (friend) – why do they actually have these different names? Because they have personalities and that is why they get the names that fit them. For example, Maggi (after Margaret Thatcher) is a bitch . . . she is out now but I bring her back home next year. She can be free one more year. She has got a big calf. And all the other reindeer are so afraid of Maggi. And I tell these things to the guests and when they are in the fence they say 'Ow I can see that she is bitchy.'

As Laila points out several times during our conversation, being fenced in is not natural for reindeer, and this might cause some problems:

> The reindeer´s welfare is number one; always. In the summer we sometimes have problems to keep the herd here because of the flies; they eat them. The first year I kept them the whole year, this was in 2010, and I had big troubles in the summertime and I had to set them free because they went crazy.

The herd counts a handful of castrated males as well. The male reindeer are larger and have bigger antlers that they use for fighting in the mating season. Many males have to be slaughtered because otherwise there would be too much fighting in the herds. However, the most beautiful and tame ones can live as tourism reindeer until they are too old or their teeth are worn down from eating lichens from stones and ice. When they are not in good condition to live a free reindeer life in the mountain anymore, their life has come to an end. This is a value that comes back in many other Sami–-animal interactions. Animals have to be able to live their natural lives. When the animal is not strong enough to take care of itself in natural circumstances, its life is ended. This happens with herding dogs also. Dogs are very important for herding the reindeer in the mountains. Most often Sami use border collies or other herding breeds. Laila talks about a pact they close with their dogs:

> You make agreements with your animals when you get a new one. For example, your dog. You talk to them and tell them that when they cannot help us anymore, their life is over. I say: 'I don't keep you as a pet. We have an agreement. You are with me in the mountains but when you don't handle this life anymore, your life has come to an end.' You talk to the dog in his eyes. That is how you make an agreement. The Norwegians they can have a dog in a wheelchair just to help them to live longer years. That is not good at all. I respect the dog. They are working dogs. That is their life.

According to Laila, the Sami people respect their animals for who they are by nature, and keeping an animal alive that cannot live a worthy life is cruel. It is animal welfare to select the weak animals and relieve them from suffering. Laila explains that keeping animals locked up is against their nature and this is a Sami-value that she communicates to her customers:

> People are very happy to hear the reindeer are set free because a zoo is a very bad thing; all these animals locked up. It is the same thing when I show them our handicraft, for example a man′s winter cape. It is made of red fox that lived here on the island and were hunted. I explain the tourists I don't use foxes from a farm because I think these farms are so sad. This is a terrible thing, I almost cry when I think about all these animals and their lives . . . I tell my guest about this and they can see that we mean it, that we care. I transmit my feelings to my guest.

After the tourists have cuddled and fed the reindeer for an hour, the group goes back to the *Lavo* to eat. Laila offers a homemade reindeer stew with potato and locally grown vegetables. Some people don't want to eat the animals they have just fed and cuddled, and they get a vegetarian plate. Laila has noticed cultural differences between groups of tourists. Muslim guests will not eat reindeer because they are not slaughtered *halal*; Asian people are very concerned with their health and would rather have a fish-soup; while northern Europeans more often tend to be vegetarian compared to southern European guests. Laila had to learn about cultural differences from the people visiting her and can now accommodate for a wide range of different people. Laila explains that she is very open in her communication with her guests and that this strategy works best:

> I always first tell them about our respect for the animals and the animals welfare. And they understand this and they are very happy to hear about it. I tell them this is not a zoo; this place is made for the Reindeer to help them. I tell them about the slaughtering, why we keep the reindeer, why we do it. They respect me for that. They understand it is necessary. I have to have an income so we have to slaughter to sell the meat, the fur, the antlers. They know the meat does not come from sausages, something you buy in the shop. Of course they can be a little bit shocked but they understand me and they have respect for the way we are living. I have never heard negative things . . . some don't like to hear about blood, they are not comfortable but I think it is important to tell everything. Why should we hide it; it is our life.

The Sami people have depended on reindeer for their survival and consider it a sign of respect to use every part of the animal. Tourism has granted new opportunities as well. For example, every reindeer has a special bone in his hoofs to spread the two toes apart in case of slippery ice or thick snow. The foot becomes wider and acts like a snow-shoe. These bones are considered to bring luck according to Sami beliefs. The lucky bones are now collected from the slaughterhouse, cooked, and used for making necklaces for charm and luck. The Inga family has a souvenir shop on their farm where they sell these handicrafts, meat, and other reindeer and Sami products like knives and crafts made of the antlers and bones.

Hence, the reindeer now help to sustain the Sami people in the twenty-first century, where the experience economy has made its entrance, from a prehistoric nomadic lifestyle to a modern tourism company in just one generation. Although other people have always been interested in what Sami culture has to offer, tourism entrepreneurship presents Sami people with the possibility of deciding for themselves what to show and sell of Sami culture. Inga Sami Siida is a company grounded in eco-tourism values of animal welfare, ecological respect, and education. Laila comments:

> This is education of adult people for many hours. You get tired in the evening and you have to go on and on. However, I love my work and it is so important to tell the right story. That keeps me going.

Discussion

The objective of presenting the case study of Inga Sami Siida was to elaborate on the ethical challenges associated with the animal–human relationship in (reindeer) tourism. One of the challenges that Laila Inga faces is that the life of reindeer has changed because of tourism. They are not roaming free anymore but are kept at the farm in order to meet tourists, at least for a period of time. This has influenced the relationship between human and reindeer that had been unchallenged for generations of reindeer herders. The starting point of this chapter was the assumption that it is morally right to use an animal as long as this animal has had a worthy life. The reindeer owners are responsible for the wellbeing of their herd, and the development of tourism means reconsidering how this new relationship between animal and man affects the quality of life of the animals involved.

The relationship between humans and non-human animals has been the object of discussion of several philosophers, like Plato, Bentham, and Mill. Western philosophical traditions have attributed a unique and elevated status to the human species. This has led to a dualistic position of humans toward other animals based on reason, language, autonomous will, or even immortal soul. This idea has been challenged by evolutionary theory, where the human species is but one in the web of life. However, in *The Life and Letters of Charles Darwin* (page 461; day 123 of 188, 1837), Darwin notes that people and animals not only have a common ancestry and are developing in mutually dependent relationships, but also that the evolutionary thesis should lead to a reevaluation of the moral character of our relationships toward other animals.

> If we choose to let conjecture run wild, then animals, our fellow brethren in pain, disease, death, suffering and famine – our slaves in the most laborious works, our companions in our amusements – they may partake [of?] our origin in one common ancestor – we may be all melted together.

This idea has led to the development of the concept of biocentric egalitarianism (Taylor, 1986) – an inherent value to all living beings that is derived from their irreplaceable role in complex, evolved, and interdependent systems. Sami-culture acknowledges these egalitarian and social relationships across species boundaries. For example, Laila tells about the bond she has with her animals and the pact they close with, as in the example of their working dogs.

The philosophy of deep ecology also takes on board the idea of biocentric equality. The term deep ecology was introduced in Arne Næss' article entitled "The shallow and the deep, long-range ecology movement: a summary" (1973) and has now been accepted as a very useful terminology to refer to a major division within contemporary environmental thought. Deep ecology is opposed to shallow ecology, which is an anthropocentric worldview. Shallow ecology focuses on fighting pollution and resource depletion. It views humans as above or outside of nature, as the source of all value, and ascribes only instrumental, or use value, to nature. According to Capra and Luisi (2014) the major problems of our time cannot be understood in isolation. We need a holistic worldview, emphasizing the whole rather than the parts, in order to deal with the social and environmental challenges the world's population is facing today. Deep ecology does not separate humans from the natural environment (metaphysical holism) and recognizes the intrinsic values of all living beings and views humans as just one particular strand in the web of life (biocentric egalitarianism). This means the core of the worldview of deep ecology is interconnectedness. Philosophers of deep Ecology like Næss, Devall, and Sessions have argued that one can apprehend ontological interconnectedness through enlightenment or self-realization. The method of self-realization is identification. By identifying and recognizing the intrinsic worth of other living beings, one recognizes the solidarity of all life forms. Hence, a following ethical norm is that every life form has in principle a right to live and blossom (Næss & Rothenberg, 1989). The "in principle" clause was inserted because any realistic praxis necessitates some killing, exploitation, and suppression (Witoszek & Brennan, 1999). Arne Næss explains that for deep ecology there is a core democracy in the biosphere:

> My intuition is that the right to live is the same for all individuals, whatever the species, but the vital interests of our nearest, nevertheless have priority.
>
> (Naess, 1995, p. 67)

Another concept that refers to a form of interconnectedness is "Ubuntu." Archbishop Desmond Tutu, who was rewarded the Nobel Peace prize in 1984, explains "Ubuntu" as connectedness, followed by the ethical norms of human rights and freedom:

> A person with "Ubuntu" is open and available to others, affirming of others, does not feel threatened that others are able and good, for he or she has a proper self-assurance that comes from knowing that he or she belongs in a greater whole and is diminished when others are humiliated or diminished, when others are tortured or oppressed, or treated as if they were less than who they are.
>
> (Desmond Tutu, *No Future Without Forgiveness*, 1999)

Could we take the idea of "Ubuntu" to the non-human world as well? Perhaps Desmond Tutu takes an anthropocentric perspective when he discusses "Ubuntu," but when we think of interconnectedness and the resulting openness, compassion, and understanding as something that transcends the human world, we could arrive at a comprehension of what it means to ethically use animals in tourism. Laila Inga tries to treat the reindeer for who they are and what they need because she is connected to them in a greater whole. However, they are used for food, entertainment, and souvenirs. How can we treat our domestic animals with "Ubuntu" while we eventually use them for our own needs? The philosophy of deep ecology points in the direction of self-realization, as does the idea of "Ubuntu." Laila Inga´s words about her treatment and concern for her livestock seem to share the same values: self-realization and seeing other creatures for what they are can be ethical guidelines for our relationship with the animals that we depend on. However, the difficulty lies in finding out who our domestic animals are and what they need in order to be happy tourism companions that can lead fulfilling lives. In the case of Sami tourism, the reindeer owners grew up with their animals and have a lot of tacit and explicit knowledge based on a lifetime of experience. Dialogue with people who are in close contact with animals, in combination with biological, veterinary, and ecological research, could provide the sources of knowledge to determine what animals working in tourism need. Hence, in all examples of human–animal interactions in tourism, independent of whether the animals are camels, cows, horses, reindeer, or elephants, a dialogue between different knowledge- and value-systems should be facilitated by tourism stakeholders. The needs of animals in order to live worthy lives should be the basis for ethical guidelines for using animals in tourism.

References

Baglo, C. (2008). Visualisations of the "Lappish race": On photos and exhibitions of Sámi in Europe in the period 1875–1910. *Acta Societatis Skytteanae*, *19*(25), 25–49.

Boswijk, A., Peelen, E., & Olthof, S. (2012). *The economy of experiences*. Amsterdam: European Centre for the Experience Economy.

Bulbeck, C. (2005). *Facing the wild: Ecotourism, conservation, and animal encounters*. London: Earthscan.

Capra, F., & Luisi, P. L. (2014). *The systems view of life: A unifying vision*. Cambridge: Cambridge University Press.

Darwin, C. (2016 [1837]). *Life and letters of Charles Darwin: The evolution*. Edited by A.C. Seward. Google Play: VM eBooks.

Fennell, D. A. (2012). Tourism and animal rights. *Tourism Recreation Research*, *37*(2), 157–166.

Fonneland, T. (2013). Sami tourism and the signposting of spirituality. The case of Sami tour: A spiritual entrepreneur in the contemporary experience economy. *Acta Borealia*, *30*(2).

Gáldu. (n.d.). Retrieved 23 March, 2017, from http://galdu.custompublish.com

Hughes, P. (2001). Animals, values and tourism – structural shifts in UK dolphin tourism provision. *Tourism Management*, *22*(4), 321–329.

Kramvig, B. (2011). Orientalisme eller kulturmøter? Tendenser i samisk turisme og kulturnæringer In M. Forbord, G. T. Kvam, & M. Rønningen (Eds.), *Smak, kultur og opplevelser: nye ideer om reiseliv i Norge* (pp. 169–188). Oslo: Fagbokforlaget.

Markwell, K. (Ed.). (2015). *Animals and tourism: Understanding diverse relationships*. Bristol, UK: Channel View Publications.

Müller, D., & Huuva, S. K. (2009). Limits to Sami tourism development: The case of Jokkmokk, Sweden. *Journal Of Ecotourism*, *8*(2).

Müller, D., & Pettersson, R. (2001). Access to Sami tourism in Northern Sweden. *Scandinavian Journal of Hospitality and Tourism*, *1*(1).

Müller, D. K., Saarinen, J., & Hall, C. M. (2009). *Nordic tourism: Issues and cases*. Bristol: Channel View.

Næss, A. (1973). The shallow and the deep, long-range ecology movement: A summary. *Inquiry*, *16*(1–4), 95–100.

Næss, A. (1995). The apron diagram. In A. Drengson &. Y. Inoue (Eds.), *In the deep ecology movement: An introductory anthology*. Berkely, CA: North Atlantic Books.

Næss, A., & Rothenberg, D. (1989). *Ecology, community and lifestyle: Outline of an ecosophy*. Cambridge: Cambridge University Press.

Pettersson, R. (2004). *Sami tourism in Northern Sweden: Supply, demand and interaction*. PhD, Umeå University, Umeå universitet, Umeå.

Pine, B. J., & Gilmore, J. H. (1998). The experience economy. *Harvard Business Review*, *76*(6), 176–+.

Richard Butler, T. H. (Ed.). (1996). *Tourism and indigenous peoples*. London: International Thomson Business Press.

Sundbo, J., & Darmer, P. (Eds.). (2013). *Creating experiences in the experience economy*. Cheltenham, UK: Edgar Elgar.

Taylor, P. (1986). *Respect for nature: A theory of environmental ethics*. Princeton, NJ: Princeton University Press.

Therkelsen, A. (2003). Imagining places: Image formation of tourists and its consequences for destination promotion. *Scandinavian Journal of Hospitality and Tourism*, *3*(2).

Tutu, D. (1999). *No Future Without Forgiveness*. 1999. London: Rider Books.

United Nations Economic and Social Council. (2009). *Committee for Development Policy – Report on the eight session*. Retrieved from http://www.un.org/en/ecosoc/docs/report.asp?id=1121

United Nations Permanent Forum on Indigenous Issues (2009). *State of the world's indigenous peoples*. Retrieved from http://www.un.org/esa/socdev/unpfii/documents/SOWIP/en/SOWIP_web.pdf

United Nations Regional Information Centre for Western Europe (UNRIC). (n.d.). Retrieved from http://www.unric.org/en/

Weaver, D. (2010). Indigenous tourism stages and their implications for sustainability. *Journal of Sustainable Tourism*, *18*(1).

Witoszek, N., & Brennan, A. (1999). *Philosophical dialogues: Arne Næss and the progress of ecophilosophy*. New York: Rowman & Littlefield.

10 The fishy ethics of seafood tourism

Max Elder and Carol Kline

Coastal tourism is a pastime that spans centuries. Early forms of travel to the sea for rest and respite are documented in Europe, North America, and Asia. Coastal tourism is a geographical subsection of the tourism industry similar to mountain tourism, urban or rural tourism, island tourism, and polar tourism; each of which has warranted much attention in the tourism literature. However, this chapter traverses new ground by examining the overlap of coastal tourism and culinary tourism, with a focus on the seafood eaten while visiting coastal or other aquatic regions. While the connection between seafood and tourism has been addressed somewhat (Deale, Norman, & Jodice, 2008; Lacher, Oh, Jodice, & Norman, 2013), this chapter seeks to view the phenomenon through a new ethical lens – focusing on issues concerning biodiversity, public health, animal welfare, sustainability, ecology, and economics – in order to demonstrate "the problem of seafood tourism," as well as to explore some possible solutions.

"Seafood" denotes a mass of swimming protein whose only end is to be consumed by humans rather than an incredibly diverse group of individual animals who are subjects of a life. The use of a mass noun, seafood, as opposed to a count noun, like aquatic animals, only further entrenches the notion that these animals are one collective mass of protein for human consumption. Similar to the problematic term "farm animals" (as opposed to "farmed animals"), the term "seafood" is rather erroneous and, in some ways, reinforces the problems on which this paper intends to shed light. We use the term seafood in this paper, but hope that in the future we move beyond it to a more equitable and accurate term.

The phrase "seafood tourism" will be used throughout this chapter in reference to the activities surrounding the catching, processing, cooking, eating, and learning about aquatic animals, regardless of whether these activities are a primary motivation for visiting the coast or merely part of a diverse coastal experience. This chapter will focus on fish, shellfish (mollusks like oysters and clams; crustaceans like lobsters and crabs; and echinoderms like sea urchins), aquatic mammals, reptiles, and jellyfish, but not sea plants or vegetables.

Drivers of seafood tourism

Seafood has been defined within a tourism context as "coastal cuisine that [is] unique to the region and culture" (Lacher et al., 2013, p. 536). These same authors found that the dining experience, including regional coastal cuisine and the availability of locally-owned restaurants, is often extremely important to the overall coastal vacation experience for tourists.

While seafood tourism is typically centered around the consumption of aquatic animals, it can also include a variety of social and cultural experiences. These experiences range from an "ordinary" meal at a local restaurant to a "catch and cook" hands-on experience, whereby the tourist is guided through each of the "ocean to table" steps in catching, killing, cleaning, and preparing a meal. The latter might involve fishing on a guided boat tour, having a harbor-side experience, or visiting a fishing village and fisher's home (Chen, 2010). Additionally, associated products beyond mealtime such as crafts, jewelry, furniture, and household decorations can be created from crab "pots" (cages), fishing poles, fishing hooks, and nets to be sold as souvenirs to tourists.

There is considerable infrastructure (e.g. wharfs, piers, marinas, fishing boats, pack houses, and outdoor markets) built around the seafood industry, which contributes to the culture, appearance, and vibrancy of the destination and, ultimately, to the tourism experience. As such, tourism marketers have linked together towns or areas of seafood significance to create driving trails. Some examples include the Top of the South Aquaculture and Seafood Trail and the Coromandel Aquaculture and Seafood Trail, both of which are in New Zealand (Sassenburg, Hull, & Jodice, 2009). Seafood festivals such as the Beaufort Shrimp Festival in South Carolina (Deale, Norman, & Jodice, 2008) and the Maine Lobster Festival (see Blankfield within this same volume) are cultural celebrations of local seafood cuisines that draw tens of thousands of tourists annually.

Tourists are also drawn to these locations by the availability of exotic or unusual foods uniquely associated with the destinations. Many types of aquatic animals are sought because of their strangeness or otherness, or because they are a severely threatened species like the sea cucumber (Conand et al., 2014). Consuming exotic foods allows the tourist to "embody" the destination and instills "bragging rights." Travel blog websites such as *Go Backpacking* offer suggestions on what regional seafood to eat (Wien, 2013) and *The Daily Meal* features information for the more daring in their post "8 Animals That Are Eaten Alive Around the World" (Govender, 2014). The latter piece alerts the reader that "[a] few of these delicacies are banned in most countries because the preparation of a live animal is considered 'torture' or 'animal cruelty';" the use of quotation marks around the words "torture" and "animal cruelty" from the original text implies that the author does not agree with this assessment and includes this heightened element of the forbidden as part of the appeal. Issues surrounding animal cruelty are treated in depth later, but for now it is worth noting that seafood tourism can be associated with, directly or indirectly, a desire to ingest or even harm aquatic animals in a way that tourists cannot in their home regions.

In addition to consuming exotic foods, some tourists are driven to eat more traditional foods that are embedded in a destination's heritage. Lowitt (2012) describes the multiple facets of this phenomenon in Newfoundland, Canada, and how seafood tourism there is a means to preserving local foodways:

> Tourism establishments are using traditional foods as a way of promoting a culinary experience attached to a particular place. For example, one restaurant operator noted that many tourists haven't heard of 'scrunchions,' a local term for crisp-fried bits of pork fat often used for cooking fish and as a garnish for such dishes as fish and brewis. . . . The restaurant also offers a single cod tongue as a tasting to people interested in trying this local delicacy. . . . At a bed and breakfast, the guests were delighted in the morning to be served fishcakes. . . . One tourism operator I spoke with referred directly to using food to tell stories about a place. He said to me, 'each product you put on your menu has a story to tell behind it.'
>
> (pp. 68–69)

Just as there are a variety of drivers for seafood tourism, so too are there a variety of impacts that are often overlooked and underappreciated.

Impacts of seafood tourism

Biodiversity problems

The ocean is being emptied of its fish. According to the latest data from the Food and Agriculture Organization of the United Nations (FAO), 89.5% of all wild fish stocks are either fully-fished or overfished (2016). In fact, a meta-analysis published in the journal *Science* projected a global collapse of fish in our oceans by 2048 (Worm et al., 2006). Although not entirely caused by seafood tourism, there is a link between seafood consumption in tourist destinations and biodiversity loss.

For example, the Mediterranean Sea is considered a major tourist destination. The Mediterranean not only houses tourists, but it also is home to over 10,000 marine species, or 4% to 18% of all known marine species (United Nations Environment Programme [UNEP], 2010). This makes the Mediterranean one of the twenty-five biodiversity centers on Earth (Meyers, Mittermeier, Mittermeier, da Fonseca, & Kent, 2000). The increased economic and recreational activity in the region "has destroyed Mediterranean fish stocks and caused marine resources to be 'over-exploited' for decades because of increased human activity, amplified demands on marine resources, and innovations in fishing technology" (Gupta, 2017, p. 318).

In 2009, the FAO declared that seafood importation in the Caribbean has been increasing faster in the high-valued groups of fish, and within countries with high tourist activity (Nguyen & Jolly, 2010). Mas (2015) cites similar preferences for expensive species consumed by tourists, which resulted in overfishing of crustaceans in the Balearic Islands in the 1970s, and more recently, a shift in social construction of seafood tourism, as cheaper imported fish products are substituted for local ones in the preparation of seafood dishes.

Additionally, overfishing is closely tied to bycatch, which results in the needless death of billions of fish, along with marine turtles, whales, dolphins, seabirds, and other species. Global bycatch levels (excluding illegal, unreported, and unregulated fishing) are estimated at 7.3 million tons annually (World Wildlife Fund, 2015). Bycatch is an inherent aspect of major fishing operations, and it not only threatens ecosystems but also kills a large number of non-target species in an unparalleled manner. In no other context of eating animals is there such unnecessary and wanton death of entirely unrelated animals.

Biodiversity concerns are only heightened by our changing climate. As water temperatures rise and acidification increases, the ocean is becoming a less hospitable place. Some projections have found climate change leading to both local extinctions and species invasions as organisms search for more congenial homes, together resulting in "dramatic species turnovers of over 60% of the present biodiversity, implying ecological disturbances that potentially disrupt ecosystem services" (Cheung et al., 2009, p. 235).

One possible solution to these disturbances is to curb the overfishing of predatory fish, which are often among the fish consumed by tourists in coastal regions. Reducing, or altogether stopping, the consumption and thus the overfishing of predatory fish could "act as a key action to stall diversity loss and ecosystem change in a high-CO_2 world" (Nagelkerken, Goldenberg, Ferreira, Russell, & Connell, 2017, p. 2177). The consumption of fish not only threatens biodiversity by pressuring wild stocks, which is an increasing problem in a high-CO_2 world, but it also contributes to a plethora of public health issues.

Public health problems

In light of the dwindling fish stocks discussed above, sometimes purveyors cannot acquire high-value fish to meet demand in coastal regions. When that happens, high-value fish are imported (Nguyen & Jolly, 2010), or different species of fish or farmed fish are substituted in the dish (Mas, 2015). In a study exploring views of marine aquaculture, Davis, Norman, and Jodice (2016) found support from both residents and tourists. Globally, more than half of all seafood consumed is now farmed (FAO, 2016), so tourists are no strangers to eating farmed fish (Grudda, 2010). Unfortunately, aquaculture poses serious risks to public health.

The rampant use of antibiotics in aquaculture raises concerns about antibiotic resistance and the threat of resulting zoonotic pathogens. An abundance of research demonstrates the link between the use of antibiotics for animal agriculture and the increased prevalence of antibiotic-resistant bacteria (see, for example, Mathew, Cissell, & Liamthong, 2007; Witte, 1998). Researchers are now realizing that aquaculture contributes to the same antibiotic resistance issues plaguing terrestrial agriculture. A 2015 review of over 650 papers compared aquaculture and land animal agriculture and found that three quarters of all antibiotics commonly used in both sectors were also important to human medicine, and that various zoonotic pathogens in both meat and seafood exhibited resistance to multiple antibiotics (Done, Venkatesan, & Halden, 2015).

Antibiotic-resistant infection is not a hypothetical threat, but the cause of illness for over two million people in the United States annually, and some 23,000 deaths (Centers for Disease Control, 2013). According to the World Health Organization,

75% of all emerging pathogens are zoonotic, meaning naturally transmittable between human and non-human animals, increasing concern around the risk that industrial animal farming poses to human health (World Health Organization, 2006).

Another public health problem regarding aquaculture is the consumption of contaminants. For farmed fish, "the main contaminants of concern are methylmercury, persistent organic pollutants (POPs), and production drugs" intended to maximize growth and stave off disease, like algaecides, antibiotics, disinfectants, herbicides, pesticides, and probiotics (Gormaz, Fry, Erazo, & Love, 2014, p. 231). Production drugs can be deadly, and at least one study has found a potential link to an increased occurrence of non-communicable diseases such as cancer (Sankpal et al., 2012). The way we raise the fish we eat has vast implications for public health that cannot be overlooked. Consumers, such as Top of the South Aquaculture and Seafood Trail visitors surveyed in 2010, "are highly concerned about sustainability issues around farmed seafood" and, as "health and safety conscious, they prefer to consume fresh seafood" (Grudda, p. 112). Despite consumer preferences, consuming fresh seafood is no solution to the public health problems outlined.

Animal welfare problems

One of the most critical issues within seafood tourism is also one of the least discussed in the literature: the ability of aquatic animals to feel pain. Although some continue to debate the issue, "in recent years most scientists do acknowledge that fish can experience at least something similar to the mammalian experience of pain" (Bergqvist & Gunnarsson, 2013, p. 75). As Sneddon (2015) explains:

> Contemporary studies over the last 10 years have demonstrated that bony fish possess nociceptors that are similar to those in mammals; that they demonstrate pain related changes in physiology and behavior that are reduced by painkillers; that they exhibit higher brain activity when painfully stimulated; and that [. . .] [t]he neurophysiological basis of nociception or pain in fish is demonstrably similar to that in mammals.
>
> (p. 967)

We will not dive deeper into making the case that fish are sentient and thus can feel pain, as others have researched this question in great detail (see Elder, 2014; Sneddon, Elwood, Adamo, & Leach, 2014; Braithwaite, 2010). Furthermore, the precautionary principle lessens the importance of the question, since much more harm comes from assuming fish are not sentient, if in fact they are, as opposed to assuming fish are sentient, if in fact they are not (Bergqvist & Gunnarsson, 2013). So, we treat fish as sentient creatures worthy of moral concern.

When mapping out the problems of seafood tourism, it becomes clear that two industries inflict unnecessary pain on an immense number of fish around the world every year: aquaculture and fisheries. Every year, it is estimated that aquaculture kills between 64–129 billion fish (Elder & Fischer, 2017) and fisheries kill between 1–2.7 trillion fish (Mood & Brooke, 2010). To put these numbers into perspective, it is likely that more fish are killed for food than all farmed land animals combined. The seafood tourism industry is not responsible for 100% of those losses, of course, but it nevertheless drives demand for seafood.

Wild-caught fishing practices inflict pain upon fish during every step of the process, from the capture to the landing and the ultimate slaughter. The capture can last for several hours and, depending on the type of fishing method employed, can result in decompression injuries like a burst swim bladder; death by suffocation as they are crushed by other fish in the net; or death from circulatory failure as their bodies shut down from injuries and stress. Once landed, fish are either left to asphyxiate (suffocate); are gutted, filleted, or otherwise cut into pieces; are frozen; or are clubbed or spiked in the brain to kill them. As Mood (2010) explains, "fish are captured and killed in a manner entirely inconsistent with the concepts of humane treatment and slaughter, and the severity and duration of suffering are likely to be high" (p. 10).

Wild-caught fisheries not only harm the fish being caught, but also other, non-target animals in the ecosystem. Birds, turtles, marine mammals, sharks, and other species are often killed unintentionally as bycatch. The Yangtze River dolphin, a freshwater dolphin native to the Yangtze and Qiantang Rivers in eastern China, was driven to extinction because it was so frequently the victim of accidental death from the fishing industry. This extinction was "the first global extinction of a large vertebrate for over fifty years, only the fourth disappearance of an entire mammal family since AD 1500, and the first cetacean species to be driven to extinction by human activity" (Turvey et al., 2007, p. 537). The vaquita are the next cetaceans on the brink of extinction largely because they too are the victims of bycatch (Jaramillo-Legorreta et al., 2007). These are just two examples of species being severely harmed because they are accidentally killed in the fishing industry.

The animal welfare issues associated with aquaculture can be generally grouped into the following three categories: "(1) physical issues of pain, disease, immunosuppression, and skeletal malformations due to breeding, (2) behavioral issues of overcrowding, aggression, abnormal behavior, and repression of natural swimming and social behavior, and (3) stress issues of fear, exhaustion, food deprivation and starvation" (Bergqvist & Gunnarsson, 2013, p. 96). During breeding, growth, capturing, handling, and slaughter, fish face pain that can parallel and sometimes exceed the plight of farmed land animals. Due to space constraints, we will focus on a few welfare concerns with farmed salmon as an illustrative example of the larger aquaculture industry.

Sea lice can be particularly parasitic for farmed fish, especially juvenile salmon who are lethally vulnerable (Torrissen et al., 2013). Sea lice bore into the flesh of fish, often eating all the way down to the skull, creating what the aquaculture industry has called "the death crown." Sea lice prevalence in farms on the west coast of Canada has been measured at about 30,000 times higher than normal levels, leading to an infection rate of juvenile salmon 73 times higher than normal (Liu, Sumaila, & Volpe, 2011). Farmed salmon are not only literally eaten alive in these farms, but they also often cannot hear – recent research on farmed salmon found a 28–50% loss of functionality of one of the primary hearing structures in the inner ear (Reimer, Dempster, Warren-Myers, Jensen, & Swearer, 2016).

These aforementioned conditions can stunt growth and produce what are called "drop out" fish, or fish whose growth is so stunted that their motor functions cease, eventually leading to their death. In 2016, researchers studied these drop out fish by monitoring their cortisol production and serotonin levels. Their conclusion was that drop out salmon exhibit depression-like symptoms due to the stressful situations they are forced to endure and as a result, become incapable of survival (Vindas et al., 2016). While it might seem clear that there are numerous concerns regarding seafood tourism, tourists can be so disconnected from the seafood supply chain that they fail to see the welfare issues of the underwater conditions that produce their meals.

Sustainability problems

Many discussions about eating meat include an analysis of the greenhouse gas (GHG) footprint, sometimes called the "hoofprint." Red meat is often criticized as having the largest GHG footprint, primarily due to the methane gas emitted by cows. A recent study on cow hoofprints found that "nationally substituting beans for beef, on an equal energy and protein basis, can achieve 25% – 50% of the reductions needed to meet the US 2020 greenhouse gas target" (Harwatt, Sabate, Eshel, Soret, & Ripple, 2016). While hoofprints are certainly a problem, it often overshadows the increasingly large and overlooked GHG "finprint" of seafood.

To assess the true GHG impact of a product, one must account for the impact that product has across its entire lifecycle. When it comes to seafood, it is important to note that the GHG finprint "does not only include emissions directly from the value chain of the product, but also from the production and distribution of material and energy commodities and infrastructure that underpins the products [*sic*] life cycle" (Hognes, Garrett, & Ziegler, 2014, p. 10). Therefore, a true finprint would take into account the emissions from the fuel used, the on-board refrigeration, and the transportation of the fish, among many other elements.

Tilman and Clark (2014) performed a meta-analysis of 555 lifecycle analyses of eighty-two different types of crops and animal products, including seafood. They found wide variation of finprints for various seafood products depending largely on the method of capture. For example, they found that seafood caught by trawling, in which nets are dragged across the ocean floor, "has emissions per gram of protein about 3 times those of non-trawling seafood" primarily due to the fuel requirements of dragging a net across the seabed (p. 518). For each variable (per gram of protein, per kilocalorie, and per USDA serving size), seafood from trawling fisheries had a higher finprint than poultry, pork, butter, eggs, and dairy. In fact, when kilocalories are the point of comparison, the upper end of the trawling finprint range and the recirculating aquaculture finprint range are both higher than the upper end of the ruminant meat (cows, sheep, and goats) hoofprint range.

Additionally, finprints are only getting bigger, especially in light of the biodiversity concerns and dwindling fish stocks already discussed. Unsurprisingly, "[m]odern commercial fisheries are heavily dependent on the input of fossil fuels throughout their supply chains, particularly diesel inputs to fishing vessels" (Parker, Vázquez-Rowe, & Tyedmers, 2015). As fish stocks shrink, vessels are forced to fish farther away from shore for longer periods of time, increasing the amount of diesel fuel used. The more fuel used to catch the same number of fish means a larger finprint. Across a multitude of environmental factors like GHG emissions, energy use, and acidification potential, a diet of seafood is from 2 to 25 times more harmful than a plant-based diet per kilocalorie (Clark & Tilman, 2017). All of this points to the importance of both production and consumption decisions, the latter being something over which the seafood tourist has significant control.

Ecological problems

The impact that fishing has on ecosystems, beyond the challenges to biodiversity previously discussed, depends largely on the fishing method. The most destructive method is trawling, introduced above. Direct effects of trawling "include scraping and ploughing of the substrate, sediment resuspension, destruction of benthos [the flora and fauna found on the bottom of the ocean], and dumping of processing waste. Indirect effects include post-fishing mortality and long-term trawl-induced changes to the benthos" (Jones, 1992, p. 59). Trawling, which damages the seafloor, has been compared to the destructive practices of both strip-mining on land and clear-cutting in forests, but the difference is "that trawling is conducted on a scale about 50 times greater" (Brown et al., 1998, p. 7). Thus, many mistakenly turn to fish farming as a more ecologically-friendly alternative.

Aquaculture is the fastest growing food production system in the world, growing at an annual rate of 8.6% (World Wildlife Fund, 2015). However, the World Wildlife Fund (2015, p. 17) reports that, "[i]n many countries, aquaculture production has depleted key ecosystems like mangroves, polluted aquatic environments and potentially reduced climate change resilience for coastal communities." Governing bodies and scientific communities have recognized these issues and called for more protective regulations and economic disincentives. However, national governments and industry partners are historically slow to respond.

In a quantitative analysis of State of the World Fisheries and Aquaculture (SOFIA) reports from 1995–2016, Lobo and Jacques (2017) found a disproportionate number of references to fishing productivity and considerably low attention to the increasing complexity of management caused by climate change, acidification, loss of biodiversity, and other key issues such as plastic pollution. The authors conducted this study within the context of recent efforts to focus more on sustainability, as the fisheries industries and the agencies that govern them are recognizing the intense peril they can suffer as the marine ecosystem continues to be compromised. They appraise the findings with an alarming summary (Lobo & Jacques, 2017, p. 32):

> However, perhaps the most surprising finding is the lack of comparative attention to fishery problems themselves, indicated by only 670 mentions from words 'depletion,' 'collapse,' 'overfishing/harvesting' within the overfishing category. Tellingly, there is almost twice as much concern for Illegal, Unreported, and Unregulated fishing. Related, subsidies – an issue that is widely held as a perverse problem in overfishing – are only brought up 249 times over the twenty-year period . . . over half of that interest was confined to 2002 and 2004 and has declined nearly every report since. This is a remarkable trend, given the increasing recognition that public funding of overfishing is comparatively low-hanging fruit for a pernicious problem, but the reticence of national interests to eliminate things like fuel subsidies to fleets in a race to the bottom of the world's fisheries shows just how much economistic values and sheer quantity of catch are working away at the marine food web.

Although clearly a complex issue, the ecological impact of seafood consumption can no longer afford to go unnoticed. It might not be visible on our plates, but it becomes clear when we look beyond our gustatory pleasures and into our oceans.

Economic problems

Within the U.S., the predominance of research on seafood tourism within the tourism literature has been conducted in South Carolina and Florida, and it has an economic focus. Positive impacts of the industry include the economic support of local fisherman (Deale, Norman, & Jodice, 2008) and, in the case of marine aquaculture, economic diversification within communities that previously relied on wild-capture fisheries (Davis, Norman, & Jodice, 2016). The development of seafood-focused tourism, such as a seafood trail, can also promote networking and collaboration within and across communities and local economic sectors (Sassenberg, Hull, & Jodice, 2009). Additionally, when this development is supported by government entities, it can increase financial investment within the community for harbors, markets, visitor centers, rest stops, lodging properties and restaurants, and subsidies to support tourism businesses, as well as aid in policy changes that lessen restrictions for fishermen and tourism providers (Chen, 2010; Cheong, 2003).

Whether the impacts of seafood tourism are viewed as positive or negative depends upon your perspective or, more accurately, your position in the supply chain. Nguyen and Jolly (2010) note that tourism has a positive impact on seafood imports whereby high-value fish are brought in for tourists. However, these imports can negatively affect domestic fisheries. Whereas typically a price increase has been shown to benefit domestic fisheries, an increase in price on all fish may have a negative effect on local resident consumer groups (Nguyen & Jolly, 2010). This means local residents who would otherwise consume this food cannot afford even so-called "low-value" fish due to the overall price increases that the tourist market engenders.

Tourism also "shapes the preferences for certain species," especially within economically developing nations (Comen & Naeher, 2017; Rodrigues & Villasante,

2016, p. 33). Additionally, Rodrigues and Villasante (2016) explain that "Tourists may start targeting seafood once consumed mostly by the local population. Such changes could result in negative impacts on local food security, considering that the access to protein sources other than fish is already reduced in the country" (pp. 40–41). Within traditional economies, tourism can greatly affect the distribution of income among stakeholders in the seafood industry. Restaurateurs who cater to tourists have high profit margins and therefore much higher average salaries than other members of the industry: fishers, traders, distributors, and market managers (Rodrigues & Villasante, 2016). Moreover, in many areas the fishing industry is now dominated by low-wage immigrants as opposed to long-time local resident fishers (Mas, 2015). Indeed, recent reports from Associated Press (2016) have uncovered a range of instances whereby the seafood sector is sustained by slave labor. The link between seafood and human trafficking cannot be ignored.

In a study set in Taiwan which examined policies related to fisheries diversification and merging of fishing with tourism, Chen (2010) documents a host of resulting social and economic challenges. Among these were wasteful spending of public funds, lack of community capacity to plan for changes, and low market penetration. Examining a similar shift to "fisheries tourism" in Korea, Cheong (2003) notes an increase in privatization of lands previously devoted to fishing, which in turn led to less local participation in tourism, less community buy-in, diminished sense of place, and higher economic leakage.

Torres (2003) studied the food system in Cancún, Mexico, and attributes the high cost of seafood to "the monopolistic market for fresh seafood, strong demand by tourists, and depleted stocks from over-fishing" (p. 554), noting specifically that the seafood industry in Mexico is controlled by a small group of powerful suppliers. These suppliers have business arrangements with fishing cooperatives and/or engage in a vertical integration of sorts by employing their own fishing fleets. Additionally, the desire to cater to tourism markets has bred a disproportionate channel in the supply chain, resulting in unsavory business practices. Torres (2003, p. 553) states that "In interviews with suppliers and chefs, the seafood supply network has been referred to as a 'mafia' that is particularly notorious for the 'incentives' they offer to chefs and food and beverage managers."

Smith and Zeller (2016) assert that the "dual demand" for seafood by residents and tourists at a destination must be carefully documented and managed. However, accounts of catches attributed to the tourist industry are lacking, making it difficult to assign an exact level of responsibility of unsustainable pressures on fisheries and aquatic environments. The demand for seafood from tourists can also put a strain on local government officials as they must attempt to regulate fishing laws designed to protect limited natural resources. Honey and Krantz (2007, p. 19) explain that "[l]ocal governments are often poorly equipped to monitor and enforce fishing guidelines – especially when demand by tourists for prized varieties of fin fish and shellfish can generate relatively high amounts of foreign currency."

Finally, fishing for seafood contributes to a phenomenon called "ocean grabbing." This term is applied to "actions, policies or initiatives that deprive small-scale fishers of resources, dispossess vulnerable populations of coastal lands, and/or undermine historical access to areas of the sea. Rights and access to marine resources and spaces are frequently reallocated through government or private sector initiatives to achieve conservation, management or development objectives with a variety of outcomes for different sectors of society" (Bennett, Govan, & Satterfield, 2015, p. 61). Ocean grabbing occurs when a governing body and/or corporate interest influences the reallocation of marine resources away from small-scale fishers or fisheries. Examples include the transfer of publicly-owned mangrove forests to private firms, the eviction of indigenous communities to provide better access to aquatic resources for global "development projects," or even the designation of marine parks that disallow small fishers from accessing waters that they have historically used.

In instances of ocean grabbing, fishing communities are denied physical or legal access to marine resources, or the resources themselves no longer provide a productive livelihood because of overfishing, pollution, or destruction of habitat by large-scale industrial firms. (See Franco, Vervest, Feodoroff, Pedersen, Reuter, & Barbesgaard, 2014 for a fascinating review of this topic). Ocean grabbing intersects with seafood tourism when the disproportionate demand for seafood creates a shift in allocation of ocean resources for fishing high-value fish. In this case, small-scale community-based fishing operations are commonly replaced with mass capture of seafood by larger companies.

Possible solutions

Methods for addressing "the problem of seafood tourism" are multi-faceted. Within the tourist product itself, an emphasis on tourism that helps, as opposed to harms, the ecosystem and animals would represent a start. Alternatives to seafood tourism would include traveling to coastal destinations and patronizing restaurants, markets, and other food businesses that focus on permaculture and other alternatives to industrial farming and fishing. Or, simply avoiding the consumption of seafood during tourist excursions altogether. Examples of additional solutions are listed below.

1 Infusing more education about aquatic animals, their habitats, and the "fishy ethics of seafood" into tourism experiences would help visitors gain awareness of the impacts they cause through their seafood demand not only while traveling but also at home. Marine conservation organizations should become more heavily involved in coastal tourism by educating consumers about the impact of their choices. As Carl Safina, famed marine ecologist, writes, we need to "extend our sense of community below the high-tide line" (1998, p. 439).

2 Emphasize maritime heritage activities and related outdoor recreation opportunities as quintessential experiential tourism products, downplaying current coastal dishes. Just as trophy hunting in some regions has shifted to non-violent safaris, so too can seafood tourism can shift toward activities like whale watching, snorkeling, or other characteristically-coastal activities.

3 Reduce portions. Putting aside the larger issue of overeating that plagues much of the west, tourists can both reduce portions and adopt a "reducetarian" diet where seafood consumption in general is reduced. Just like the 'beans for beef' scenario discussed earlier, tourists can substitute local plant-based foods for fish as center-of-plate items. Those plant-based foods can still be aquatic; seaweed, oysters, and other potentially carbon-neutral products are considered a delicacy in some regions of the world.
4 Focus on bivalve consumption. Bivalves – oysters, scallops, clams, and mussels – already play a significant role in seafood tourism. Either farmed or wild-caught, bivalve consumption is better than other aquatic animals when considering the animal welfare, food security, and environmental impacts (Jacquet, Sebo, & Elder, 2017).
5 Consume plant-based and cultured (or "clean," meaning real fish tissue grown outside of fish bodies) seafood whenever and wherever possible. Plant-based and cultured seafood offer the opportunity to decouple aquatic food production and consumption from coastal regions. In the future, people might travel to a landlocked region to sample fresh seafood acquired that day (or hour) from plants or bioreactors. Both plant-based and cultured seafood companies already exist. (See, for example, Good Catch or New Wave Foods for plant-based seafood products, and Finless Foods or Hampton Creek for development of cultured seafood products.)
6 Promote vegan or vegetarian menu and restaurant options in coastal destinations. An aversion to animal products does not mean an aversion to travel (vegans like the beach too). Vegan coastal tourism circumvents most, if not all, of the problems of seafood tourism discussed here.
7 Abstain from travel. While certainly the most extreme solution to the effects of seafood tourism, abstaining from taking a seafood vacation provides a two-fold benefit to global issues. First, it reduces the demand for seafood, thereby diminishing overfishing and the myriad of related ethical problems. Second, the emissions saved from staying at home will prevent further damage to the atmosphere and resulting climate change.

Any attempt to solve some of these problems will likely involve a portfolio approach of many of the solutions above. However, the first step in combating these issues is the recognition of their existence. The second step is aligning one's values with one's actions. Tourists, as well as everyday consumers for that matter, often claim to be anti-animal cruelty or pro-environmental sustainability, but their actions rarely align with those values. While traveling, there is a real opportunity for ethical frameworks to align with ethical behavior. There is also a real urgency, as the global diet in 2050 is expected to contain 82% more fish and seafood than diets in 2009 (Tilman & Clark, 2014).

The decision of what to eat is an ethical choice made at least three times a day, every day. As far back as 1826, the French gastronome Jean Anthelme Brillat-Savarin said: "Tell me what you eat, and I will tell you what you are" (2009, p. 15). The travel choices we make, and correspondingly the food we consume while traveling, are expressions of who we are and the kind of world in which we want to live. We can align our values to reflect that world every time we sit down with a plate in front of us. The problem of seafood tourism has historically been underappreciated, but every tourist can be empowered to help turn the tides to create a more humane, sustainable, and ethical future.

References

Associated Press. (2016). *Seafood from slaves*. Retrieved from www.ap.org/explore/seafood-from-slaves/ (Reference note: The Associated Press team consisted of Martha Mendoza, Robin McDowell, Esther Htusan, and Margie Mason).

Bennett, N. J., Govan, H., & Satterfield, T. (2015). Ocean grabbing. *Marine Policy, 57*, 61–68.

Bergqvist, J., & Gunnarsson, S. (2013). Finfish aquaculture: Animal welfare, the environment, and ethical implications. *Journal of Agricultural and Environmental Ethics, 26*, 75–99.

Braithwaite, V. (2010). *Do fish feel pain?* Oxford: Oxford University Press.

Brillat-Savarin, A. (2009). *The physiology of taste: Or, meditations on transcendental gastronomy* (M. F. K. Fisher, Trans. & Ed.). New York: Alfred A. Knopf.

Brown, L., Flavin, C., French, H., Abramovitz, J., Bright, C., Dunn, S., . . . Tuxill, J. (1998). *State of the world 1998: A Worldwatch Institute report on progress toward a sustainable society*. New York: W.W. Norton & Company.

Centers for Disease Control, U.S. Department of Health and Human Services. (2013). *Antibiotic resistance threats in the United States, 2013*. Retrieved from www.cdc.gov/drugresistance/pdf/ar-threats-2013-508.pdf

Chen, C. L. (2010). Diversifying fisheries into tourism in Taiwan: Experiences and prospects. *Ocean & Coastal Management, 53*(8), 487–492.

Cheong, S. M. (2003). Privatizing tendencies: Fishing communities and tourism in Korea. *Marine Policy, 27*(1), 23–29.

Cheung, W., Lam, V., Sarmiento, J., Kearney, K., Watson, R., & Pauly, D. (2009). Projecting global marine biodiversity impacts under climate change scenarios. *Fish and Fisheries, 10*(*3*), 235–251.

Clark, M., & Tilman, D. (2017). Comparative analysis of environmental impacts of agricultural production systems, agricultural input efficiency, and food choice. *Environmental Research Letters, 12*, 1–11.

Comen, T., & Naeher, E. (2017). Sustainable food sourcing. In M. Honey & S. Hogenson (Eds.), *Coastal tourism, sustainability, and climate change in the Caribbean, Volume II: Supporting activities*. New York: Business Expert Press.

Conand, C., Polidoro, B., Mercier, A., Gambao, R., Hamel, J., & Purcell, S. (2014). The IUCN red list assessment of aspidochirotid sea cucumbers and its implications. *SPC Beche-de-mer Information Bulletin, 34*, 3–7.

Davis, J., Norman, W. C., & Jodice, L. W. (2016, February 22–26). Support for mariculture among residents and tourists in South Carolina and Florida coastal communities. Presentation at the *World Aquaculture Society meeting, Aquaculture 2016*, Las Vegas, Nevada.

Deale, C., Norman, W. C., & Jodice, L. W. (2008). Marketing locally harvested shrimp to South Carolina coastal visitors: The development of a culinary tourism supply chain. *Journal of Culinary Science & Technology, 6*(1), 5–23.

Done, H., Venkatesan, A., & Halden, R. (2015). Does the recent growth of aquaculture create antibiotic resistance threats different from those associated with land animal production in agriculture? *The AAPS Journal, 17*(3), 513–524.

Elder, M. (2014). The fish pain debate: Broadening humanity's moral horizon. *Journal of Animal Ethics*, *4*(2), 16–29.

Elder, M., & Fischer, B. (2017). Focus on fish: A call to effective altruists. *Essays in Philosophy*, *18*(1), article 7.

Food and Agriculture Organization of the United Nations (FAO). (2016). *The state of world fisheries and aquaculture 2016: Contributing to food security and nutrition for all*. Rome: Food and Agriculture Organization of the United Nations.

Franco, J., Vervest, P., Feodoroff, T., Pedersen, C., Reuter, R., & Barbesgaard, M. C. (2014). *The global ocean grab: A primer*. Transnational Institute. Retrieved July 10, 2017, from www.tni.org/en/publication/the-global-ocean-grab-a-primer.

Gormaz, J., Fry, J., Erazo, M., & Love, D. (2014). Public health perspectives on aquaculture. *Current Environmental Health Reports*, 1(3), 227–238.

Govender, S. (March 7, 2014). 8 animals that are eaten alive around the world. *The Daily Meal*. Retrieved July 24, 2017, from https://www.thedailymeal.com/animals-eaten-alive-around-world/3714

Grudda, M. (2010). *Understanding visitor attitudes towards seafood and tourism in the Nelson/Marlborough and Golden Bay Region in New Zealand to foster innovative sustainable forms of tourism*. Doctoral dissertation, Auckland University of Technology.

Gupta, A. (2017). There's something fishy in the Mediterranean: The harmful impact of overfishing on biodiversity. *Duke Environmental Law & Policy Forum*, *XXVII*, (Spring), 317–344.

Harwatt, H., Sabate, J., Eshel, G., Soret, S., & Ripple, W. (2016). Eating away at climate change – substituting beans for beef to help meet US climate targets, *The FASEB Journal*, *30*(1), Supplement 894.3.

Hognes, E., Garrett, A., & Ziegler, F. (2014). *Handbook for green house gas assessment of seafood products*. Norway: SINTEF Fisheries and Aquaculture.

Honey, M., & Krantz, M. A. (2007, December). *Global trends in coastal tourism* [presentation]. Prepared by the Center on Ecotourism and Sustainable Development for the Marine Program of the World Wildlife Fund, Washington, DC.

Jacquet, J. Sebo, J., & Elder, M. (2017). Seafood in the future: Bivalves are better. *The Solutions Journal*, *8*(1), 27–32.

Jaramillo-Legorreta, A., Rojas-Bracho, L., Brownell, R., Read, A., Reeves, R., Ralls, K., & Taylor, B. (2007). Saving the vaquita: Immediate action, not more data. *Conservation Biology*, *21*(6), 1653–1655.

Jones, J. (1992). Environmental impact of trawling on the seabed: A review. *New Zealand Journal of Marine and Freshwater Research*, *26*(1), 59–67.

Lacher, R. G., Oh, C. O., Jodice, L. W., & Norman, W. C. (2013). The role of heritage and cultural elements in coastal tourism destination preferences: A choice modeling – based analysis. *Journal of Travel Research*, *52*(4), 534–546.

Liu, Y., Sumaila, U., & Volpe, J. (2011). Potential ecological and economic impacts of sea lice from farmed salmon on wild salmon fisheries. *Ecological Economics*, *70*, 1746–1755.

Lobo, R., & Jacques, P. J. (2017). SOFIA'S choices: Discourses, values, and norms of the World Ocean Regime. *Marine Policy*, *78*, 26–33.

Lowitt, K. (2012). The reinvention and performance of traditional Newfoundland foodways in culinary tourism in the Bonne Bay region. *Newfoundland and Labrador Studies*, *27*(1), 63–78.

Mas, I. M. (2015). The fishing footprint of a tourism-based economy: Displacing seafood consumption from local to distant waters in the Balearic Islands. *Journal of Political Ecology*, *22*, 212.

Mathew, A., Cissell, R., & Liamthong, S. (2007). Antibiotic resistance in bacteria associated with food animals: A United States perspective of livestock production. *Foodborne Pathogens and Disease*, *4*(2), 115–133.

Meyers, N., Mittermeier, R., Mittermeier, C., da Fonseca, G., & Kent, J. (2000). Biodiversity hotspots for conservation priorities. *Nature*, *403*, 853–858.

Mood, A. (2010). Worse things happen at sea: The welfare of wild-caught fish. *Fishcount.org*. Retrieved from www.fishcount.org.uk/published/standard/fishcountfullrptSR.pdf

Mood, A., & Brooke, P. (2010). *Estimating the number of fish caught in global fishing each year. FishCount.org*. Retrieved from http://fishcount.org.uk/published/std/fishcountstudy.pdf

Nagelkerken, I., Goldenberg, S., Ferreira, C., Russell, B., & Connell, S. (2017). Species interactions drive fish biodiversity loss in a High-CO2 world. *Current Biology*, *27*(14), 2177–2184.

Nguyen, G. V., & Jolly, C. M. (2010). Aggregate seafood import demand in selected tourism-reliant Caribbean countries. *Tropical Agriculture*, *87*(2), 40–51.

Parker, R., Vázquez-Rowe, I., & Tyedmers, P. (2015). Fuel performance and carbon footprint of the global purse seine tuna fleet. *Journal of Cleaner Production*, *103*, 517–524.

Reimer, T., Dempster, T., Warren-Myers, F., Jensen, A., & Swearer, S. (2016). High prevalence of vaterite in sagittal otoliths causes hearing impairment in farmed fish. *Scientific Reports*, *6*.

Rodrigues, J. G., & Villasante, S. (2016). Disentangling seafood value chains: Tourism and the local market driving small-scale fisheries. *Marine Policy*, *74*, 33–42.

Safina, C. (1998). *Song for the blue ocean*. New York: Henry Holt and Company.

Sankpal, U. T., Pius, H., Khan, M., Shukoor, M. I., Maliakal, P., Lee, C. M., . . . Basha, R. (2012). Environmental factors in causing human cancers: Emphasis on tumorigenesis. *Tumour Biology: The Journal of the International Society for Oncodevelopmental Biology and Medicine*, *33*(5), 1265–1274.

Sassenberg, U., Hull, J., & Jodice, L. (2009). Exploring the impact of innovation in promoting sustainable tourism development: The role of key stakeholders on the top of the south aquaculture and seafood trail in Nelson/Marlborough, New Zealand. In Proceedings of the Environmental Research Event 2009, Noosa, QLD. *Environmental Research Event 2009*, Noosa Heads, Queensland, pp. 1–12, May 10–13.

Smith, N. S., & Zeller, D. (2016). Unreported catch and tourist demand on local fisheries of small island states: The case of The Bahamas, 1950–2010. *Fishery Bulletin*, *114*(1), 117–132.

Sneddon, L. (2015). Pain in aquatic animals. *The Journal of Experimental Biology*, *218*, 967–976.

Sneddon, L., Elwood, R., Adamo, S., & Leach, M. (2014). Defining and assessing animal pain. *Animal Behavior*, *97*, 201–212.

Tilman, D., & Clark, M. (2014). Global diets link environmental sustainability and human health. *Nature*, *515*(7528), 518–522.

Torres, R. (2003). Linkages between tourism and agriculture in Mexico. *Annals of Tourism Research*, *30*(3), 546–566.

Torrissen, O., Jones, S., Asche, F., Guttormsen, A., Skilbrei, O., Nilsen, F., . . . Jackson, D. (2013). Salmon lice – impact on wild salmonids and salmon aquaculture. *Journal of Fish Diseases*, *3*, 171–194.

Turvey, S., Pitman, R., Taylor, B., Barlow, J., Akamatsu, T., Barrett, L., . . . Wang, D. (2007). First human-caused extinction of a cetacean species? *Biology Letters*, *3*, 537–540.

United Nations Environment Programme (UNEP). (2010). *Mediterranean action plan, Regional Activity Centre for Specially Protected Areas*. The Mediterranean Sea

Biodiversity: State of the Ecosystems, Pressures, Impacts and Future Priorities, UNEP-MAP RAC/SPA.

Vindas, A., Johansen, I., Folkedal, O., Höglund, E., Gorissen, M., Flik, G., Kristiansen, T., & Øverli, Ø. (2016). Brain serotonergic activation in growth-stunted farmed salmon: Adaption versus pathology. *Royal Society Open Science*, *3*.

Wien, M. (January 2, 2013). *Countries for Seafood Lovers. Go Backpacking*. Retrieved July 14, 2017, from https://gobackpacking.com/countries-seafood-lovers/

Witte, W. (1998). Medical consequences of antibiotic use in agriculture. *Science*, *279*, 996–997.

World Health Organization. (2006). *The control of neglected zoonotic diseases: A route to poverty alleviation: Report of a joint WHO/DFID-AHP meeting*, September 20 and 21, WHO Headquarters, Geneva, with the participation of FAO and OIE.

World Wildlife Fund. (2015). *Living blue planet report*. Retrieved June 13, 2017, from www.worldwildlife.org/publications/living-blue-planet-report-2015

Worm, B., Barbier, E., Beaumont, N., Duffy, J., Folke, C., Halpern, B., . . . Watson, R. (2006). Impacts of biodiversity loss on ocean ecosystem services. *Science*, *3*(314), Issue 5800, 787–790.

11 Melbourne, the food capital of Australia

Human and animal encounters in the contact zone of tourism

Jane Bone and Kate Bone

Introduction

Food and tourism inevitably go together on city holidays and in places where historical artefacts in the "new" cities of Australia are not the drawcard. There is an emphasis on Aboriginal culture (the oldest living culture in the world) in the Northern territories; walking and outdoor activity in Tasmania; Sydney has the iconic Opera House and Bondi beach; in Melbourne the tourist emphasis is on eating. Food may be the main reason for a "foodie" trip (Wilkinson, 2016) or just a sideline – in either case, it is of interest in terms of production, marketing, destination profiling, and sustainability. In this chapter we highlight the ethical issues involved in not only making a certain species a tourist attraction but also on making them "killable" (Haraway, 2008, p. 80). In the context of the Melbourne food and tourism industry we discuss some aspects of interspecies encounters that are often unspoken and invisible. These encounters take place in what Haraway (2008, p. 214) calls "contact zones." These are sites where human and animal meet, are entangled, and have competing interests. In this chapter we refer to wild contact zones where animals are in their usual habitat and are not tamed or domesticated like pets or farm animals. The latter contact zone is where the subjugation of the animal in relation to the human is accepted and normalized.

Melbourne is a large city situated on the South Eastern coast of Australia with a population of 4.5 million (Australian Bureau of Statistics, 2016), and it has been rated the world's most livable city (The Economist Intelligence Unit, 2016). Melbourne is in the State of Victoria, an area with the highest ecological footprint in Australia, and food waste and the consumption of meat are identified as factors that need to be reduced if the target to reduce ecological degradation by 25% is to be achieved by 2020 (Environment Victoria, 2014). The Victorian State government released statistics indicating that Melbourne had 2.6 million visitors who spent $6.7 billion AU dollars in the previous year ending September 2016 (Victoria State Government, 2016). Melbourne is a large inland city noted for its art galleries, food culture and coffee. To be a foodie in Melbourne is to fit in.

There are issues, however, with living in a place that is a foodie tourist destination. Residents of Melbourne are bombarded with messages about food and according to one website "you know you are a Melburnian when you find it harder to decide which café to go to for brunch than which house to buy" (Pieces of Melbourne, 2016). Weekend newspapers have a substantial supplement about travelling and tourism, there are the usual back-to-back food programs and food channels on television, and information about food is emphasized on all tourist websites. In this "food porn" culture there seems to be very little that is off limits for people to consume in terms of graphic descriptions, images, and eating experiences (Dejmanee, 2016, p. 429). In the *Traveller* supplement of a Melbourne newspaper details were given of a top experience in Korea; this involves eating "raw octopus tentacles that are so fresh they're still moving . . . writhing, wriggling legs that have to be chewed quickly lest they attach themselves to the inside of your mouth" (Traveller, 2016). From a critical, rather than curious, perspective, we wonder if these descriptions are designed to be desensitizing, to make one accept what sounds like an unpleasant experience because eating living insects and animals is often considered the ultimate foodie experience. At the very least it implies a readership that is open to such shock factor experiences.

In this chapter we refer to food tourism rather than culinary tourism, as the latter implies that the emphasis is on cooking and kitchen skills rather than on the product. There is a crossover, and we acknowledge the point emphasized by Chatzinakos (2016, p. 111), who describes culinary culture as "a strategic pillar for stimulating a sustainable way of 'consuming' and promoting a city's identity." Melbourne has built an identity around art and food. Both aspects are contributing factors to its attraction as a tourist venue as well as its reputation as a city that values diversity. Waves of migrants have ensured that food is a key contributor to this reputation, and the diversity of food available is interesting from the tourist perspective. We also wondered, what was seen as uniquely Australian in terms of food and tourism?

Methodological approach

In our work we constructed searches of websites that are easily available to tourists wanting information about Melbourne. We read guides, biographies, animal rights research, and policy documents, and we engaged with the literature about tourism and food. We also shared our own experiences as tourists (now residents) in Melbourne. Our perspective is not value-free; we are vegetarians and interested in animal rights, especially in terms of gender and equity (see Bone & Bone, 2015), and we concur with Fennell (2012) that not enough attention is paid to animal welfare in relation to tourism. We like to work with theory that supports new thinking, and here we construct an assemblage (Bone & Blaise, 2015; Bone & Bone, 2015) composed of information from our media searches and an analysis of visual images. 'Assemblage' implies a gathering of materials in a way that Fox and Alldred (2015, p. 401) describe as "unpredictable." This approach reflects our method and the focus on the theories of new materialism and posthuman theory (Haraway, 2008). From the perspective of this theory, notions of ethics are not separate but intimately linked to issues about our connections in the world: the material, human, and more-than-human world. We also use the ideas of Donna

Haraway (2008) in order to focus on human–animal entanglements and to discuss what she describes as "the lives and deaths of differentially situated humans and animals" (p. 38). The work of Adams (2015) also underpins our inquiry into what makes some animal flesh more desirable than others and what constructs a "delicacy" in cultural terms. In our analysis we make particular use of Adams' notion of the "absent referent" (Adams, 2015, p. 20). Adams (2015, p. xxiv) explains "behind every meal of meat is an absence: the death of the animal whose place the meat takes. The 'absent referent' is that which separates the meat eater from the animal and the animal from the end product." This lies at the heart of what makes us uneasy and constitutes the basis for our discussion: the absence of the dead animal and the absence of the animal as 'meat' in tourist resource materials. These ambiguities and challenges are presented below by theme; we turn first to a wild animal, endemic to Australia, and then to a domesticated animal, to engage with some of these complexities.

Findings

Wild contact zones

Haraway (2008, p. 4) describes the contact zone as a site of our "world-making entanglements," a space where power relations and diversity can be grappled with. Tourist encounters with animals are a potential site for negotiating difference and there are distinct cultural differences in the way animals are perceived. Sometimes tourists are confused about what the host nation is prepared to offer, as in the following example. National animals, such as the lion and the unicorn in the UK, are usually mythic and revered beasts. We are challenged by the propensity of Australians to encourage tourists to regard Australia's national icons, the emu and kangaroo, as items on the menu.

In her food blog the UK based writer Fuchsia Dunlop (2013) references "Skippy" in relating her tourist experience of Australian cuisine. Skippy, the bush kangaroo, was a much-loved children's television character, and Dunlop describes a reluctance to eat Skippy on the part of many Australians. She however, in her role as tourist notes that "like many foreign cooks and food writers visiting Australia, I was dying to try some of the country's unique local ingredients, and none of them more than kangaroo" (Dunlop, 2013, np). Ms. Dunlop is dying to try it but not as often as the kangaroos and wallabies who occupy an ambiguous place in the hearts and minds of Australians. As Dunlop (2013, np) explains, "although kangaroos are a protected species, there are so many of them that they are widely regarded as pests." This is an example of a tourist text highlighting "a struggle of conscience" as "the adulation of animals, juxtaposed with the culinary enjoyment of meat, creates a paradox, from which cognitive dissonance occurs" (Mkono, 2015, p. 223). Dunlop (2013) uses the words "protected species," and she also describes the kangaroo as a "unique local ingredient." In an effort to absolve herself from the moral dilemma of eating a protected and unique species, she adds the word "pest." Ultimately the kangaroo is simply an object of desire. This objectification may result in conservation efforts or may mean that the animal is on the menu, rationalized, and imagined into a unique experience of consumption. Dunlop explains that none of the restaurants she visited in Southern Australia served kangaroo except one, where the chef said that many of the restaurant's customers are tourists for whom "kangaroo is a bit of a novelty meat, like crocodile and emu . . . most local people wouldn't have it at home" (Dunlop, 2013, np).

In Melbourne eating kangaroo is not seen as a problem, and according to one website (Melbourne Restaurants, 2017) the Top Ten eateries in Melbourne all serve kangaroo as stew, burger, steak and fillet. They also dish up "tantalisingly succulent Crocodile and the deliciously gamey Emu." It is quite common for this kind of language to be used in describing Melbourne's indigenous meats. Yudina and Fennell (2013) state that in their analysis of eating camel in Australia's Red Centre, the words are often "highly possessive, violent and pornographic." In this way, the Melbourne site makes it clear to tourists that the national animals are edible and available. On websites the word "sourced" elides terms like shot, trapped, and hunted. Kangaroos are described as "wild game" (Paroo Premium Kangaroo, n.d.). This implies that out there in the outback something playful might be going on, this is far from the case. Kangaroos are shot with impunity and are a staple of the pet food trade. In 2012 the Australian government gave permission for 5 million kangaroos to be slaughtered for commercial purposes (Animals Australia, 2016).

Kangaroo supply chains

A supplier of kangaroo meat (Paroo Premium Kangaroo, n.d.) mentions on their website that they only target male kangaroos. Because baby roos, or joeys, spend a long time in their mothers' pouches, the image in the mind of consumers of roo babies being bludgeoned next to the body of their dead mothers would reduce appetite for the meat. Research carried out indicates that in fact when "chillers" (freezers) at kangaroo meat suppliers were investigated, 70–80% of the carcasses were female (Animals Australia, 2016). Another report estimates that the kangaroo trade results in 440,000 young kangaroos being clubbed to death or left to starve annually (Ben-Ami, 2009).

A supplier of kangaroo meat to restaurants asserts that they "manufacture" kangaroo meat (Paroo Premium Kangaroo, n.d.), thus divorcing it from the animal that has its habitat in regional Australia. Indeed, the attraction of these exotic animals is that they originate in the outback, the colonized domain of white, macho-Australia, the great outdoors, the venue for hunting down or trapping any animal that might interfere with the main "crops" of sheep and cattle. Mahood (2000, p. 51) describes her father's life managing cattle stations as "a constant struggle with broken down vehicles and bores and equipment, of stock perishing and of men pulling out," and yet nostalgia persists through maleness and meat. Adams (2015, p. 4) points out "meat eating societies gain male identification by their choice of food." Hunting and meat eating has long been associated with hegemonic masculinity and valued male traits such as strength, domination, and superiority (Sumpter, 2015). The stereotypical image of this masculine and brutal Australia persists and infiltrates the city through meaty foods which reflect a feeling of entitlement and dominance.

In food tourism the exotic is desirable and marketing is key to maintaining tourist interest. Bell and Lyall (2002, p. 139) note that that "for the commercial suppliers of artefacts and food, it is a matter of recontextualizing products so the tourists will buy and eat." In terms of kangaroo the suppliers have worked with chefs "to capture flavour and texture profiles that have never been achieved in kangaroo" (Paroo Premium Kangaroo, The story, n.d.). Thus, the wild is tamed and modified to suit the consumer palate, and any disturbance to the sensibilities of tourists who inquire where they might eat this meat in Melbourne are soothed. Marketers resist the usual appeal to the palate of eating the young of others (tender, milk fed, suckling). Kangaroo is one of the few meats where the youth of the meat is not mentioned. This is despite the fact that a study carried out over two years found that most of the dead animals were barely in the low 13kg end of the scale and had not reached maturity (Animals Australia Kangaroo shooting, 2016). An argument is sometimes made that eating kangaroo is ethical because it is a sustainable source of meat. However, the number of large male kangaroos is in decline, to the extent that some research suggests that the gene pool will be limited in the future (Animals Australia Kangaroo shooting, 2016). Another drawback of eating kangaroo is that investigators found kangaroo meat to be contaminated by bacteria including E. coli, streptococcus, and staphylococcus (Ben-Ami, 2009). These problems make it hard to understand the attraction of eating kangaroo and the ethics of promoting it as suitable for tourist consumption. Another ambiguity lies in the fact that tourists can be presented with kangaroo on a plate, and yet kangaroos are also a major tourist attraction at wildlife sanctuaries.

The wildlife sanctuary

Another ambiguity in Melbourne is in the "contact zone" between tourist and animal found at a premier tourist site: the Healesville wildlife sanctuary. Here a number of tourists go in order to feed and have close contact with kangaroos. This place is described as "a bushland haven for Australian wildlife" (Zoos Victoria, 2017, Healesville Sanctuary), and each day there is a talk where children and their families can "meet some reds and greys, and learn some amazing facts about one of Australia's most iconic marsupials." In this way the kangaroo (and wallaby) is also put to work for the tourist industry as a heart-warming attraction.

In this contact zone that focuses on conservation and education, tourists learn about kangaroos and have the opportunity to think about them as important to the ecosystem of Australia. Many animal-focused organizations think that unless something is done about the widespread hunting of kangaroos they will join the long list of creatures who have become extinct in Australia – what Tim Flannery (2012) has called Australia's extinction crisis. Nowhere is it pointed out that eating kangaroo (or wallaby) is a strange activity. These unique animals attract tourists to Australia and is it not then weird to want to eat them? Again, the undertone of food culture as pornographic and violent is implicit in this desire to possess and destroy the object whether it be material, human, or animal (Adams, 2015; Yudina & Fennell, 2013). Melbourne is implicated in a worldwide activity whereby animals are commodities to be viewed, petted, and also eaten.

Haraway asks "how can animal labour remain (or become) for the animals as well as human beings vital, value making practice" (Potts & Haraway, 2010, p. 322). This question touches on the ethics of, on one hand, a population protecting its wildlife and, on the other hand, promoting killing and eating it. Any challenge to eating Australian animals touches on the right to hunt, indigenous rights and, in terms of tourism, has the potential to be economically damaging as it might make tourists think that their desire for novelty may be denied.

Novelty is of course very high on the tourist agenda, and a primary reason to travel is to contact the new and unusual, and in terms of food, to experience what one will not be eating at home. Melbourne ranks higher than any other state in Australia in terms of food as a tourist attraction (Victoria's Tourism Plan Summary, 2004–2007), and in 2014, 61% of tourists who visited regional Victoria put eating first in their Top 15 activities (Tourism Victoria, 2014). Tourists come to Melbourne to either look at animals (Melbourne Zoo; Healesville) or to go to the laneways, Victoria Market, and docklands where they eat animals. The emphasis is on the cultural experience and the freshness of the product that comes from rural Victoria and the ocean.

Animal encounters on the farm

An aspect of our methodological approach was to talk about first visits to Australia. We both remembered going to Queen Victoria Market and taking photos of the sign outside. This sign in pastel colors features farm animals with a sheaf of corn. The animals invite the visitors to enter, always an irony (Adams, 2015); the cuteness of the animals on the sign in contrast to the raw slabs of meat and dead and live fish and crustaceans (seafood) on display inside. The market is always full, always popular, and like other markets in the world, a prime tourist site, similar to the Tokyo fish market and Smithfield's meat market in London. Again, the dead animal is not present; the animal is alive, as represented, or parts of the animal are objects of consumption. The intermediate process is not detailed and to our knowledge abattoirs are not a feature of the tourist scene. This is because the masses are sheltered from the "abhorrent processes of slaughter" as they experience an "(in) visibility of connection" (Henderson, 2015, p. 595). Adams and Calarco (2016, p. 35) suggest that "the function of the absent referent is to allow for the moral abandonment of a being.," Any violence is hidden, and conscience is protected in order "to render the idea of individual animals as immaterial in the face of someone's specific and selfish desires to consume them" (p. 36). This becomes obvious when tourists go on visits to the farmyard.

In some views, the ethics of eating farmed animals is worse than eating wild animals. The argument is that at least the wild animal has been free to enjoy life, even if only for a brief period. Farmed usually means that animals are kept in sheds and factories, confined and suffering, their lives and deaths an ongoing reproach to the lack of empathy by the human for their animal other (Singer, 1985). In tourist terms this is glossed over in favor of a romantic vison of life in rural Australia. The realities of farm life in terms of the economic bottom line – pesticides, trapping, separating young animals from their mothers, confining animals in sheds, artificial insemination, shit shoveling, and sadly, the depression and suicide of farmers – are not aspects of agricultural life that tourists are exposed to. Websites show that tourists are attracted to the spectacle of the farm as a rural idyll.

The farm visit

A visit to a Yarra Valley Farm is a Top 10 experience on one of the Melbourne tourist sites, and the work of animals in these spaces is an invaluable contribution to the picture of romantic Melbourne. One of Melbourne's largest tourism campaigns that ran interstate since 2001 (Victoria's Tourism Plan Summary, n.d., p. 24) was based on romance; this combined with food contributes to the desire for tourists to have memorable and sensory experience (Bell & Lyall, 2002). On these trips it is important for tourists to be able to touch animals with fur and animals who are young. In one of the promotional photos on the website a woman looks delighted to be stroking the nose of a calf. Later, a similar group of tourists is shown tucking into a roast dinner as part of the experience. This links to an aspect of heritage tourism, the desire to connect with the history of the country, and in this case by sitting down to a "traditional roast." One site recommends Warrook Farm in its Top 15 must visits in Melbourne – it is a place to have "some lovely time up close with animals" and also to eat "Warrook cattle farm award winning pies and delicious country cooking" (Tommy OOI Travel Guide, Warrook Cattle Farm, 2017).

Tourists can milk a cow in the dairy, crack a stockwhip, feed baby calves, and stay on for lunch. A sheep is shown being sheared with children nearby. There is no record of whether the animals are stressed in these encounters, and it is made clear that the human is in charge, with or without the stockwhip. Beef or chicken is on the roast menu, and especially popular, according to the farm website, is "spit roast lamb" (Warrook Farm, n.d.). In this contact zone the encounters with animals can be followed up by eating them, and the pictures show a laughing human adult or child in each frame. The restaurant is called The Homestead, and all bases are covered as it also features "halal meats and Chinese meals" (Warrook Farm, n.d.). The traditional roast dinner has a colonial and gendered aspect, and the "hero of the meal" is of course the roast meat. Carol Adams quotes Inez Irwin (Adams, 2015, p. 153):

> That plethoric meal – the huge roast, the blood pouring out of it as the man of the house carved; the many vegetables, all steaming; the heavy pudding. And when the meal was finished- the table a shambles that positively made me shudder- the smooth replete retreat of the men to their cushioned chairs, their

Sunday papers, their vacuous nap, while the women removed all vestiges of the horror.

The males in the photos (shearing sheep, playing the guitar) are all wearing cowboy hats, and tourists take a "wagon ride" and are urged to return to a mythical romantic outback past and "take a step back in time" (Warrook Farm, n.d.). This strange mix of diversity and the old Wild West is mystifying and denotes that this is an entertainment tourist venue despite being also a "premier working farm." This direction is very much in line with Tourism Victoria's policy to increase the volume of tourists and encourage diversification and development of rural agribusinesses (Tourism Victoria, 2014).

In 2015, a media release noted that after the mining boom Melbourne could lead a "dining boom" (Victorian Agribusiness Council [VAC], 2016). The term "agribusiness" on the whole is about branding and marketing agriculture and increasing the profitability of businesses. What is not mentioned is anything about animal welfare, ethical considerations, or how many of them will be needed in order to keep up with demand. Like the farm visit, a profitable type of agribusiness, there is no mention of how the animal passes from field or pen or cage to plate and how many of them are needed to satisfy the appetites of increasing numbers of tourists. One of the most controversial aspects of Australia's appetite for making animals profitable has been the live export trade. Here we consider the animal who travels.

Live export – the animal travels

Live export is the practice in Australia whereby millions of farm animals are sent to countries, usually without animal welfare legislation, for meat, religious sacrifice, and breeding purposes (Bone & Blaise, 2015). These animals endure long boat journeys, and if they survive being crushed and overheated they are then at a destination that affords yet more "brutal treatment and conscious slaughter" (Ban Live Export, 2017). It has been shown to be more expensive to ship a live animal than to slaughter the animal in Australia and export the meat, so even in economic terms we are not sure why this miserable trade persists. There is also (periodically) an outcry if a whistle blower brings back visual evidence of wide scale abuse and suffering to the animal in the host country. Then there is public outcry as the cruelty and suffering involved in live export cannot be ignored by Australians, whose vote supports these practices. These exposés signify a breakdown of the "Zones of spatial confinement" that "render slaughter processes out of sight and out of mind" (Henderson, 2015, p. 595). In these multiple movements and strange parallels of experience the boundaries between the human and more-than-human animal as traveler is blurred. The outcome is different because no matter how herded we might feel in airports or how objectified as we are processed through customs, it remains a fact that human tourists retain certain privileges and do not have the same experiences as their animal other: to be tortured, hung, have tendons slashed, to be suffocated, tied to the roof of cars, starved, thirsty, and eventually killed and eaten (many thousands die onboard during the harrowing journey). Ironically this trade might be expanded by the tourist experience and promoted by agribusiness. Someone who comes to Melbourne where meat is such a norm, where it is pushed at every point of the tourist experience, may well feel a sense of entitlement to the same "protein" when they return home. Haraway (2008, p. 72) writes that:

> We are in the midst of webbed existences, multiple beings in relationship, this animal, this sick child, this village, these herds, these labs, these neighbourhoods in a city, these industries and economies, these ecologies linking nature and culture without end.

In these existences and relationships, in the contact zone of tourism, what does suffering look like, and is enough done to bring this suffering to the attention of the tourist who has the power and the tourist dollars? Might one be accused of wrecking what is otherwise an innocent and pleasant experience for the tourist by pointing out the paradoxes? These include making connections between the cute baby animal and the body on the BBQ; the animal on the ship and the tourist cruise; the animal on the national shield; and the low-fat fillet on the plate. By drawing these comparisons we do what is only ethical in the circumstances, and that is, become responsible/response-able and share in the suffering (Haraway, 2008) by advocating for change.

These touristic connections are a way of making it clear that as kin, we (humans and animals), have shared experiences, and we share other attributes, for example, the ability to feel pain. Tourist consumption creates a demand for more resources and products. Cities like Melbourne position themselves uncritically as places that are cornucopia of plenty, where food overflows and all desires can be met. Haraway notes that we "eat and are eaten at Earth's table together" (Haraway, 2010, p. 54), and this is what makes us kin. We are kin but not kind to those we are entangled with. She names various contact zones between human and animal, zones of "breeding, agriculture, sports, war, pet relations, pastoralism, technology, medicine, and science" (Haraway, 2010, p. 54). We add tourism as a primary site of entanglement and a major contact zone to consider in ethical terms.

Conclusion: becoming kin/d/er

Our position as academics, sometime tourists, always animal advocates, is to bring forward scenarios for consideration, and we argue that tourism could be kin/d/er. The commodification of the human is bound up with the role of tourist, and the animal is not passive but is actively part of the tourist experience. Animals are not paid, they are not rewarded in any way for their participation, and the odds are stacked against them when profit is put before animal rights and welfare (Fennell, 2012). Ethically the people who give information, run tourist sites, and promote food in tourism could provide more information about the animal. They could avoid untruthful claims about sustainability and tradition. However, as Adams (2015) points out, this would make the connection clearer, would make the absent referent visible, and maybe spoil the tourist experience, as she says "when we turn an animal into 'meat' someone who has a very particular, situated life, a unique being, is converted into something that has no distinctiveness, no uniqueness, no individuality" (p. 190). This is the description of the animal as commodity, with all individuality erased, and certainly this is the animal that most tourists are comfortable with.

Tourists could argue that this form of commodification also happens to them; they are commodities and statistics with their money and passports and privileges. However, the difference is that they are not killed and made into meat. The average tourist survives with photos and new narratives to share, very often stories that involve tasting different and exotic animals (Yudina & Fennell, 2013). Tourists are influenced by context, and in Melbourne it quickly becomes apparent that pleasure and the satisfaction of appetite is on offer rather than an emphasis on ethical food practices or ecotourism. This is despite recommendations by Environment Victoria (2014) to reduce consumption, particularly of meat.

Melbourne is a meeting point, a place of diversity, and, in terms of its food culture, too often heartless. It is a city that participates in the culture of food porn to attract tourism and that benefits from animals in the bush, desert, in wildlife sanctuaries and zoos, on the farm, in factories, on plates, and on ships bound elsewhere. It has the potential to be a place that, from its rich and privileged position, could lead the world in considering ethical approaches to food, and this could be an inestimable benefit to tourism worldwide. Melbourne is a desirable city – but it could also be kin/d/er.

References

Adams, C. J. (2015). *The sexual politics of meat: A feminist-vegetarian critical theory* (4th ed.). New York: Bloomsbury.

Adams, C. J., & Calarco, M. (2016). Derrida and the sexual politics of meat. In A. Potts (Ed.), *Meat culture* (pp. 31–54). Leiden: Brill.

Animals Australia. (2016). *Kangaroo shooting*. Retrieved from www.animalsaustralia.org/issues/kangaroo_shooting.php

Australian Bureau of Statistics (ABS). (2016). Retrieved from www.abs.gov.au/ausstats/abs@.nsf/mf/3218.0

Ban Live Export. (2017). Retrieved from www.banliveexport.com/

Bell, C., & Lyall, J. (2002). *The accelerated sublime: Landscape, tourism and identity*. Westport, CT: Praeger.

Ben-Ami, D. (2009). *A shot in the dark: A report on kangaroo harvesting*. New South Wales: Animal Liberation.

Bone, J., & Blaise, M. (2015). An uneasy assemblage: Prisoners, animals, asylum seeking children and posthuman packaging. *Contemporary Issues in Early Childhood*, *16*(1), 420–417.

Bone, K. D., & Bone, J. E. (2015). The same dart trick: The exploitation of animals and women in Thailand tourism. In K. Markwell (Ed.), *Animals and tourism: Understanding diverse relationships* (pp. 60–75). Bristol: Channel View.

Chatzinakos, G. (2016). Exploring potentials for culinary tourism through a food festival: The case of Thessaloniki food festival. *Transnational Marketing Journal*, *4*(2), 110–125.

Dejmanee, T. (2016). "Food Porn" as postfeminist play: Digital femininity and the female body on food blogs. *Television & New Media*, *17*(5), 429–448. doi:10.1177/1527476415615944

Dunlop, F. (2013). Eating Skippy: Why Australians have a problem with eating kangaroo meat. *BBC blog*. Retrieved from www.bbc.com/news/magazine-23086541

The Economist Intelligence Unit. (2016). Retrieved from www.eui.com

Environment Victoria. (2014). One planet living. Retrieved from http://environmentvictoria.org.au/2014/03/30/one-planet-living/

Fennell, D. A. (2012). Tourism and animal rights. *Tourism and Recreation Research*, *37*(2), 157–166. doi:10.1080/02508281.2012.11081700.

Flannery, T. (2012). After the future: Australia's new extinction crisis. *Quarterly Essay*, *46*, 1–81.

Fox, N. J., & Alldred, P. (2015). New materialist social inquiry: Designs, methods and the research-assemblage. *International Journal of Social Research Methodology*, *18*(4), 399–414. doi:10. 1080/13645579.2014.921458.

Haraway, D. J. (2008). *When species meet*. Minneapolis, MN: University of Minnesota Press.

Haraway, D. J. (2010). When species meet: Staying with the trouble. *Environment and Planning D: Society and Space*, *28*, 53–55. doi:10.1068/d2706wsh.

Henderson, J. (2015). Out of sight, out of mind: Global connection, environmental discourse and the emerging field of sustainability education. *Cultural Studies of Science Education*, *10*(3), 593–601. doi:10.1007/s11422-014-9614-z

Mahood, K. (2000). *Craft for a dry lake*. Sydney: Doubleday.

Melbourne Restaurants. (2017). Retrieved from www.melbournerestaurants.com.au/kangaroo/

Mkono, N. (2015). 'Eating the animals you come to see': Tourists' meat-eating discourses in online communicative texts. In K. Markwell (Ed.), *Animals and tourism: Understanding diverse relationships* (pp. 211–226). Bristol: Channel View.

Paroo Premium Kangaroo. (n.d.). Retrieved from http://parookangaroo.com.au/

Pieces of Melbourne. (2016). Retrieved from www.piecesofvictoria.com/2016/08/you-know-youre-a-melburnian-when/

Potts, A., & Haraway, D. (2010). Kiwi chicken advocate talks to Californian dog companion. *Feminism & Psychology*, *20*(3), 318–336. doi:10.1177/09593535103681 18.

Singer, P. (1985). *In defense of animals*. New York: Basil Blackwell.

Sumpter, K. (2015). Masculinity and meat consumption: An analysis through the theoretical lens of hegemonic masculinity and alternative masculinity theories. *Sociology Compass*, *9*(2), 104–114. doi:10.1111/soc4.12241

Tommy OOI Travel Guide. (2017). Retrieved from www.tommyooi.com/melbourne-attractions/

Tourism Victoria. (2014). *Regional Victoria: Market profile*. Retrieved from www.tourism.vic.gov.au/component/edocman/?view=document&task

Traveller. (2016, December 10). Top food experiences. *The Age*, 16.

Victorian Agribusiness Council. (2015). *Media release: The dining boom agribusiness summit*. Retrieved from www.vicagsummit.com.au

Victoria State Government. (2016). *International visitor survey results*. Retrieved from www.tourism.vic.gov.au/research/international-research/international-visitation.html

Victoria's Tourism Plan Summary. 'Food and wine 2004–2007'. Retrieved from www.tourismvictoria.com.au/foodandwine

Warrook Farm. (n.d.). Retrieved from www.warrook.com.au/

Wilkinson, P. (2016). Foodies and food tourism. *Annals of Leisure Research*, *19*(1), 139–141. doi:10.1080/11745198.2015.1072729.

Yudina, O., & Fennell, D. (2013). Ecofeminism in the tourism context: A discussion of the use of other-than-human animals as food in tourism. *Tourism Recreation Research*, *38*(1), 55–69.

Zoos Victoria. Retrieved from www.zoo.org.au/healesville

12 Munch, crunch, it's whale for lunch

Exploring the politics of Japanese consumption of whales, whaling, and whale watching

Stephen Wearing, Michael Wearing, and Chantelle Jobberns

> Now, because of severe heat waves, deplenishing water tables, crops such as maize and sugar beet being diverted from human consumption to produce fuel, plus a growing and in places more carnivorous population, food is once again at the top of the political agenda and source of conflict.
>
> (Sloan, Legrand, & Hindley, 2015, p. xiv)

Introduction

The culinary relationship between Japan and whale meat is complex and controversial as the following recent press stories indicate. Notwithstanding the controversy, the Japanese government continues to invest heavily in the industry ($50 million USD in 2014) (Zhang, 2015). Despite the global opprobrium directed toward the country for what many see as the needless slaughter of an iconic and endangered species, and even the majority of Japanese consumers turning away from consuming whale products, it is still being served in restaurants all over the country (Agence France-Presse in Tokyo, 2015). Food festivals in Ebisu, one of Japan's famous gastronomic hubs, has been keen to demonstrate "how they really feel about eating the animal (whale)" by attracting foreign tourists to experience it. Lhuillery (2014) reports that tourists are either reluctant or indifferent toward consuming whale meat. A few expressed their moderate willingness to try it as long as the animals have not suffered in the process. Lack of tourist interest has not stopped Japanese producers remaining at the ready to export the product overseas. They have been luring new customers from Malaysia and Indonesia and are producing a *Halal* variety of the product.

The Japanese whaling industry remained small-scale until the end of World War II, where it was seen as one of a number of ways to feed a hungry country, after which time it grew into a significant industry (Zhang, 2015). For the generation that lived and were born straight after World War II, eating whale meat was a staple, and today it is bound up with a certain amount of nostalgia. The younger generation, however, view it largely as a curiosity. The Nippon Research Centre indicates that only 5%of Japanese consume whale meat. Since 1986, the International Whaling Commission has issued a ban on commercial whale hunting, with a legal loophole allowing an exception for gathering scientific data. Japan attempts to obey "the spirit" of the ban by announcing that it only intends to kill a few hundred each year (333 in 2014). In other countries such as Iceland and Norway, however, whale hunting remains without using scientific research as the excuse. In general, there is an ambivalent attitude toward whaling as a political issue among the Japanese as well as indifference toward whale meat as food. Zhang (2015) concludes that with or without international interference, whale meat is already declining in Japan.

History

In 1907 chemist Wilhelm Norman hydrogenated whale oil, converting it into an edible solid fat for margarine. The new technologies opened a new industrial era in whaling, which proved calamitous for the species (Ziegelmayer, 2008). Prior to the twentieth century, whale meat was usually only a staple diet of indigenous communities closer to the Arctic such as the Inuit; after this, whaling attracted both commercial and amateur hunters through the eighteenth and nineteenth centuries. By the mid-twentieth century, many countries had realized the limits to whaling, the possibility of hunting whales to extinction, and the failing whaling industry. The new perception, at least in the 1980s, was that the International Whaling Commission (IWC) moratorium had, and would into the future, put an end to commercial whaling across the globe with every OECD country except Norway and Japan signing on. In 1987, the Japanese fisheries introduced the concept and discourse of "scientific" whaling, as what was seen as a tactical maneuver around the moratorium on commercial whaling. In response to this, close scrutiny was given to the scientific research relied upon by Japanese authorities, and it was suggested that it was more likely an excuse to supply whale meat to the Japanese market for consumption even thought it was predicted that the market would soon die out (Nyack, 2011). Whale meat is sold in Japanese restaurants, including for the consumption of international tourists who desire an exotic and culturally novel food.

In 2009, the growth of whale watching internationally was seen to be spectacular. It was occurring in more than 100 countries, and its economic value was estimated to be worth in excess of $2.1 billion USD per annum in revenue (O'Connor, Campbell, Cortez, & Knowles, 2009). Whale watching had become a valuable resource for tourism, and the destination communities that are able to develop it, with a few indigenous communities still engaged in its consumption (Cunningham, Huijbens, & Wearing, 2012) both historically and currently. With the growth in food tourism (Hall, Sharples, Mitchell, Macionis, & Cambourne, 2003) and the commodification of nature and particular animals through ecotourism (Wearing & Jobbins, 2011), it would seem logical to put whale back on the global menu at least in certain developed countries. Arguments for whale meat and slaughter disguised as "cultural consumption" are at the forefront of the Japanese whaling debate. Consumption is still very active in Japan, Norway, Iceland, the Faroe Islands, and by Basques, the Inuit and other indigenous peoples of the United States (including the Makah people of the Pacific Northwest), Canada, Greenland; the Chukchi people of Siberia, and Bequia in the Caribbean Sea (McGlynn, 2012). In recent times we find a move in Japan to introduce it to tourists with thirty restaurants in the district of Ebisu offering whale dishes at a festival (Agence France-Presse in Tokyo, 2015).

For now, Japan has lost the "whaling for research" debate. This research has supposedly shown that one of the main reasons for hunting the whales is that they eat commercially important fish, and that it is important then to cull the population to save fisheries (Nyack, 2011). The research done consists of such tasks as DNA sampling, physical measurements such as ear bone size, age ID, and most importantly, the contents in the digestive tract. This data on what whales eat has been established in research and it appears there is little need to do further research; a strongly worded resolution to suggest this at IWC was directed at Iceland's whaling industry which commenced a "scientific hunt" as a reason to hunt whales. What is clear from this information it that the consumption of whale meat is central to the debates around whales and whaling.

This chapter will argue that neoliberal models of tourism continue to hold dominance in tourism theory and practice, and hence the ways in which whales are used and valued within tourism. Tourism in the free market economy represents the commercialization of the human desire to travel and exploits natural and cultural resources as means to profit accumulation. Nonetheless, tourism can conserve and preserve an ethic and counter strategies for anti-whaling by showing a different way to understand the lives of these creatures and their relationship with other beings, including humans. For some, the way forward is to support consumption based on traditional cultural use, which is seen as a growing market (Boonpienpon, Maneenetr, Siriwong, & Kovathanakul, 2015). We suggest that the next market for whale meat is potentially in the area of food tourism; other countries have pursued similar directions, such as Australia, where the consumption of kangaroo and crocodile meat is evident in restaurants and supermarkets. The debate around indigenous rights (or cultural rights) as a justification for the consumption of native animals has been extensive in the area of ecotourism; it has been a central platform for continuing to exploit hunting with many supporters suggesting that the indigenous stewardship can be assumed, and so sustainable harvesting will occur; this has been contested (Fennell, 2008) but is used in the debate for the continued hunting of whale meat (Orams, 2001).

This chapter suggests a need to examine the continuing consumption of whale meat in tourism and examines the frameworks that might be used to generate discussion. We suggest the "Global Code of Ethics for Tourism" as a mechanism to ensure the provision of social equity for local community tourism as a shift away from commodified and neo-liberalist approaches to tourism. This code advocates both an ethical and political framework as a mechanism to change the paradigm of practice and analysis. Nonetheless we could also ask what voice within this has been given to the care, protection, welfare, and needs of animals that ecotourism bases much of its commercial enterprise? Does the Japanese argument for whaling based on a traditional cultural consumption of whale meat further open up this debate? What role does food tourism play in this? The discussion raises issues and the consumption of whale meat provides an interesting example and given the likely growth in food tourism and the reintroduction of novelty cultural foods in tourism particularly those associated with traditional indigenous cultures (see for example Selwood, 2003, p. 163), there is some need to examine it.

The chapter presents the ways in which the commodification of animals in tourism has fostered the unethical treatment and valuing of these animals through the production and consumption process. It maintains that without ethical valuing through something like a "Global Code of Ethics for Tourism" the handling of animals in tourism can reach a high level of mistreatment, and it is essential to discuss this especially with the growth of food tourism. There is a catch-22 in the use of whale meat for food tourism; as animals like whales are commodified as food for tourists, this creates a demand and an associated view of whales as meat, so while it also ensures that tourists are aware of whales and issues relating to their existence, they can come to value them as a commodified food source rather than as a protected species. This commodification of species as food for tourism has manifested within food tourism around the world, and as Hall et al. (2003) suggest, a more diverse menu, for tourists supporting local communities and business who can come to rely on ensuring the continued existence of the animals used for that food. This is the particular case in ecotourism, where we find that the approach is even more closely aligned to animals as food, where communities and producers can be found to sell directly to the consumer "via farm shops, direct mail, farmers" and produce markets, local events, and food and wine festivals (Hall et al., 2003, p. 29), thereby seeing food tourism creating a direct link to the communities valuing of animals.

Values

We ask if ethical values are found in the debates surrounding food and tourism, especially within and against the dominant and globalized economic paradigm of utilitarian economics and pragmatism in tourism as the determinant of animals as objects for food. If animals are not treated humanely and ethically in the production of food, or this production contravenes accepted international conventions on animal rights, then a new charter and social action is needed to change the exploitation of animals.

Van Vark (2013) suggests that customers want food they can trust and generally expect the providers to undertake the ethical and environmental sourcing for them. In this chapter we are interested in discussing issues around the idea that if Japan enters the cultural tourism marketplace, will it be able to convince consumers of its cultural right to kill whales and that its supply of whale meat fits within current ethical and environmental parameters? There is no doubt that food tourism at a tourism destination can be classified as a component of cultural tourism (Corigliano, 2002; Richards, 1996); the question for us is would a tourist be happy to consume whale meat with the images that have been viewed internationally of the harvesting of whales by the Japanese whaling fleet, and how would this weigh up against the alternative of whale watching? As mentioned previously, the whale watching industry is worth $ 2.1 billion USD per annum (O'Conner, Campbell, Cortez, & Knowles, 2009) while a report on the estimate of expenditure on food services in 2012 found it was nearly a quarter of all travel expenditure, and that food service was the highest category of travel spend (Liu, Norman, & Pennington-Gray, 2013); this suggests a considerable opportunity for food tourism in terms of economic return. In the global economy of consumption, the brand equity of sushi as Japanese cultural property adds to the cachet of both the country and the cuisine. Bestor (2000) suggests that if whale meat could be added to this brand there may be potential to market it as a part of the cultural tourism experience of Japan.

Use and conservation

The wider discussion that contextualizes this chapter pertains to the ideas of and theories around associating ethical conduct with animal welfare and wellbeing. There is also much discussion pertaining to the classification of activities where whales are the central focus and where we consider whale watching, whaling, and whale meat consumption, and we find that the discussion can be centralized around the activity as either consumptive or non-consumptive (Butcher, 2005; Lemelin, 2006; Ryan & Saward, 2004). Definitions typically refer to consumptive tourism as the removal of an animal, for example through forms of hunting, and conversely, non-consumptive ecotourism where the wildlife is not removed (Meletis & Campbell, 2007). Butcher (2005) believes ecotourism to be non-consumptive; however he refers to hunting as an acceptable form of sustainable tourism. Ryan and Saward (2004) state that non-consumptive forms of viewing ecotourism, such as bird watching, may have negative impacts for the species, and they therefore highlight the zoo as an appropriate alternative. The animals viewed in zoos generally have at one point been removed from the wild, and the zoo could therefore be considered a consumptive form of tourism. It can be said, however, that additionally the term "eco" has become in many ways little more than a marketing ploy to appease the environmentally conscious traveler, which seem to satisfy tourists' needs, if only superficially (Dolnicar, Crouch, and Long (2008), and which has led to the mislabeling of consumptive tourism as forms of ecotourism, particularly hunting and by extension the use of animals for food consumption, which will be discussed in greater detail below.

We suggest that the labeling of ecotourism as non-consumptive, or a benign form of tourism, does not acknowledge its impacts, and it is disregarding and placating the negative impacts forms of ecotourism have on animals and their surrounding environments (Ananthaswamy, 2004; Lemelin, 2006); in this case the use of animals for consumption, and here specifically whales. We would further advocate that without some form of inclusiveness of the rights of animals into the fundamental philosophy and ethic of ecotourism, and by extension food tourism, they are at risk becoming just a commodified product. This then ignores the centrality of animals in the area of food tourism in a tourism industry where traditionally we find concern for the environment rarely the first consideration for those in controlling major elements of the industry – an industry not known to stand at the cutting edge of ethics and ethical practice. (Holden, 2015; Köseoglu, Sehitoglu, Ross, & Parnell, 2016; Sin, 2017).

As the popularity of for example "eco" and nature-based tourism continues to rise, and the ecotourism market establishes itself as a mainstream segment (Cole, 2007; Wight, 1993), so too do the negative impacts of tourism, even the theoretically environmentally conscious ecotourism, have on the surrounding environment and wildlife, and ecotourism could potentially become another form of mass tourism destroying local communities and environments (Butcher, 2005). For untouched areas, the arrival of ecotourism signals change, and while ecotourism, particularly through conservation, is thought to economically benefit the local community, the change may not be supported by all. Ecotourism, no matter how small, will impact the environment. Supporters or beneficiaries of ecotourism may purport that it is an environmentally benign form of tourism with no adverse environmental impacts; however, while scientists and researchers study and document short term changes and impacts from ecotourism, the long-term effects of these activities on a particular ecosystem, species or habitat is unknown (Ananthaswamy, 2004).

Here we examine the rise of sustainable food tourism with books such as the *The Routledge Handbook Of Sustainable Food And Gastronomy* (Sloan et al., 2015) and how this might be reflected in discussion around whalc meat consumption. For example, if we create a market for a certain animal we must allow the supply of it in the marketplace, perpetuating the hunting of wildlife, which then creates an impact on the behavior of the hunted wildlife, this in turn impacts on the breeding patterns as well as a defensive reaction to interactions with humans on the part of the wildlife. Therefore, the hunting of whales (in this case by the Japanese whaling fleet), can make whales wary of interaction with all ships, which can then impact the experience of whale watching tourists. In this dual market of whaling and whale watching there may be a need to compromise the way whales are hunted to ensure the whale watching industry is not jeopardized.

Therefore the change to whale hunting may occur through the tourism industries' consumption of whales for both watching and eating; this discussion raises issues around how food tourism might influence the practices of obtaining animals for this market and may ensure a more ethical or sustainable approach to whale hunting (c.f. Fennell, 2008 on ethics and practice). Examples of this can be seen in the area of ecotourism which generally occurs in locations where accommodation is located close to the animals that are there for viewing, and often those animals are on the menus. In Australia, local operators try to include local product including animals such as kangaroo and sometimes crocodile meat, which obviously encourages the hunting or breeding of kangaroos and crocodiles and makes the human–nature interaction more complex.

Further to this we raise questions around the common view of animals as commodities in the tourism industry, and ethical questions regarding the dilemma of increasing this through placing them on a tourism menu – "view them, consume them" – could be the motif, and where does that leave the welfare of each individual animal? It can already be seen in the tourism industry where canned hunts in South Africa are becoming increasingly popular, and in order to meet demand, underground breeding facilities have been established, where an estimated 3000 lions are held captive. Cheetahs and wild dogs, both endangered, are captured illegally and held captive. This market is fueled by the large sums of money involved; a small lioness is worth R5000 (approx. $625 USD), a large black manned lion is worth R25,000 (approx. $1,327 USD), and a white lion is worth R680,000 (approx. $85,000 USD). The South African government, becoming concerned about their image, is attempting to ban captive breeding not contributing to conservation (Yeld, 2005). Where and how would an increase in this market evolve if food tourism put animals on the menu – a place that whales already find themselves?

Consuming whales

The overnight growth of the whale watching industry has "industrialised the ocean" (Corkeron, 2004, p. 848), and while short term impacts such as increased boat noise and traffic is affecting the whales, the long-term consequences remain debatable (Anonymous, 2004; Corkeron, 2004; Jelinski, Krueger, & Duffus, 2002; Milius, 2004). The validity of whale watching as a non-consumptive form of ecotourism is questioned by Jelinski et al. (2002) and Corkeron (2004), as this implies that it has no impact upon the environment or the wildlife. Changing whale behaviors in the presence of tourist boats indicate impacts and questions this classification. Jelinski et al. (2002) highlight the need for uniform and acceptable levels of interaction between humans and whales, and they predict that the continuation of the whale watching industry in its current form will contribute to the displacement of, and harm to, whales. Due to limited scientific research regarding the type of recreational activities that impact killer whales in particular, disturbance levels will continue to be generalized amongst many activities (Corkeron, 2004; Jelinski et al., 2002).

The whale watching industry has exploded, with significant economic benefits for countries involved (Corkeron, 2004; Jelinski et al., 2002). Hoyt (2001) estimated that the international whale watching industry is valued at over $1 billion USD, and it attracts oven 9 million people annually. As the industry grows, however, so does the number of vessels trailing whales (Anonymous, 2004; Jelinski et al., 2002). Killer whale populations, especially off British Columbia and Washington State, have been the targets of tourist boats (Jelinski et al., 2002), and as potential economic profit entices the involvement of pro-whaling countries such as Japan, Norway, Iceland, and Russia (Gillespie, 2003), whale watching is now being viewed by some as "an acceptable form of benign exploitation" (Gillespie, 2003, p. 408).

There is still much debate regarding the long-term impacts of whale watching. Jelinski et al. (2002) highlight serious impacts of whale watching, such as stress responses and the disruption of their movement patterns, which may affect their ability to locate suitable food. The long-term consequences may be as serious, as decreasing activity and reproduction levels affect the survival of pods (Jelinski et al., 2002). Corkeron (2004) on the other hand suggests that compared with threats and dangers facing whales, such as extinction through whaling – "deaths in nets, prey removal by fisheries, chemical and acoustic pollution" (Corkeron, 2004, p. 848) – the effects and impacts of whale watching seem miniscule and insignificant. Commercial vessels deliberately follow and track the whales, which in some cases lead to whales altering their movements (Jelinski et al., 2002). Off Washington State, the number of vessels trailing only three pods of whales has risen from zero to seventy in just over twenty years, and research indicates that each pod may be trailed by an average of twenty-two vessels on any given day (Anonymous, 2004). Pods in Canada still recovering from live captures for captivity have now been listed by the government as "threatened" and of "special concern" (Morton & Symonds, 2002, p. 71).

Ethics and whales

Environmental ethics often examines and challenges the validity of human behavior toward the natural environment and proposes that human behavior be based on ethics and morals – that is what we believe the right behavior to be – not what human behavior has historically been. Environmental ethics is concerned with defining the obligations and responsibilities we as humans have toward the environment, including all animals, plants, and humans (Holden, 2003). There are different environmental ethics perspectives, including conservation ethics, the ethics of the environment, and anthropocentric ethics. Conservation ethics is the idea that the environment and its resources should be conserved and maintained for future generations. Conserving the environment is a byproduct of ensuring that humankind will thrive and have the same access to natural resources in the future. The ethics of the environment is a view whereby the environment is given the same respect and moral considerations afforded to humans. Finally, anthropocentric ethics is the view that acknowledges humans as the only beings worthy of moral considerations. It is the latter view that dominates the tourism industry, a view which does not advocate equal consideration for animals, and which facilitates and perpetuates animal cruelty.

Animals in the tourism industry are regarded as commodities to be traded, transferred, loaned, sold, and killed. They are large investments, and large returns are expected. The argument for justifying captive animals is wavering in light of a more knowledgeable society educated through wildlife films, television channels dedicated solely to animals such as Animal Planet, and other channels such as National Geographic and The Discovery Channel (Bulbeck, 2005). As was highlighted in an Association of Zoos and Aquariums (AZA) study (Falk et al., 2007), the public is more knowledgeable about environmental and conservation issues; this has raised questions about whether the modern urban zoo's role of bringing the public into contact with animals is obsolete, and if its role is to achieve this and it is occurring through other forms of interaction. Added to this, the success of educating through signage at animal exhibits is ambiguous. It seems questionable to classify zoos as educational platforms, when the transfer of knowledge is reliant upon two factors; the visitors reading, and how they absorb the information with this being also aligned to the quality and depth of the information.

Conservation

The threat of extinction through hunting, poaching, and loss of habitat has pushed conservation to the forefront of environmental issues; zoos in particular have been quick to voice their contributions to validate their existence (DeGrazia, 2002). The group (AZA) that represents them points out that since the 1990s they have changed their focus from captive breeding programs with the intent of preserving captive zoo populations, to the preservation of wild animals and their natural habitats (Kuehn, 2002). This statement conflicts with the number of breeding programs and captive births at zoos (Appleton, 2008; San Diego Zoo Website, 2008).

Breeding endangered species in particular is common practice among zoos, however there is also a common problem of surplus animals, particularly deer, tigers, and lions (PETA, 2006a), which may be sold to inferior zoos and hunting ranches, or fed to other zoo animals (DeGrazia, 2002; Jamieson, 1985; Newkirk, 1999). AZA has acknowledged this issue and now has extensive guidelines to ensure an appropriate balance of animals and to reduce the number of unwanted animals (Kuehn, 2002; AZA, 2017). A tracking system of animals held in AZA facilities has been developed, and the International Species Identification System (ISIS) seeks to stop the transfer of animals to substandard facilities and hunting ranches (Kuehn, 2002; Shephard et al., 2006; Henn, 2016). In order to preserve captive populations with strong genetic diversity, animals continue to be captured from the wild to support such breeding programs (Olive & Jansen, 2017); however, more animals are captured than are released (DeGrazia, 2002; Jamieson, 1985).

So . . . why not put animals on the menu?

Conservation is a legal requirement of all aquariums in the UK, however aquariums play a role in promoting the keeping of exotic fish as pets and indirectly contribute to the destruction of coral reefs and over fishing. Aquariums in Europe send mixed signals regarding conservation and the importance of protecting wildlife, as visitors can purchase souvenirs of corals, shells, and dried starfish and seahorses in gift shops. Successful captive breeding programs in aquariums are difficult due to the susceptibility of fish to diseases, and captive breeding often produces behavioral and genetic problems, and it is recommended that wild fish breed only once. Casamitjana (2004) found no evidence of aquariums contributing to *in situ* conservation. Conservation claims by aquariums are misleading, as only 1.8% of individuals displayed in UK aquariums are threatened. For example, the Humboldt penguin is the only animal part of the European Endangered Species Program, and none have been released (Carrell, 2004).

However, there is little evidence supporting the contribution of marine parks to the survival of whales, dolphins, and seals. Education is limited, teaching little or nothing relevant to the survival of particular species, such as the current status of the natural environment their animals should inhabit, and the threat caused by human activities, namely pollution (Singer, Dover, & Newkirk, 1991). The contribution to *in situ* projects is miniscule, with SeaWorld funding around $4 million on conservation and stranding efforts (Kestin, 2004). The whaling industry has heavily lobbied the International Whaling Commission in an effort to keep small whales and dolphins outside their "jurisdiction." The inclusion of whales and dolphins would give them international protection under the International Whaling Commission, which could prevent marine parks from capturing whales and dolphins in the future (PETA, 2006b).

Critics of conservation disagree with the common sentiment that the benefits of animals in zoos, aquariums, and marine parks outweighs the cost of the individual welfare and rights of the animal, in order to educate, protect, and conserve wild populations and habitats (DeGrazia, 2002; Kuehn, 2002). The conservation of animals through captive breeding programs, and the establishment of captive populations, are viewed as human desires. If a species becomes extinct, the animal itself is not harmed, and they are unaware of their species impending extinction. There are ethical considerations involved in conservation, and we must remember that conservation is not concerned with the individual rights or welfare of an animal. Famed conservation group, The World Wildlife Fund (WWF), was founded by a group of trophy hunters concerned with declining numbers of game animals. The WWF supports sustainable hunting, including the Canadian Seal hunt, trophy hunting, sustainable culling of elephants for trophy hunters and the ivory trade, trapping with steel-jaw leghold traps, and wolf hunting as part of a WWF tourism program in Alaska, United States (Mullin, 1999; Wicked Wildlife Fund Website, 2008).

We contend that it is the government's role to be at the forefront of engraining a conservation (animal rights) ethic into the industry, through an increasing amount of regulation and legislation. Concern by ecologists and activists over the ethical and cultural treatment of animals needs to be brought to bear on government policy. Intervention by the state is necessary to compensate for the failures of a free market system that is exploitative of these animals. In the context of ecotourism, this intervention is required due to the inability of the free market (including industry self-regulation) to successfully deliver in tourism a balance of economics and ethics. Just as it is a social responsibility of economically developed and economically developing governments to address the issue of abuse of human rights for indigenous and local communities around the globe, it is equally the social responsibility of the governments where ecotourism is concerned to provide a just balance between economic and environmental goals, and these environmental goals must include the rights of animals. We have suggested that discussion of decommodified principles applied to animals in ecotourism will lead to a more sustainable approach in this industry.

Conclusion

Would we be better off promoting a cultural consumption of whales where they are used in tourism as a novel form of food based on the cultural traditions of those countries that cite it as a cultural tradition? Or are we just recreating in both whale watching and food consumption a "tragedy of the commons" and a failure to protect and care for the species? In moving in this direction of cultural food consumption through food tourism, we must be careful of the further objectification which can perpetuate animal commodification in general and diminish the ethical and practical gains we have made for rights of whales and other species. The new global awareness and perception of the need to protect whale species since the 1980s with the IWC moratorium has given the planet an opportunity to bring back many of the species of whale almost hunted to extinction. In 1930 and 1931 alone tens of thousands of blue whales, the largest animal on the planet, were killed in Australia for commercial use (Australian Geographic, 2016). Given humans' track record, we do not want any return to even a limited and completely unnecessary hunting of whales for food or any other commercial consumption. We argue that unless decommodifying criteria of the kind offered through "Codes of Ethics" can include the "right of animals," then the stories outlined above will continue to haunt ecotourism and draw it into the commodified regimes of mainstream tourism by organizations seeking to be called ecotourism operators. Such factors require implementation in governments' and operators' policies if a more sustainable ecotourism is to develop the dual strategies of benefiting both local communities and the rights of animals. With modern tourism creating multi-national economic investment, which means economics is predominant in tourism practices', any change that might impact on animal welfare will not occur in a short period of time. Thus, it may be unrealistic to expect that full scale responsible tourism practices within organizations will be embraced or endorsed immediately. However, if ecotourism is effectively regulated and practices of sustainability established, a more viable and rich tourist experience from ecotourism is possible using animals in a role that is ethically acceptable.

References

Agence France-Presse in Tokyo. (2015). *Whale meat on the menu at Japanese food festival*. Retrieved February 26, 2015, from www.theguardian.com/world/2015/oct/09/whale-meat-on-the-menu-at-japanese-food-festival

Ananthaswamy, A. (2004). Beware the ecotourist. *New Scientist, 181*(2437), 6–7.

Anonymous. (2004). Boats drown out Orcas' cries. *New Scientist, 182*(2445), 19.

Appleton, K. (2008). *Zoo babies 2008: New kids on the block*. Retrieved May 19, 2016, from http://btsrv.budgettravel.com/bt-srv/zoobabies2008/index.html

Association of Zoos and Aquariums (AZA). (2017). *AZA Population Management Center (PMC)*. Retrieved 21 April 2017, from www.aza.org/population-management-center.

Australian Geographic. (2016). Antarctica's blue whales are split into three populations. *Australian Geographic*. Retrieved June 30, 2016, www.australiangeographic.com.au/news/2016/03

Bestor, T. C. (2000). How Sushi went global. *Foreign Policy*, (121), 54–63.

Boonpienpon, N., Maneenetr, T., Siriwong, P., & Kovathanakul, D. (2015). Indigenous Islamic food: An ideal product innovation for creativity in cultural tourism: A case study of Khao Tung Pla (Thai crispy rice crackers with anchovies). *Mediterranean Journal of Social Sciences*, *6*(5), 445–453.

Bulbeck, C. (2005). *Facing the wild: Ecotourism, conservation and animal encounters*. London: Earthscan.

Butcher, J. (2005). The moral authority of ecotourism: A critique. *Current Issues in Tourism*, *8*(2–3), 114–124.

Carrell, S. (2004). *Aquarium fish suffer abuse and ill – health*. Retrieved September 26, 2016, from www.independent.co.uk/environment/aquarium-fish-suffer-abuse-and-ill-health-5351872.html

Casamitjana, J. (2004). *Aquatic zoos: A critical study of UK public aquaria in the year 2004*. Retrieved September 26, 2016, from www.captiveanimals.org/aquarium/aquatic zoos.pdf.

Cole, S. (2007). Implementing and evaluating a code of conduct for visitors. *Tourism Management*, *28*(2), 443–451.

Corigliano, A. (2002). The route to quality: Italian gastronomy networks in operation. In A. M. Hjalager & G. Richards (Eds.), *Tourism and gastronomy* (pp. 166–185). London: Routledge.

Corkeron, P. J. (2004). Whale watching, iconography, and marine conservation. *Conservation Biology*, *18*, 847–849.

Cunningham, P. A., Huijbens, E. H., & Wearing, S. L. (2012). From whaling to whale watching: Examining sustainability and cultural rhetoric. *Journal of Sustainable Tourism*, *20*(1), 143–161.

DeGrazia, D. (2002). *Animal rights: A very short introduction*. Oxford: Oxford University Press.

Dolnicar, S., Crouch, G. I., & Long, P. (2008). Environment-friendly tourists: What do we really know about them? *Journal of Sustainable Tourism*, *16*(2), 197–210.

Falk, J. H., Reinhard, E. M., Vernon, C. L., Bronnenkant, K., Deans, N. L., & Heimlich, J. E. (2007). *Why zoos & aquariums matter: Assessing the impact of a visit to a zoo or aquarium*. Silver Spring, MD: Association of Zoos & Aquariums.

Fennell, D. A. (2008). Ecotourism and the myth of indigenous stewardship. *Journal of Sustainable Tourism*, *16*(2), 129–149.

Gillespie, A. (2003). Legitimating a whale ethic. *Environmental Ethics*, *25*(4), 394–410.

Hall, C. M., Sharples, L., Mitchell, R., Macionis, N., & Cambourne, B. (Eds.). (2003). *Food tourism around the world: Development, management and markets*. Oxford: Butterworth Heinemann.

Henn, C. (2016). *The shocking truth about what happens to 'Surplus' zoo animals*. Retrieved April 21, 2017, from www.onegreenplanet.org/animalsandnature/the-shocking-truth-about-what-happens-to-surplus-zoo-animals/.

Holden, A. (2003). In need of new environmental ethics for tourism? *Annals of Tourism Research*, *30*(1), 94–108.

Holden, A. (2015). Evolving perspectives on tourism's interaction with nature during the last 40 years. *Tourism Recreation Research*, *40*(2), 133–143. doi:10.1080/02508281.2015.1039332.

Hoyt, E. (2001). *Whale watching 2001: Worldwide tourism numbers, expenditures, and expanding socioeconomic benefits*. London: International Fund for Animal Welfare.

Jamieson, D. (1985). Against zoos. In P. Singer (Ed.), *Defense of animals* (pp. 108–117). New York: Basil Blackwell.

Jelinski, D. E., Krueger, C. C., & Duffus, D. A. (2002). Geostatistical analyses of interactions between killer whales (Orcinus Orca) and recreational whale-watching boats. *Applied Geography*, *22*, 393–411.

Kestin, S. (2004). *Other stories from marine attractions: Below the surface.* Retrieved May 17, 2012, from www.sun-sentinel.com/sfl-marinestorygallery-storygallery.html

Köseoglu, M. A., Sehitoglu, Y., Ross, G., & Parnell, J. A. (2016). The evolution of business ethics research in the realm of tourism and hospitality: A bibliometric analysis. *International Journal of Contemporary Hospitality Management, 28*(8), 1598–1621. doi:10.1108/IJCHM-04-2015-0188.

Kuehn, B. M. (2002). *Is it ethical to keep animals in zoos?* Retrieved December 1, 2012, from www.avma.org/onlnews/javma/dec02/021201d.asp

Lemelin, R. H. (2006). The gawk, the glance and the glaze: Ocular consumption and polar bear tourism in Churchill, Manitoba, Canada. *Current Issues in Tourism, 9*(6), 516–534.

Lhuillery, J. (2014). *Halal whale meat? Muslim tourism takes off in Japan Muslim Village.* Retrieved May 10, 2016, from https://muslimvillage.com/2014/11/19/59232/halal-whale-meat-muslim-tourism-takes-off-in-japan/.

Liu, B., Norman, W. C., & Pennington-Gray, L. (2013). A flash of culinary tourism: Understanding the influences of online food photography on people's travel planning process on Flickr. *Tourism, Culture & Communication, 13*, 5–18.

McGlynn, D. (2012, June 29). Whale hunting. *CQ Researcher, 22*, 24. Retrieved April 20, 2017, from http://library.cqpress.com/cqresearcher/document.php?id=cqresrre2012062900.

Meletis, Z. A., & Campbell, L. M. (2007). Call it consumption! Re – conceptualizing ecotourism as consumption and consumptive. *Geography Compass, 2*, 850–870.

Milius, S. (2004). Din among the Orcas. *Science News, 165*(18), 275–276.

Morton, A. B., & Symonds, H. K. (2002). Displacement of *Orcinius orca* (L.) by high amplitude sound in British Columbia, Canada. *Journal of Marine Science, 59*, 71–80.

Mullin, M. H. (1999). Mirrors and windows: Sociocultural studies of human-animal relationships. *Annual Review of Anthropology, 28*, 201–224.

Newkirk, I. (1999). *You can save the animals: 251 ways to stop thoughtless cruelty.* London: Prima.

Nyack, C. (2011). *Why Japanese whaling is NOT scientific research.* Retrieved February 26, 2016, from www.care2.com/c2c/groups/disc_list.html?gpp=61

O'Connor, S., Campbell, R., Cortez, H., & Knowles, T. (2009). *Whale watching worldwide: Tourism numbers, expenditures and expanding economic benefits* A special report from the International Fund for Animal Welfare, Yarmouth, MA. Prepared by Economists at Large.

Olive, A., & Jansen, K. (2017). The contribution of zoos and aquaria to Aichi Biodiversity Target 12: A case study of Canadian zoos. *Global Ecology and Conservation, 10*, 103–113. doi:10.1016/j.gecco.2017.01.009.

Orams, M. B. (2001). From whale hunting to whale watching in Tonga: A sustainable future? *Journal of Sustainable Tourism, 9*(2), 128–146.

People for the Ethical Treatment of Animals (PETA) Website. (2006a). *Marine Mammal Parks: Chlorinated prisons.* Retrieved December 1, 2012, from www.peta.org/mc/factsheet_display.asp?ID=63

People for the Ethical Treatment of Animals (PETA) Website. (2006b). *Zoos: Pitiful prisons.* Retrieved December 1, 2012, from www.peta.org/mc/factsheet_display.asp?ID=67

Richards, G. (1996). The scope and significance of cultural tourism. In G. Richards (Ed.), *Cultural tourism in Europe* (pp. 19–45). Wallingford: CAB International.

Ryan, C., & Saward, J. (2004). The zoo as ecotourism attraction – visitor reactions, perceptions and management implications: The case of Hamilton zoo, New Zealand. *Journal of Sustainable Tourism, 12*(3), 245–266.

San Diego Zoo Website. (2008). Retrieved December 1, 2012, from http://zoo.sandiegozoo.org/

Selwood, J. (2003). The lure of food: Food as an attraction in destination marketing in Manitoba, Canada. In M. Hall, L. Sharples, R. Mitchell, N. Macionis, & B. Cambourne (Eds.), *Food tourism around the world: Development, management and markets* (pp. 187–191). Oxford: Butterworth Heinemann.

Shephard, R., Aryel, R. M., & Shaffer, L. (2006). Animal health. In M. M. Wagner, A. W. Moore, & R. M. Aryel (Eds.), *Handbook of biosurveillance* (pp. 111–128). Burlington, MA: Elsevier Academic Press.

Sin, H. L. (2017). Selling ethics: Discourses of responsibility in tourism. *Annals of the American Association of Geographers*, *107*(1), 218–234. doi:10.1080/24694452.2016.1218266.

Singer, P., Dover, B., & Newkirk, I. (1991). *Save the animals! 101 east things you can do*. Sydney: Collins, Angus & Robertson.

Sloan, P., Legrand, W., & Hindley, C. (2015). *Routledge handbook of sustainable food and gastronomy*. Oxon: Routledge.

Van Vark, C. (2013). *Shoppers stick to ethical principles despite financial pressures*. Retrieved September 26, 2016, from www.theguardian.com/sustainable-business/shopppers-stick-to-ethical-principles

Wearing, S. L., & Jobbins, C. (2011). *Ecotourism and the commodification of wildlife: Animal welfare and the ethics of zoos in zoos and tourism: Conservation, education, entertainment?* (pp. 47–58). Clevedon: Channel View Press, Channel View Publications.

Wicked Wildlife Fund Website. (2008). Retrieved December 1, 2012, from www.wicked-wildlifefund.com/abuse.html.

Wight, P. (1993). Ecotourism: Ethics or eco – sell. *Journal of Travel Research*, *31*(3), 4–14.

Yeld, J. (2005). *The horror of captive breeding exposed*. Retrieved November 16, 2012, from www.iol.co.za/index.php?click_id=13&set_id=1&art_id=vn20051116111126310C675688.

Zhang, S. (2015). *The Japanese barely eat whale: So why do they keep whaling?* Retrieved May 9, 2016, from www.wired.com/2015/12/japanese-barely-eat-whale-whaling-big-deal/.

Ziegelmayer, E. J. (2008). Whales for margarine: Commodification and neoliberal nature in the Antarctic. *Catalism Nature Socialism*, *19*(3), 65–93.

13 Animals and food

Transcending the anthrocentric duality of utility

Carol Kline

Food is routinely given attention in tourism research as a motivator of travel and examined through studies on food festivals, destination images centered on food, the development of food trails, food-based experiences such as cooking classes, and through market studies of foodies and the culinary traveler. Within the agritourism literature, a few investigations have touched on the education provided at farms regarding food sourcing, and the propensity of tourists to choose sustainable food options including grass fed meats and free-range poultry products after visiting a farm. Regardless of whether tourists travel with a primary motivation for experiencing local food, eating is required during the course of their trip, and therefore the condition of inputs that go into the making of their meals – the soil and water, the workers, and the animals – raise the eating of food while traveling to the level of a moral act regardless of whether tourists are cognizant of this or not. *Animals, Food, and Tourism* integrates topics previously independent: animal welfare and tourism, animal welfare and food production, and ethical consumption.

Animal welfare as a critical consideration within the tourism industry was illuminated in 2012 with David Fennell's book *Tourism and Animal Ethics*. Additionally, a growing body exists within peer-reviewed journals, however the majority of these published works address the topics of zoos and marine animals in tourism, with lesser attention paid to elephants and primates. Issues surrounding the eating of animals is being addressed within philosophical, spiritual, economic, anthropological, psychological, political, and feminist scholarship, however, the specific issue of *animals as food* for tourists, and the ethical associations, has to date been neglected. *Animals, Food, and Tourism*, while making a contribution to the increased importance being placed on socially responsible and sustainable tourism development, also joins a broader interdisciplinary social science literature that examines the entangled relationships between humans and non-human animals.

The chapters are grounded in ethics-related theories and frameworks including critical theory, ecofeminism, gustatory ethics, environmental ethics, ethics within a political economy context, cultural relativism, market construction paradigm, ethical resistance, and the Global Sustainable Tourism Criteria. Several chapters explore contradicting and paradoxical ethical perspectives, whether those contradictions exist between government and private sector, between tourism and other industries, or whether they lie within ourselves. Like the authors in *Tourism Experiences & Animal Consumption: Contested Values, Morality, & Ethics*, the authors in this volume struggle with a range of issues regarding *animals as food* – in terms of animal sentience, the environmental consequences of animals as food, viewing animals solely as an extractive resource for human will, as well as the artificial cultural distortion of *animals as food* for tourism marketing purposes.

While the terms aquatic and terrestrial are sometimes inadequate classifications, I will have used them here as a general way to distinguish between animals who spend their lives above land and below water. As such, this volume contains a nearly equal split between aquatic (fish, lobster, whales, and seals, the latter considered a semiaquatic mammal) and terrestrial animals (goat, reindeer, kangaroo, farmed animals, domestic and wild). Blankfield begins the compilation of chapters by examining David Foster Wallace's 2004 Gourmet essay "Consider the Lobster." He contends that the essay "functions simultaneously as a treatise on tourism, a theorization of gustatory ethics, and a rhetorical performance," inviting readers of the essay to consider their own consumption habits in a more holistic manner. For those who love food, Blankfield warns that adopting gustatory ethics is not easy:

> Much like a connoisseur of fine wine, a gourmet abiding by Wallace's gustatory ethics revels in slowing down, embracing complexity, and savoring all the details. The flipside, of course, is whether one can fully savor their meal upon having researched it thoroughly. This is the pleasure and peril of being a gourmet. It goes beyond pleasing one's taste buds by enlisting one's mind.

Simply learning more about where our food comes from brings with it a sobering responsibility. Once we know about unsavory or unethical practices, we must then decide how that knowledge will translate into our own actions. Max Elder and I deconstruct the phenomenon of "seafood tourism" through an ethical lens that focuses on issues of biodiversity, public health, animal welfare, sustainability, and ecology, as well as explores some possible solutions to the "problem of seafood tourism." We similarly assert that as (ethical) eaters, we have individual accountability to learn what impacts are made by our eating choices: "It might not be visible on our plates, but it becomes clear when we look beyond our gustatory pleasures and into our oceans." Albert Bandura (2015) addresses the pervasiveness of moral disengagement, or rather how people "do harm" and are able to "live with themselves." It seems the study of *animals as food* would be ripe for a deeper exploration of moral disengagement.

In a twist on *animals as food*, Fung studies the use of fish to provision the Amazon river dolphin (*boto*) for the purposes of tourism. While the fish are not eaten by tourists, they are nonetheless *animals as food* because they are used to lure dolphins to tourist platforms so that visitors can view the dolphins up close and swim with them. Fung argues that this particular use of fish, which is largely unregulated resulting in estimates exceeding 42,000 kg of fish used annually at the seven sites in her sample, incites conflict between the *boto* tourism operators and fishers in the region. Additionally, there are ethical considerations to the *boto*, who may be overfed and whose natural migration patterns are disrupted. She concedes that "a preliminary utilitarian view of the situation would suggest that the benefits do not outweigh the costs for a majority population (human and more-than-human); the immediate benefits seem to only apply to [*boto* tourism] operators and their families. However, the potential for BIP tourism to serve as a conservation education tool or alternative economic activity still holds some hope."

Burns, Öqvist, Angerbjörn, and Granquist address the duality of "consumptive" versus "non-consumptive" interactions (this is the duality I refer to in the title of this chapter). They discuss the individual and global ethical considerations of viewing animals as a resource simultaneously in both capacities. They dissect the cognitive dissonance of this practice using case studies on whales and seals and add to a necessary body of literature regarding our ability to reconcile seemingly opposing or distressing realities. Understanding human cognition is critical within the tourism context as our rationale for engaging or not engaging in a behavior is vulnerable to amplification. Their study addresses this contradiction head on by seeking to understand "why some tourists who object to hunting these species, and appreciate the opportunity to observe them in their natural habitat, also have interest in eating whale and seal meat." Their empirical investigation lays the groundwork for (I hope) a cadre of future studies which will have implications that challenge the marketing of *animals as food* and/or charts new courses for de-marketing *animals as food*.

A juxtaposition of chapters on Icelandic and Japanese whaling emphasizes the importance of cultural context in all of the cases portrayed in this book. Wearing, Wearing, and Jobberns approach the eating-vs.-watching whales tension "through the ecological and economic developmental model of ecotourism, [noting] how whale watching has influenced the local and global discourses on conservation." Even as eating whale is declining among the Japanese, it is promoted to tourists at the local and regional levels. The authors note that while the whale conservation discourse is making advances, Japan continues its whaling program with the underlying tenet of its use for consumption. Wearing and colleagues contemplate on its promotion as a novelty food for tourists, questioning if any form of "ethical valuing" can be developed to combat the economics of utilitarianism that is predominately determining "use" outcomes.

Some of the chapters focus on farmed animals and/or are set on farms. Certainly implied in studying *animals as food* is the continuum of animal production systems, ranging from the most highly industrialized confined animal feeding operation, as described in Bricker and Joyner's chapter to a pasture-based setting, where animals graze even at times without fences, such as when the reindeer are turned out to roam documented in Hoarau-Heemstra' s account of the Sami culture. Bertella applies a variation to this by offering a look at what a farm might look like without farmed animals. In her study of ecofeminism and veganism, Bertella deconstructs the foodscape as it applies to the region of Parma, Italy, offering a space where veganism can reside within a tourist area known for its animal-based gastronomy. Just as Blankfield's chapter calls for an ethic that spans the supply chain of one's meal, Bertella also spreads before us the expansive landscape where animals and food do, but don't necessarily have to, intersect. By enumerating the ways in which *animals not as food* are found in her two vegan holiday house cases, she reminds us of the many the ways animals can come into play in tourism, albeit not on our plate. Within her chapter is an explicit connection of veganism to a broader environmental ethic; she notes: "The absence of animals from the menu is a marker of the ethical position of the hosts and, often, also of the guests," and "the hosts argued for a broader view of veganism, such as that in relation to environmentalism, practiced by the adoption of eco-friendly products and methods."

The chapter by Bricker and Joyner also offers an environmental slant, however this time the focus is confined animal feeding operations. They frame their chapter using the Global Sustainable Tourism Criteria as a formalized code of ethics and practice, detailing the potential linkages between sustainability in tourism to sustainable food production. Using the triple-bottom line approach and adding sustainable management and animal welfare, their chapter provides a comprehensive treatise of why tourism operations cannot use factory farmed meat and still consider themselves sustainable. Their declarations that "Sustainable tourism cannot ignore animal welfare, including within food industries" and "Sustainable tourism enterprises should and can be congruent with international standards for animal welfare" should serve as a mantra for those attempting to make the tourism industry more sustainable.

Sayre and Henderson viewed the farms within their study from a marketing standpoint, exploring "the extent to which visitor interaction with farm animals is associated with a positive impression of a farm, ostensibly by fostering a sense of authenticity and a consumer–producer relationship that is increasingly sought after by ethical consumers." They embedded their study within the notion of ethical consumption and the understanding that "consumption is an act of identity-construction whereby consumers routinely make choices that reinforce their understanding of themselves and the world." They justify their study as contributing to understanding the ethical "attitude-behavior gap" whereby consumers espousing ethical consumerism principles do not always purchase with their conscience. Analyzing the online reviews of animal farms, they noted the impressions made and shared by consumers/visitors related to animals and related ethics. While this included animal welfare, comments moreover reflected an idealized ethic of authenticity and an ethic of local "as an attribute with self-evident virtues."

The chapters by Quintero Venegas and López López and by Bone and Bone combine animal sentience with cultural distortion to form the basis of their ethical critiques. While in Australia the kangaroo is portrayed as a symbol of national pride, an important megafauna, and a "cute" wild animal found in zoos in addition to a unique meal to sample, the *cabrito* is only celebrated as a quintessential meal for tourists visiting the Monterrey region of Mexico (hailed as "food for kings, not to be missed"). Quintero Venegas and López López address the dish as "an element of identity," connected to social prestige, machismo, and human domination over non-human animals. The authors detail the animal welfare issues related to serving baby goat juxtaposing these offenses with the tourist who desires a superficial experience to check it off their list of things to do to experience the culture. Bone and Bone demonstrate cultural ironies and welfare dilemmas through their examination of various contact zones where species meet: farms, sanctuaries, restaurants, and in the "wild." Additionally, they address the animal as traveler. In each case, the authors portray the ethical considerations.

Hoarau-Heemstra provides a case of reindeer and indigenous tourism within the Sami culture of Northern Europe. She presents the ethical challenges associated with the human–animal relationship in reindeer tourism and embeds the chapter within the assumption, as part of Sami culture, "that it is morally right to use an animal as long as this animal has had a worthy life." Because the owners are responsible for the wellbeing of their herd, the development of reindeer tourism operations means considering how it affects the quality of life of the reindeer. She reflects on the Sami practice of keeping reindeer through the lens of deep ecology and "Ubuntu" and concludes that the Sami people acknowledge the "egalitarian and social relationships across species boundaries."

Each of the authors in this volume approach their discussion of *animals as food* from a foundation of respect. It is out of this respect that feelings of uneasiness, disgust, or horror are conjured when confronted with human treatment of other species, in this case, as it relates to transforming their living bodies into a product for us to ingest that is not always necessary for survival. Other ethical byproducts of industrial meat consumption include a host of environmental degradations, biodiversity loss, a warping of local culture, placing tourist needs above resident needs, and widespread public health problems. While some approached *animals as food* conceptually, and others used an applied or empirical approach, they each exposed a particular conflict occurring in a particular place. These conflicts – between tourist and local, between industry and community, between exploiting and stewarding naturel resources, between various "uses" of animals, and within ourselves – are the manifestations of ethics. The ethical lenses employed within the book are just a start. Supply chain transparency ethics, environmental and conservation ethics, marketing ethics, and the ethic of government oversight are all a matter of your perspective and vantage point. Ethics of animal sentience, moral ordering of species, and intrinsic vs. use-value are largely matters of your worldview. Whether viewing the phenomena of *animals as food* through a lens of deep ecology, gustatory ethics, or principles of sustainability, it is evident that there are a myriad of ethical considerations to take into account, and not all ethical considerations are receiving the requisite review.

The chapters in this volume were set in Japan, Brazil, Mexico, Italy, Norway, Iceland, Australia, the United States, and areas providing seafood. Future studies on *animals as food* must represent broader geographical, cultural, and touristic contexts in order for us to have a more unified understanding. For example, visiting friends and relatives (VFR) is one of the most common reasons for travel, and food is often at the center of holidays, celebrations, and even death rituals. Are the conflicts and ethical decisions of *animals as food* altered within the VFR context? Are there other forms of tourism that would yield different knowledge: volunteer tourism, festival and event tourism, business and meeting tourism, or rural tourism are some examples. Bone and Bone began chronicling the contact zones where humans and *animals as food* meet; what are other contact zones within tourism that merit investigation? And while this book is part of an Ethics of Tourism series, throughout these cases, the overlap with hospitality is obvious. Studying *animals as food* is yet another bridge between the sister fields of hospitality and tourism.

For readers who feel affection toward animals, it could be difficult to read this selection of chapters. These narratives moreover incite more questions than solutions, for example:

1 What should our role with animals be?
2 How do our beliefs about animal agency or animal autonomy shape our view of this role?
3 Because the overarching human view of animals is embedded in their utility to us, is there any hope for assigning them any meaningful value beyond our need?
4 When and how early in our development is a "continuum of animals" constructed in our minds, whereby some are deemed acceptable as food and others as not?
5 To what extent should animal welfare transgressions be tolerated in the name of cultural practices? What if any policy responses are available to those inclined to mitigate animal suffering?
6 How much and in what ways are our psychological coping mechanisms influenced by the presence of animals, either live or presented as food on a plate?
7 What does any of this to have to do with tourism? (Cooney, 2010; Donovan & Adams, 2007; Joy, 2011; Thomas, 2016)

In response to the last question, there are several reasons why *animals as food* is an important consideration for tourism studies. Culinary tourism is an ever-increasing area where neo-localism and "consuming the place" intersect. Animals as well as (meat) cuisine represent places in marketing campaigns. The topic of *animals as food* within the context of tourism calls into question the boundaries of cultural relativism. Additionally, human behaviors can change when traveling. Tourism experiences have an opportunity to change minds because people are open to receiving new information, but also tourism can amplify a sense of moral disengagement. Certainly, the principles of sustainability relating to animal production pollution and waste, destruction of habitat, and environmental justice and public health concerns (e.g. antibiotic resistance) are a concern for the tourism industry. And within the field of tourism, ethics are a growing consideration (see Fennell, 2015; Macbeth, 2005; Tribe, 2002). Work in animal ethics exists beyond animal studies, and includes work in philosophy, religion, psychology, and economics; why would it not be a part of tourism ethics? On a pragmatic note, while some codes of ethics exist that address animals within tourism, it is too often an afterthought or more often not regarded with enough significance for consideration.

Confronting the uglier nature of humans takes courage. Further, even attempting to contribute to the solution (of any of the world's greatest issues) or choosing to not contribute to the problem is more than an intellectual exercise. I learned this from Drs. David Manuel-Navarrete and Christine Buzinde at the 2017 Critical Tourism Studies Conference (Manuel-Navarrete, Papenfus, & Buzinde, 2017). Leading a workshop on the place of contemplative meditation in pedagogy, they articulated something I had been witnessing for some time in my classes, but had not quite risen to the surface in my mind where I knew what to do about it. When students are confronted with climate crises, pervasive and continuing global and local racial and ethnic tensions, the clashes of religions that manifest in violence and hate crimes, or news about myriad animals being trafficked to extinction – and only taught to deal with them on an intellectual basis – it can be too much to bear. If we do not develop a multitude of tools to deal with all that awaits us in the world, then a natural and self-protective reaction is to escape and ignore. And if we do choose to engage in solutions, without taking care of ourselves, not only might we not be strong enough, rested enough, and smart enough to fight another day, but we could easily come to the conflict unprepared, uncentered, and unclear on where we stand. Identifying and describing the ethical considerations in *animals as food* is a necessary first step in processing and dealing with any collective solutions.

So, as I end this concluding chapter, I emphasize some hopeful ideas offered within the ethical dilemmas presented in *Animals, Food, and Tourism* (Pritchard, Morgan, & Ateljevic, 2011). In the chapters by Hoarau-Heemstra, Bone and Bone, and Bertella, the authors seem to suggest an "egalitarian" or "kin/d/er" or "absent referent" relationship with animals. Considering our relationship with animals is critical in both inferring and shaping the ethical view we choose.

Ecofeminism in tourism, gustatory ethics, and the Global Sustainable Tourism Criteria offer solid foundations from which to evolve further theoretical contributions or frameworks. And like other tourism studies, borrowing from and collaborating with scholars in other disciplines can only make our understanding deeper and richer. Examples where tourism can offer hope run through this volume. For example, Joyner and Bricker offer a case study on pasture-raised pigs, contrasting this method of production with the CAFOs described in their chapter. Sayre and Henderson offer a pragmatic perspective on how interactions with animals may alter the view of agritourism farms and may attract the ethical consumer. Max Elder and I suggest a range of solutions for the "problem of seafood tourism." Fung suggests that *boto* tourism might lead to environmental education. Bertella teaches us the important role that animals have in the vegan food experience. Wearing suggests ways for the stakeholders within ecotourism to take a more ethical stance resulting in "a more viable and rich tourist experience from ecotourism is possible using animals in a role that is ethically acceptable." Hoarau-Heemstra highlights how tourism can foster a sharing of knowledge between tourist and operator regarding animal ethics through open discussion of value systems. Through her case on Sami culture she reminds us all: "The needs of animals in order to live a worthy life should be the basis for ethical guidelines for using animals in tourism."

References

Bandura, A. (2015). *Moral disengagement: How people do harm and live with themselves*. New York: Macmillan Higher Education.

Cooney, N. (2010). *Change of heart: What psychology can teach us about spreading social change*. New York: Lantern Books.

Donovan, J., & Adams, C. J. (Eds.). (2007). *The feminist care tradition in animal ethics: A reader*. New York: Columbia University Press.

Fennell, D. A. (2015). Ethics in tourism. In *Education for sustainability in tourism* (pp. 45–57). Berlin, Heidelberg: Springer.

Joy, M. (2011). *Why we love dogs, eat pigs, and wear cows: An introduction to carnism*. San Francisco: Conari Press.

Macbeth, J. (2005). Towards an ethics platform for tourism. *Annals of Tourism Research*, *32*(4), 962–984.

Manuel-Navarrete, D., Papenfus, J., & Buzinde, C. (2017, June 28). Performance and contemplation to inspire tourism sustainability [workshop]. *Critical Tourism Studies VII Conference*, Palma de Mallorca, Spain.

Pritchard, A., Morgan, N., & Ateljevic, I. (2011). Hopeful tourism: A new transformative perspective. *Annals of Tourism Research*, *38*(3), 941–963.

Thomas, N. (2016). *Animal ethics and the autonomous animal self*. London: Springer.

Tribe, J. (2002). Education for ethical tourism action. *Journal of Sustainable Tourism*, *10*(4), 309–324.

Index